TO ALL WHO ASPIRE

"While those around us are looking for the key, we, having been handed the key, are looking for the door. We know the door will open inward and as we get closer, we sense approval from somewhere beyond. In this sport we are beckoned, rather than driven, to extremes. It is not worth dying for but it is worth risking dying for."

DEVILS TOWER NATIONAL MONUMENT CLIMBING HANDBOOK

Richard Guilmette, Renée Carrier
and
Steve Gardiner

Devils Tower Natural History Association

©1995 by Devils Tower Natural History Association

Formerly published in 1986 by The Mountaineers
1995 Revised Edition

Published by Devils Tower Natural History Association
Devils Tower National Monument
PO Box 37, Devils Tower, WY 82714

Maps by B. Adams and Newell Cartographics
Cover photos from National Park Service files
Frontispiece: Sun on Tower
  (Bob Kolbrener photo)

ISBN 1-881667-01-4

Disclaimer:
  The information in this book has been compiled by the authors from National Park Service files and interviews with hundreds of climbers. It constitutes a consensus of a climbing route's difficulty and description. Difficulty may vary with the size, stature, and strength of an individual climber.
  The authors' reason for compiling this book is to produce a compendium of climbing at Devils Tower which is readily available to the public. This book is not to encourage people to trust in route difficulty ratings, route descriptions, equipment lists, approaches, finishes or rappel routes, nor is it meant to encourage climbing at Devils Tower National Monument.
  Climbing is a dangerous sport and those who climb do so at their own risk.

Richard A. Guilmette

CONTENTS

ACKNOWLEDGMENTS
FOREWORD
INTRODUCTION

PART 1 **GENERAL INFORMATION**
    Creation of Devils Tower National Monument
    Reaching the Tower
    General Regulations
    Wildlife
    Geology
    American Indians

PART 2 **HISTORICAL INFORMATION**
    The Naming of Devils Tower
    A Game of High Stakes
    A Magnificent Piece of Climbing
    An Island in the Sky

PART 3 **CLIMBING INFORMATION**
    General Climbing Information
    Ratings of Routes
    Climbing Statistics
    Approaches to the Routes
    Standard Meadows Finish
    Rappel Routes
    Popular and Recommended Climbs
    Route Descriptions
        South Face
        East Face
        Northeast Face
        North Face
        West Face
        Southwest Face

APPENDIX **CLIMBING CHRONOLOGY**

CLIMBING ROUTE INDEX

Acknowledgments

Many thanks to the National Park Service for full use of their facilities, records and photo file. Grateful acknowledgment is made by the authors to the following for their aid in preparing this book: Betty Wilson, Jim Schlinkmann, George San Miguel, and Steve Norton.

We would also like to express our appreciation to past and present superintendents of Devils Tower National Monument for their contributions, and to Terry Rypkema, Curt Haire, Dingus McGee, and the Last Pioneer Woman for their early work in recording climbing events at the Tower.

Bruce Adams did an excellent job of preparing the preliminary topographical and area maps. We thank him along with the many climbers through the years who have submitted route descriptions or commented on route information.

FOREWORD TO
DEVILS TOWER CLIMBING HANDBOOK

For those whose first glimpse of the Tower raises both articulate and inarticulate questions, and for those who have the heart to follow in the foot and hand-holds of others who have made their way up its fluted sides, this handbook is written for you. It provides information combining the practical aspects of climbing the Tower—as it is affectionately known in these parts— with a historical, geological and cultural perspective.

May it serve...

—Renée Carrier
Crook County, Wyoming
1994

Todd Skinner leading first ascent of Animal Cracker Land (Route 56), 1984 (Beth Wald photo)

INTRODUCTION

Variously described as "the most unique and fascinating phenomenon I have ever seen," to tribute as the eighth wonder of the world, this singular, awe-inspiring, silent sentinel of a rock, Devils Tower, commands the landscape in the northeastern corner of Wyoming. It is a natural attraction to tourists and wayfarers. To some it is a revered shrine. For rock climbers the Tower is simply there... to be climbed.

During the more clement months, climbers scale its nearly vertical sides virtually every day. While walking around its base, one may encounter people from all parts of the United States and several other countries. In 1994, 6,035 individuals scaled the Tower. Those who reached the summit numbered 2,108. To date, records show that 34,961 total ascents have been made. About 450,000 visitors tour the monument annually.

As a geological formation, the Tower is an exceptional feature and absolutely unique in North America. The columnar jointing of its fluted sides formed as molten rock cooled, creating near-vertical walls. Cracks of various sizes formed, offering years of challenge for climbing enthusiasts.

With this in mind, this book has been written in a format that serves as a comprehensive climbing history and current route description.

To keep the handbook up-to-date and to facilitate a revision should one be necessary in the future, climbers who free climb existing aid routes are requested to submit written descriptions of their activities to a ranger or the superintendent prior to leaving the area. A Route Description Checklist is available at the registration desk for climbers to fill out. A sketch or photo of the climb marking important points would be appreciated.

Welcome to the Tower and Safe Climbing!

PART ONE

General Information

FIRST NATIONAL MONUMENT

By presidential proclamation dated September 24, 1906, Theodore Roosevelt declared that "the lofty and isolated rock in the State of Wyoming, known as the 'Devils Tower', situated upon the public lands owned and controlled by the United States, is such an extraordinary example of the effect of erosion in the higher mountains as to be a natural wonder and an object of historic and great scientific interest and it appears that the public good would be promoted by reserving this tower as a National monument."

The president, using the power of the Act for the Preservation of American Antiquities, set aside Devils Tower as America's first national monument. To declare the rock a national park would have taken an act of Congress, and rumors were circulating indicating interest in the rocks surrounding the Tower for use in building and for souvenirs. President Roosevelt, not wishing to take time for a Congressional act and following the requests of Wyoming Representative Frank W. Mondell, reportedly chose the more expedient method for protecting the area. The proclamation warned "unauthorized persons not to appropriate, injure, or destroy any feature of the natural tower," and prohibited settling or living on any of the lands within the boundary of the monument.

REACHING THE TOWER

The monument is entered from state highway 24 nine miles southwest of Hulett, Wyoming, 33 miles northeast of Moorcroft, Wyoming, 27 miles northwest of Sundance, Wyoming, and 52 miles west of Belle Fourche, South Dakota. The nearest scheduled air services and rental cars are available at Gillette, Wyoming and Rapid City, South Dakota.

Opposite: Beth Wald rappelling after first ascent of Avalon, Route 147 (Todd Skinner photo)

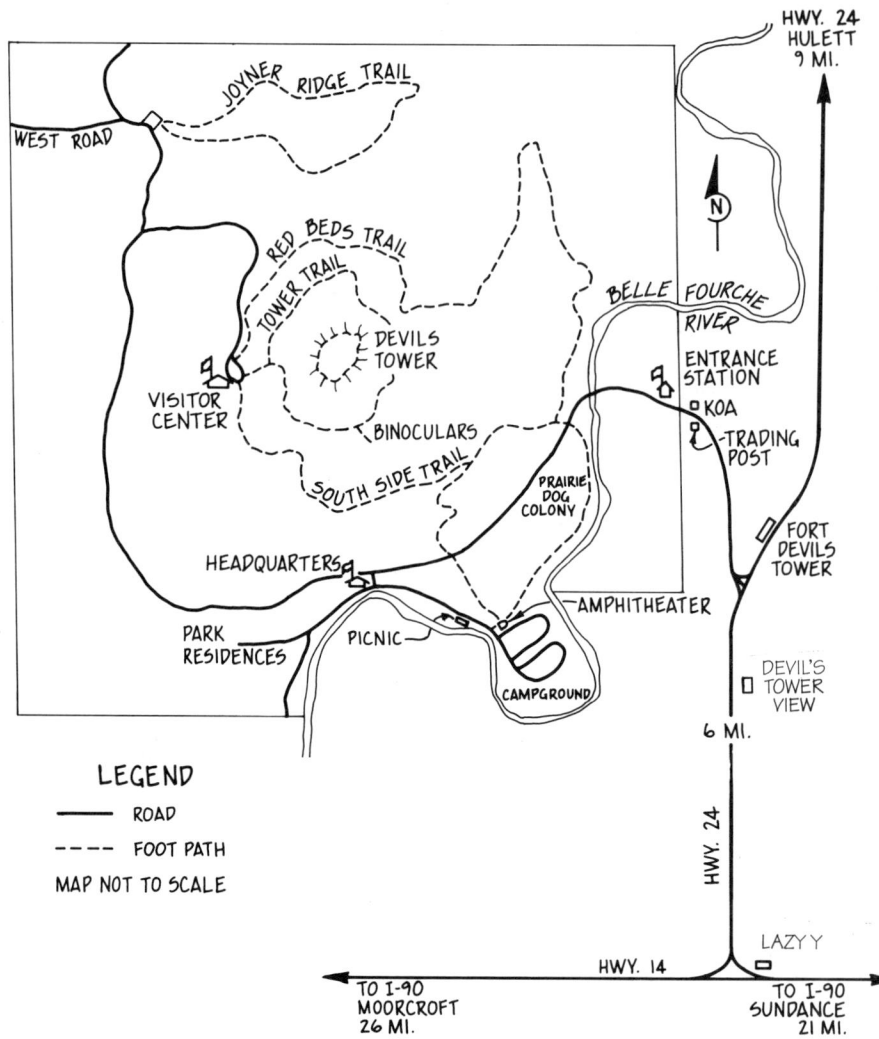

GENERAL REGULATIONS

An entrance fee will be charged when entering the monument. Those staying overnight at the campground must also pay a camping fee. Information regarding fees and camping is available at the entrance station, by phone (307-467-5283) or by writing to Devils Tower National Monument, P.O. Box 10, Devils Tower, WY 82714. Camping is permitted only in the campground and not on the Tower itself. Backcountry camping is not available in the monument.

Climbers must register with a ranger prior to climbing and must sign in after completing a climb according to established regulations. All accidents and injuries must be reported to a ranger.

Vehicles must comply with all state and federal regulations. Driving a motor vehicle off park roads is prohibited as is riding bicycles on trails or cross-country.

No alcoholic beverages (open containers) may be possessed on the main park road, in the visitor center parking area, or on the Tower Trail. No ground fires are permitted. Pets must be physically restrained (leash, cage, etc.) at all times and may not be left unattended and tied to an object.

WILDLIFE

Abundant wildlife thrives in the Tower area. The animals, when left alone, don't seem to mind the curious gaze of park visitors and can be easily photographed. The monument supports habitat for prairie dogs, deer, wild turkey, chipmunks, squirrels, rabbits, porcupines, and an occasional fox, bobcat, bull snake (non-poisonous), and rattlesnake (poisonous). The rattlesnake frequents the prairie dog holes and rocky ground.

Large soaring birds of the area include the bald and golden eagle, turkey vulture, and red-tailed hawk. Other raptors include the northern goshawk, American kestrel, and great horned owl. The upper sections of Devils Tower are home to rock doves. These are preyed upon by prairie falcons that nest on the Tower. As with most birds of prey, these falcons may attack climbers who approach their nests. Most reported attacks have occurred primarily on the west face and occasionally on the north face. Park managers close certain routes and areas on the Tower during the falcon's nesting season.

View south from the top of the Tower (Dick Guilmette photo)

Park visitors have the opportunity to spot wild turkeys, yellow-rumped warblers, red-headed woodpeckers, cordilleran flycatchers, black-capped chickadees, western meadowlarks, mountain bluebirds, and over 100 other species.

For your own safety and that of wildlife, the National Park Service prohibits the feeding or disturbance of the animals.

Naturally, hunting and trapping are also prohibited inside the monument.

GEOLOGY

Devils Tower rises 1,270 feet above the Belle Fourche River to an elevation of 5,117 feet. From the talus slope at its base it rises 867 feet. Its base diameter is approximately 800 feet. The top of the Tower is relatively flat, with the high point at the center. The summit measures 300 feet across from north to south, 180 feet from east to west, and comprises nearly an acre and a half.

During the Cretaceous and Jurassic Periods, some 213 to 65 million years ago, dinosaurs roamed the region. The weather and vegetation were subtropical. Over millions of years, the land rose and subsided several times. Large inland seas covered the region during these episodes of subsidence, only to drain away again as the land rose once more. Sediments deposited in the ancient seas hardened to form the widespread horizontal layers of sandstone, shale, gypsum, and siltstone that today surround Devils Tower. The last of these great seas was drained by the Black Hills uplift, which most geologists agree occurred sometime after the birth of the Rocky Mountains, about 70 million years ago.

Top of the Tower showing vegetation and summit marker in upper left (Dick Guilmette photo)

The Tower formed when molten rock (magma) rose up through the earth to harden either at the surface or just beneath it. This occurred about 60 million years ago. The surrounding sediments were then eroded away to expose the Tower as it appears today.

There are two main geological theories concerning the formation of Devils Tower. One suggests that both the Little Missouri Buttes and Devils Tower are volcanic necks, the lava-filled cores of extinct volcanoes. The magma hardened in the cores and was later exposed by erosion. The second theory suspects that Devils Tower is an "igneous intrusion," meaning the magma never reached the surface as with volcanoes. The igneous (once molten) rock that makes up the Tower is phonolite porphyry, a very hard rock in which large crystals of white feldspar are embedded in a finer-grained groundmass.

Aside from standing nearly vertical, Devils Tower is most striking for its large four, five, and six-sided columns, which formed as the magma cooled. These columns are four to eight feet in diameter and hundreds of feet long. The cracks separating the columns may run straight for their full lengths or meet at the bottom, middle or top. Many cracks run for long distances at a uniform width.

Climbers have their choice of many crack widths on the Tower and can choose finger, hand, fist and foot width cracks, chimneys and even face climbs. This, plus easy access to many difficult climbs, is what sustains the Tower's appeal with climbers.

AMERICAN INDIANS

Many of the Northern Plains Indian tribes consider the Tower to be "wakan," meaning holy or sacred in the Lakota language. When a place is described as "wakan" it indicates that the locality is particularly remarkable and reflects The Great Mystery or "Wakan Tanka."

Ethnographic research to date suggests that at least six American Indian tribes include the great rock in their ideology and have passed down beliefs concerning its origin. These tribes include the Lakota and Dakota people, the Kiowa, Cheyenne, Arapahoe, Shoshone and Crow nations. At some time, each claimed the surrounding countryside as territory. The Tower served as a landmark from which to guide them across the plains as it could be seen from a far distance in many directions.

When a story is told in the Indian tradition, it is offered as "straight and true," often with witnesses to concur. This practice has contributed to the collection of unadulterated stories that were handed down orally and which have only recently been recorded.

One such story about the origin of the Tower was recounted in 1897 by I-See-O, meaning "Plenty Camp Fireplaces," a Kiowa scout and soldier stationed at Fort Sill, Oklahoma. The following dictation is from the notes (Vol.1 p.99, 1897) of Maj. Gen. H.L. Scott (Ret.):

> Before the Kiowa came south they were camped on a stream in the Far North where there were a great many bears—many of them. One day, seven little girls were playing at a distance from the village and were chased by some bears. The girls ran toward the village and the bears were just about to catch them, when they jumped up on a low rock about three feet high. One of them prayed to the rock, "Rock, take pity on us, Rock, save us! And it heard them. It began to elongate itself upward pushing the children higher and higher. When the bears jumped at them, they scratched the rock, broke their claws and fell down on the ground. The rock rose higher and higher, the bears still jumping at them until the children were pushed up into the sky, where they are seven little stars in a group (the Pleiades). In winter, when they are just overhead, it is the middle of the night. The marks of the bears' claws are there yet. The Kiowas call this rock "Tso-ai" or Tree Rock.

The Dakota and Lakota called the Tower "Mato-Tipi" or Grizzly Bears' Lodge or more correctly, "dwelling place of the bears," due to the unusually great number seen. "Broken Standing Buffalo Horn" is yet another name, though not as common as the others.

Army Sgt. Samuel S. Gibson, in a letter concerning the Black and Yellow Trail, mentioned that "the Indians (also) say that during thunderstorms, the Thunder God (or Being) takes his mighty drum to the top of the tower where he beats it, thus causing the thunder." Anyone who has ever experienced a thunderstorm in the Black Hills would appreciate this conclusion.

Traditional ceremonies still take place within the monument boundaries. Ceremonies include the vision quests, the Sun Dance, the sweat lodge rites, and prayer offerings. The National Park Service consults with climbers and American Indians on how best to manage a climbing program at a sacred site. All monument users can help the situation by showing respect for the beliefs and practices of Indian people.

Much of the ceremonial use is by small groups or individuals who go unnoticed by most visitors. Left behind in the clefts of rocks or hanging on a tree limb may be seen ceremonial articles such as prayer bundles and ribbons. Tradition requires that these articles be left in place to continue the spiritual effect of the ceremony. If such an offering is found, kindly leave it undisturbed.

Opposite: Painting showing Indian legend of how the Tower was formed (National Park Service file photo)

PART TWO

HISTORICAL INFORMATION

THE NAMING OF DEVILS TOWER

Devils Tower was originally known by many names, depending on the Indian nation. Historians believe that since the late 1700's the Lakota and Dakota people inhabited the area and they referred to it as the "Grizzly Bears' Lodge."

In the years 1855-1857 Capt. G. K. Warren, of the U.S. Army Corps of Topographical Engineers, led three separate surveying and mapping expeditions to the outskirts of the Black Hills. In 1857, when he reached the area of Inyan Kara Mountain, he was stopped from going further by Dakota Indians who didn't want the Army company to scatter a herd of buffalo they were following. His company didn't reach the Tower, but Capt. Warren reported seeing the "Bears' Lodge" and Little Missouri Buttes by using a "powerful spy-glass." He was the first to officially note the Tower on a map and record the aboriginal name.

Gen. W. F. Raynolds was assigned to explore the Yellowstone and Missouri Rivers in 1859-60. On July 19, 1859, Raynolds' company reached the "Bears' Lodge" and his journal entry describes "an isolated rock on the bank of the river, striking from the fact that it rises in a valley...."

Raynolds mapped out his route, including his camps and the features he found interesting. The "Bear Lodge" rock is so noted.

It was nearly fifteen years before another explorer, Lt. Col. Richard Irving Dodge of the U.S. Army, again mapped the Tower and recorded his observations:

> An immense obelisk of granite, eight hundred and sixty-seven feet at base, two hundred and ninety-seven feet top, rises one thousand one hundred and twenty-seven feet above its base, and five thousand one hundred feet above tidewater.
>
> Its summit is inaccessible to anything without wings. The sides are fluted and scored by the action of the elements, and immense blocks of granite, split off from the column by frost are piled in huge, irregular mounds about its base.
>
> The Indians call this shaft "The Bad god's Tower", a name adopted with proper modification, by our surveyors.*

---

*Dodge, Richard Irving, THE BLACK HILLS (New York, 1876, 95.)

Opposite: Tower view from the southwest (Dick Guilmette photo)

It is not known if this change in name was intentional. Many believe it was a mistranslation by an interpreter. Nevertheless, when Lt. Col. Dodge completed his report and maps, he had called the rock "Devils Tower."

With many people moving into the area at that time, the new name became common, and in 1906, when President Roosevelt proclaimed the first national monument, he used the name "Devils Tower." It should be noted that in 1920, Maj. Gen. H. L. Scott, cited previously in reference to the Tower legend, wrote a letter to the Historical Society of Wyoming charging that "good taste and historical precedent will appeal to the people of Wyoming to give its most remarkable rock its own aboriginal name." He further stated that he was outraged that Col. Dodge "would so violate precedent or explorers' ethics as to change the name in 1876 to 'Devil's Tower', a name without taste, (or) meaning."

Maj. Gen. Scott's appeal was strongly supported by Chief Luther Standing Bear of the Dakota people. In a letter to historian Dick Stone, Chief Standing Bear wrote:

> Col. Dodge was, as were so many white men in meddling with Indian history, wrong in saying the Indians called the place the bad god's tower. The Sioux had no word for Devil, for the devil and hades of the white man had no place in Indian thought. It is much like the changing of the name of the entrance to the Black Hills from "Gate of the Buffalo" which Sioux called it, to the inelegant term of the white man, Buffalo Gap.

Despite the protests of Maj. Gen. Scott, Chief Standing Bear and others, "Devils Tower National Monument" remains the "official" name. Even today, American Indians petition the National Park Service to change the rock and monument's name back to a more appropriate aboriginal name.

A GAME OF HIGH STAKES

"THE RAREST SIGHT OF A LIFETIME WILL BE OBSERVED AND THE 4TH OF JULY WILL BE BETTER SPENT AT THE DEVILS TOWER THAN AT THE WORLD'S FAIR"

Such is what readers learned from the posters and bulletins dispersed in the spring of 1893 by William Rogers and Willard Ripley. The pair of ranchers (ages 35 and 28, respectively) were planning a daring, some called it foolhardy, attempt to be the first men to stand at the summit of the Tower.

Handbills promised that the observers would see "Old Glory flung to the breeze from the top of the Tower, 800 feet from the ground by Wm. Rogers." Moreover, there would be "plenty to eat and drink on the grounds!...lots of hay and grain for the horses!...and dancing day and night!"

The advertisement was successful as one thousand to three thousand curiosity seekers journeyed over unimproved roads and trails as far as 125 miles on horseback and by wagon to the Tower.

The idea for the climb has been credited to two sources. One version gives the notion to Col. Willard Ripley. His front porch enjoyed a view of the Tower and evidently he wondered what it might be like to stand on top. He proposed the idea of a climb to his son, Willard.

Another version of the story credits William Rogers with the thought. In 1891, while he and his brother-in-law, G. A. Knowles, were riding near the Tower, Knowles recalls, "Roger told me that he was 'going to be on top of that tower in three years.' I told him, 'You are going to break your neck, too,' and Bill said, 'No, I won't, but I am going to be up there.'"

In the end, the two men agreed to pool their resources. According to Newell F. Joyner, who became superintendent of the monument in 1932, the project had a

Willard Ripley (above) and William Rogers (left) scaled the summit by stake ladder in 1893 (National Park Service file photos)

double purpose, thus the relationship between Ripley and Rogers was one of business.

To John P. Harrington of the Smithsonian Institute, Joyner later wrote:
> Rogers and Ripley were two local ranchers. They were not partners in the ranch, merely being partners in this venture. I have always used the term "commercial celebration" to differentiate from a public non-profit picnic, and also to introduce the idea back of their climb. It is granted that the venture was primarily for the purpose of doing something which no one else had ever done. But the year, 1893, was one of hard-times in this agricultural region. At no time in this region which was then just being settled have there been persons so affluent as to finance an undertaking such as the construction of the ladder. This job required most of a month for several men. Naturally Rogers and Ripley saw where they could gain financially by using the proposed climb as the free attraction to a celebration where refreshments, stands, and amusements were under their control.

In preparation for their climb, Rogers and Ripley had carefully looked over the faces of the Tower. Knowles explained that his brother-in-law first constructed a large kite in order to pull a heavy cord up and over the Tower, which in turn would pull a climbing rope up to the summit. Unfortunately, the kite failed to fly high enough.

Rogers then looked for a crevice into which stakes could be driven, and thereby climb to the top. Using field glasses he finally spotted one on the southeastern corner, a continuously open vertical crack between two columns, which appeared (to a person standing at the base) to reach the full height of the Tower. This illusion, caused by foreshortening, would later present a problem.

Work began about June 1, 1893 by cutting stakes from native oak, ash, and willow. As the two men were not experienced mountain climbers, they planned to use the stakes as rungs for a ladder, rather than use alpine climbing techniques. The stakes were cut twenty-four to thirty inches in length and sharpened on one end so they could be driven and wedged into the deep crack.

National Park Service records indicate that the first pegs were heavy, long, and placed close together. Higher on the ladder, however, they were made lighter, shorter, and put farther apart. A dwindling source of wood and/or time may have caused the difference. As the stakes were driven into the rock they were supported by a wooden strip on the outer ends forming a continuous 350 foot ladder.

During the six weeks before the Fourth of July, Rogers and Ripley experimented with building methods. They made one valuable discovery which was dictated by the nature of the rock. The left-hand column was flat, but on the right side of the crack the rock protruded outward. Because Willard Ripley was left-handed, he could stand on one stake, lean his right shoulder and hip against the rock, and have his left arm free to swing his hammer. Consequently he wedged most of the stakes.

Mrs. Alice Mae "Dolly" Ripley explained the process. The men "used a pulley rope and a pulley to get the stakes up to where they were driven into the crevice. Rogers and Col. Ripley cut the pegs and pulled them up to Willard, who drove them into the crevice."

The construction of the ladder proved to be difficult and dangerous. The crack containing the ladder ended below a large ledge called "the bench" (now referred to as the Meadows). Above the ladder they had to complete a "hair-raising" leap to get to the bench. Ripley and Rogers reached the summit after another 175 feet of scrambling.

Although some disagreement exists about which of the two actually first stood on top of the Tower, most sources support Mrs. Ripley's assertion that it was her husband, Willard. The FRONTIER TIMES reported:

Superintendent Newell Joyner (left) and local resident George Grenier by old stake ladder, 1932. (National Park Service file photo)

Rogers usually is given credit for being the first man to ascend the Tower, but there are those who contend Willard Ripley was first. They base their contention on the fact that the crack in which the ladder was built curved and because Ripley was left-handed it was easier for him to drive the pegs into the crack. He completed the top of the ladder and it is logical that he was first to reach the top, probably before the designated day of July 4th.

Joyner's research concurred, "I am inclined to the belief that he (Ripley) was actually the first to reach the top and that he did most of the work in the actual construction of the ladder, altho' there are two contending factions and claims." In his report for the historical files Joyner added:

> All this procedure can be told in a sentence or two-but imagine the time and patience (and some say, nerve) required to accomplish the construction of the 350-foot ladder. These pegs had to be selected, cut, and conveyed to the base of the Tower. At least the last quarter mile no wagon could enter. Then began the somewhat precipitous climb over a talus slope of small rocks which ended in maneuvering along several ledges and up over an eight-foot face. Very few people today in attempting to gain the location of the original bottom peg are successful, although it is no trick for anyone who knows the route and has a fair amount of nerve.

On the evening of July 3 a crowd gathered at the Tower. The entertainment included music and dancing. A rain shower forced everyone to seek shelter. The next morning, after several orations, a recitation and choir music, Rogers was presented with a suit donated for the occasion by several ladies from Deadwood, South Dakota.

Citizens from Sundance had purchased an 8 X12-foot length of muslin, on which was painted the stars and stripes. Rogers was to carry it to the top of the Tower. The SUNDANCE REFORM reported:

> (At the Bench) the Tower has a slight incline for 200 feet to the summit, and here Mr. Rogers had placed a rope which he had placed (sic) at the top of the Tower. His first climb over this 200 feet (before the rope had been placed in position) required an amount of coolness and nerve possessed by few men. Here in the air 400 feet from the ground, with only rugged pieces to assist him, he climbed and carried his rope. It was well he had the rope to assist him on the 4th, for if he had not, some of the ladies no doubt would have fainted. This climb is the most wonderful ever witnessed in America and Mr. Rogers deserves all the glory he will undoubtedly receive in making it possible for man to reach the summit of one of nature's greatest wonders.

In the meantime, Ripley's earlier ascent of the Tower had not been made public, and Joyner has recorded that "quite a few large bets were made by those 'in the know' after the ascent had actually been made. They found plenty of persons who were skeptical that it could be done, and who were willing to back up their skepticism with cold cash."

Amid much cheering, Rogers made his climb in approximately one hour. On the summit he secured the flag to the staff and then descended. That afternoon an unexpected wind blew the flag off the Tower and it was cut up and sold as souvenirs.

The celebration continued until the daylight hours on the morning of the fifth.

Exactly two years later, on July 4, 1895, Mrs. Rogers repeated her husband's climb for what Joyner has termed "a similar commercial celebration."

In the years to follow, many persons claimed to have made the trip up the Tower. An article in the May 4, 1944 edition of THE RAPID CITY JOURNAL vividly described a climb by C.W. Whiffin and Herman Harden, who claimed to have reached the summit in 1895. The recollection reportedly "made him shudder 49 years later."

> Sun reflections made eyes ache. The rock cast off heat. C.W. sweat from every pore. His mouth became dry. He had brought no canteen. "I happened to glance

down, my grip tightened on the pegs. A lump bobbed into my throat." They climbed on in grim silence. "I locked jaws and shut my mouth tight. That look downward had weakened me more than the exertion. Finally, after a torturous eternity, Herman said he had reached a ledge. There we could rest just below the top." The view was grand. Ridges, hills and gulches all seemed ironed out flat below them. The Belle Fourche river was a silver snake crawling under cottonwood groves.

They were only able to climb on to the top after an "agonizing" jump.

The National Park Service has confirmed that possibly as many as 200 climbs were made to the top by use of the ladder.

The last known ascent employing the ladder was made in 1927 by Babe "The Human Fly" White of San Francisco. He spent two days repairing the structure and, following his climb, recommended the lower stakes be removed to discourage subsequent climbs. The Park Service soon after removed the lower 100 feet of the ladder. The upper 250 feet remains as a monument to the human spirit.

Mrs. William Rogers, the first woman to climb the Tower, 1895 (National Park Service file photo)

Fritz Wiessner belaying Lawrence Covney on 1937 first ascent of the Tower using mountain climbing methods (National Park Service file photo)

A MAGNIFICENT PIECE OF CLIMBING

When Rogers and Ripley climbed the stake ladder in 1893 Devils Tower was solely a rock in the wilderness. They had only to devise a way to climb it and carry out their plan. By the time alpine mountaineering techniques had progressed to the level necessary to ascend the Tower, it had been declared a national monument. This was beneficial in protecting the Tower and a boon for surrounding communities, but a hindrance to Fritz Wiessner and his companions in their attempt to reach the summit.

For nearly two years a round of letters passed between New York, Washington D.C., and Devils Tower National Monument. Wiessner was confident he could make a successful technical ascent, but the National Park Service wanted to be sure that Wiessner's experience and equipment were adequate to ensure safety.

On May 13, 1937, Fritz Wiessner was granted permission for a party of three to attempt the first ascent of the Tower by mountaineering methods.

Wiessner, from New York, brought his companions Lawrence Coveny, also from New York, and William P. House, of Pittsburgh. All three were members of the American Alpine Club. Wiessner had climbed in the Alps, the Himalayas, and the Rocky Mountains of Canada, the United States, and Mexico. Coveny had experience on smaller routes in the East and the Tower would be his first major climb. House had experience in the Alps, the Grand Tetons, and in Mexico. On route to the Tower they stopped in the Needles area of South Dakota and scaled two spires in training for the Devils Tower climb.

Wiessner had proposed the ascent for June 28, 1937. They arrived at the Tower the day before and spent several hours examining the face before choosing an appropriate route.

The three set out at 6:30 the next morning. According to Coveny, they were wearing "ordinary hiking clothes with wool socks and low canvas climbing shoes with heavy hempen soles, which not only gave them sure footing, but allowed them to feel the crevices with their feet. Each climber carried a thirty-five meter safety rope made of the best quality Italian hemp, which is tested to 1-1/2 tons and will stretch twenty to twenty-five feet, thus acting as a cushion to the climber in case of a fall."*

The party scrambled up the talus slope to the base of a wide crack. Wiessner led up a broken column, upon which all three could stand. "Wiessner looked over the crack when we got to the overhanging ledge, and said 'I think it goes,'" said Coveny. "I wasn't so sure, but Wiessner led us up as magnificent a piece of mountain climbing as I have ever seen."

Wiessner used a chimney technique to ascend the wide crack. Coveny later described this lead:

> In the crack Fritz climbed at first with effort, but after some 15 feet all seemed well. A shoulder and elbow, thrust into the crack, provided the friction hold which enabled him to raise a knee. By a turn of the ankle sufficient pressure was maintained with heel, toe and knee to straighten his body upward and again jam shoulder and arm in the crack a few inches higher. He was now climbing rhythmically with his characteristic flawless technique. Only two regular gasps of breath which sounded like the panting of locomotive interrupted the steady cycle of upward movement. A bulge in the edge of the column forced his shoulders back but did not delay him more than a minute. At this point the intensity of preparedness on the part of Bill and myself gave way to spontaneous and complete but soft-spoken admiration. We knew that we were watching an exhibition of leading such as few climbers ever see.*

---

*(Coveny, Lawrence, "Ascent of Devils Tower", Appalachia, 84 December, 1937: 481.)

In the middle of this long crack, Wiessner halted to hammer a piton into a smaller horizontal crack for protection. This was the only preventive measure he employed, but he later admitted the piton was unnecessary and wished he had not placed it. "Every bit of the climb was made under our own power, "Wiessner said. "We used no artificial means whatsoever."

At the end of the chimney, the climbers scrambled to the Meadows and then onto the summit, arriving at 11:18 a.m. The ascent had taken 4 hours, 48 minutes. They spent twenty minutes taking photographs and gathering specimens requested by Superintendent Joyner, including tufts of grass, cactus in full bloom, ferns, small samples of rock, a Mormon cricket, and droppings from a small mammal which was assumed to be chipmunk. They measured the summit area, then built a small cairn to hold a container for their names.

They observed that the summit of the Tower is dome-shaped rather than flat as had previously been believed. They also confirmed that the summit is oval and that the north-south axis is the longer one, as had been surmised by an earlier geological survey team.

Coveny related the descent of the party as follows:

> We took a last view of the panorama and twenty minutes after our arrival began the descent by the same route. From the top of the steep slab, where we had unroped, we began a series of six rappels almost in a straight line to the bottom. When projecting rocks or chockstones made it possible we used ropeslings through which to pass the rope. In other places a piton was driven in and we took precautions against a fouled rope by sacrificing a carabiner on each **piton**.

William House (left), Lawrence Coveny (center), and Fritz Wiessner (National Park Service file photo)

---

* Ibid., p. 483.

The climbers reached the base of the Tower at 1:30 p.m. and Joyner brought them canteens of water. "Three cans of grapefruit juice and orange juice doesn't (sic) go so very far," House said, "but if we had carried up all the water we wanted, we wouldn't have had any strength left to climb the Tower."

All three were visibly proud of their accomplishment and agreed it was a difficult climb. "I wouldn't recommend that anyone except an experienced mountain climber attempt the trip we made," Wiessner admitted. "It is an extremely difficult climb for 200 feet, and to one who does not know mountain climbing it would be practically impossible to reach the top. A serious accident would be very likely to result. There is only one pitch on the north face of the Grand Teton in Wyoming which is as difficult in its way as this crack is on the Devils Tower."

The climb had not been advertised and only a small crowd was present to watch. But among the spectators was Mrs. Alice Heppler whose first husband was Willard Ripley. She was the only person to have witnessed both historic events.

Wiessner donated his climbing shoes, a piton, a carabiner, and a short piece of the climbing rope to the Devils Tower Visitor Center Museum.

AN ISLAND IN THE SKY

On October 1st, 1941, at 8:15 in the morning, Charles George Hopkins, a thirty-year-old former R.A.F. parachute instructor from Oregon known for movie stunt-flying, barn-storming and risky sky-diving, parachuted from a sixty horsepower Aeronca monoplane, and landed on top of Devils Tower. At the time, Hopkins held world records for the most jumps (2,347) and for the longest delayed jump (20,800 feet). In addition, he had broken the American record for the jump from the greatest height in the United States at 26,400 feet.

Park Superintendent Joyner had heard a rumor regarding the stunt on the previous day, "I could not believe that he actually was there instead of at a point beyond until I saw Hopkins standing on the edge." The unscheduled landing was only the first scene of a drama that would capture the imagination of the entire country.

Joyner reportedly yelled up at Hopkins, asking how he planned to get down. "Why worry about that? It is no problem, is it?" he answered.

The Tower jump was heralded as a publicity "stunt" to promote a forthcoming thirty-jump day in Rapid City the following week to win back his recently broken record for the most consecutive jumps in one day. The Rapid City Chamber of Commerce was sponsoring that event and all proceeds were to benefit the Black Hills General Hospital. The media attention, however, was now riveted on the Tower.

Yet why did Hopkins do it? He said he "wanted to let the people know just what a person can do with a parachute if they (sic) really know their parachutes. I had always wanted to get a 'chute so I could prove that I could hit the impossible and this is it and I could do it again."

The Park Service had not granted permission for the jump. To discourage such attention-getting stunts in the future Joyner was ordered to stop all publicity. This proved to be impossible. Earl Brockelsby, who was backing Hopkins, had phoned New York and four hundred radio stations were informed moments after the landing.

Brockelsby detailed the plan to Joyner. Rapid City pilot Joe Quinn had dropped Hopkins from 2,000 feet up and just slightly to the south of the Tower summit. The pilot had then made subsequent passes over the Tower and assistant Jack Gensler had dropped equipment, including a pulley, a sledge hammer, a pin made from a Ford axle sharpened on one end, and one thousand feet of half-inch manila rope.

Hopkins was to take the steel pin, drive it into a crevice, and using the pulley and rope, lower himself over the edge and descend to the base. Knowing nothing of technical climbing, he planned to use a hand-over-hand method. When Gensler tossed the rope from the plane, however, it struck the top of the Tower and bounced, landing on a ledge on the southeastern side.

Hopkins was unable to retrieve it and was stranded. Plans were drawn to effect a rescue.

Quinn had already left for Rapid City and could not be reached. Brockelsby located a Spearfish, South Dakota pilot, Clyde Ice, who arrived at the Tower late in the afternoon and dropped another rope and grappling hook. Hopkins used it to pull up the original rope, but found it hopelessly tangled. George Hopkins resigned himself to a night on the Tower while Clyde Ice dropped blankets and food to him. By six in the evening the weather had turned windy and cloudy, thus preventing further spoken communication between Hopkins and the ground.

"I was up at 5:30 a.m.. The morning was dreary," wrote Joyner on October 2. "Fog was rolling around the top of the Devils Tower. Some moisture fell during the night. I spent a few bad hours until around nine o'clock when Hopkins first appeared. I was fearful that he had fallen victim to exposure."

The wind currents which made conversation impossible also hampered written communication. Hopkins wrote a note and threw it off, only to have it float back up to the top and eventually out of sight. He thought to attach the note to a rock and toss it off. It said:

> Earl or Boyd—Please get enough rope so as it will double so as you folks can lower me from the ground or help, as I feel okay but pretty week (sic) in my arms, thanks for the grub also everything else, sure am causing you lots of trouble aren't I
>
> —"Devils Tower George"

By afternoon he saw the humor in his situation. A second note commenting on goods dropped during the day said, "What, no cross-word puzzle?" and closed with, "Send that blond yet?"

Even before his rescue, Hopkins' plight was the subject of cartoons in journals and magazines across the nation.

Meanwhile, Joyner phoned Superintendent David Canfield of Rocky Mountain National Park and requested a rescue team. Canfield sent park ranger Ernest K. Field and Warren Gorrell, a licensed guide. Pilot Clyde Ice continued to drop supplies including a tent, but a thousand-foot rope rolled off the northwestern face and landed on the talus slope, so George Hopkins made ready to spend, as the RAPID CITY JOURNAL reported, "a second night on his tight little island a quarter of a mile in the Wyoming sky."

That evening Joyner received a telegram from Jack Durrance in New Hampshire, who had led the second ascent of the Tower in 1938. It read, "Unique first descent need any help completing it? Regards." There was agreement on the ground that Durrance's route would be the best for a rescue mission.

Climbers Field and Gorrell from Rocky Mountain National Park drove most of their way in a blizzard. When they arrived on October 3rd the Tower's sides were coated with ice. They looked over the route and were climbing by eleven. Field and Gorrel managed to reach the top of a broken column but found they didn't have the training and experience to climb the next pitch, the most difficult of the route. Moreover, Field had slipped and fallen ten feet before the safety rope had caught him thus bruising his ribs. The two returned late in the evening and admitted they wouldn't be able to complete the climb.

Field persuaded Joyner to take Durrance's offer of help. They realized now that it could be several days before Hopkins' rescue. Durrance was contacted and his

Charles George Hopkins, 1967 (National Park Service file photo)

travel to the Tower was arranged. Joyner questioned a helicopter manufacturing company as to the feasibility of a helicopter rescue.

Expenses were mounting. As the Park Service had not authorized the jump, they wouldn't take financial responsibility. The burden fell on Hopkins' sponsors. Brockelsby wrote the following note to Joyner: "This is to say that I promise to see all expenses paid in connection with the rescue of Charles George Hopkins from the top of Devils Tower saving the Government from all such obligations."

On October 4th, Durrance was en route to Wyoming. Field and Gorrell carried up such equipment and supplies as to help Durrance complete his climb as easily and quickly as possible. They hauled an extension ladder to the top of the broken column, and by four in the afternoon, it was secured in place. This would enable Durrance to pass half of the most difficult pitch, and according to Joyner:

"...would lessen the length of time and the amount of work required when Durrance arrived to lead the climb. The action of Field and Gorrell throughout the balance of the rescue was the greatest display of sportsmanship which I have ever witnessed. Having been hailed as the rescuers and failing to make the climb which they thought could be done without too much difficulty, they whole-heartedly bent every effort toward making the route easier and safer for Durrance."

Durrance telephoned from Chicago in the afternoon. His plane had been grounded due to bad weather, but he would take the train to Denver. Brockelsby made arrangements for getting Durrance from Denver to Devils Tower.

The weather hadn't dampened Hopkins' spirits. He dropped a note directing Brocklesby to "phone my landlady and tell her I still want my room. P.S. If you get a chance, send up my morning paper."

That evening, Joyner received a call from Paul Petzoldt, then guide and climbing instructor in Grand Teton National Park. Petzoldt volunteered to help with the rescue. Joyner explained that Durrance was on his way, thanked him for the offer but discouraged the travel.

On the morning of October 5th, a heavy fog shrouded the Tower. Joyner called through the mist to Hopkins to relay the latest developments. In a note, Hopkins had mentioned the rats and chipmunks on the summit. Joyner asked if he would trap some as scientific specimens. "I did this to provide a diversion for his mind, as well as to take steps to procure specimen that might have scientific value. He told me that he would hate to trap any of those rodents because he had been feeding them and they had become real pets. In this feeling I could sympathize and pressed the matter no further."

Later in the morning, Paul Petzoldt arrived with Grand Teton park ranger Harold Rapp, who at 6'10", went by the nickname "Altitude." They were led to the base where Field and Gorrell were still working on insuring a safe route for Durrance.

National press coverage had brought thousands of sight-seers and reporters. The Highway Patrol and area Boy Scouts steered people away from the base of the Tower and clear of the rescue team's efforts. Joyner later wrote, "Our best estimate of the number of people here that day was 3500. This was in spite of the bad weather. Had the day been fair, I am certain that there would have been at least five times as many visitors."

Letters and telegrams poured into park headquarters from all over the United States offering suggestions on how to get Hopkins down. "Drop Hopkins four quarts of whiskey, get him drunk. Then he'll fall off the edge. The Lord takes care of drunken people." And there were drawings and diagrams of various contraptions. Still others offered to sell their ideas to the Park Service or to rescue Hopkins for a price.

By late afternoon heavy rain and snow moved into the area. Tourists left and the climbers retired for the day. Durrance arrived at the Tower at 11:30 p.m., so Hopkins was stranded for a fifth night.

"We all had a feeling of anticipation in regards to the efforts of Durrance and his party on the following day," recorded Joyner.

Early on October 6, Hopkins "airmailed" a letter to the ground crew:

> Dear Folks: Pardon my fancy stationery, but they are just out of it up here and don't know if they will stock any or not as they don't have many customers especially at this time of the year. Boy, it got so cold up here last night and so dern dreary with all that fog I would have gladly settled for a brunette or even a red head.
>
> All I worry about is someone getting hurt trying to help me, and I don't want that to happen. If I had realized how much it was putting everyone out, you can bet your bottom dollar I wouldn't have landed here, but I wanted to prove you can do damn near anything with a 'chute if you had someone that knew them—so here I am. Hope to see you all.
>
> "Devils Tower George"

Snow flurries slowed the start of the rescue climb, but by 7:30 in the morning, the team set out with Jack Durrance in charge. The team included Petzoldt, Rapp, Feild, Gorrell, Merrill McLane (a Dartmouth student with Durrance), Chappell Cranmer, and Henry Coulter, both friends of Durrance who had joined him in

Opposite: Hopkins's rescue party around model of the Tower (Black Hills Studios photo)

Hopkins's rescue made headlines across the country (Black Hills Studios photo)

Denver. When the sun appeared at 11:00, Durrance had just topped the crux pitch and the climb was completed without incident.

Joyner herein recounts the climb:

> Durrance led the climb most of the way, except for two short stretches which Petzoldt led. All eight climbers had reached the shoulder about three o'clock and at 3:15 Durrance and Petzoldt, with former leading, reached the top of the Devils Tower and shook hands with Hopkins. Soon thereafter there were nine men on top. "House cleaning" was had and such supplies and equipment as could be brought down without hazard were bundled together and started down the side. One package lodged while the parachute and a roll containing bedding, etc., reached the bottom of the columnar portion and were retrieved the following day. The balance of the supplies were cached under rocks to relieve the unsightliness. I agree with the decision to dispose of them in this manner for time was becoming an important element at this stage in operations.

And from Hopkins' point of view:

> I heard the climbers making their way slowly up the sides. I wasn't able to see them until they were within seventy-five feet of me. Durrance stopped several feet below me and waited out of reach. He talked with me and I knew he was looking me over carefully, trying to decide whether I was going to lose my head at the thought of being rescued. When he was satisfied I was completely rational, he came over the top. That was the greatest moment! I knew for the first time I was really safe!

Joyner continues:

> The descent of the men was started at 4:35 p.m.. Petzoldt came down first on the entire route and Durrance came down last. Hopkins had no experience in mountain climbing or rappelling (sic); but the climbers were high in their praise of the alacrity with which he took to it, and by the time he reached the bottom he was causing them no more concern than another member of the party.

The sun set at approximately 6:00, and floodlights from trucks lighted the rest of the descent. They were safely down by 8:20.

More observations from Joyner's files reveal:

> Hopkins' condition was remarkable, I believe, in view of the hazards which he could not escape. The wind blew continuously; he was unprotected from the weather except such protection as he could get on the lee side of a small boulder; his blankets were sopping wet; he had gotten little rest or sleep; and he had had very little drinking water. It is my belief that a normal person would have been affected by the thought of being marooned, but Hopkins' nature is such as to make him take things as they come...

The rescue had taken six days to organize, during which Clyde Ice had made 73 drops from his airplane to Hopkins. The climbers had collectively traveled 16,000 miles, and expenses of approximately $2,000 were incurred.

On the following morning, the crowds dispersed, reporters packed up their equipment to go write their stories, and the climbers departed for their respective schools, work, and families. "Devils Tower George" and Joyner drove to Sundance for an interview with NBC. Hopkins then proceeded to Rapid City to prepare for his parachuting engagement. As it happened, he was forced to abort his thirty-jump attempt after the thirteenth bail-out because of a sore ankle and bruises.

Newell Joyner returned to his headquarters at Devils Tower to document the incredible event for the U.S. Department of the Interior. It began, "One Charles George Hopkins landed on the top of Devils Tower by parachute from a plane at 8:11 a.m. October 1, 1941. Such an occurrence, with its manly ramifications, surely calls for a special report which is presented herewith." He continued for twenty single-spaced, typewritten pages.

After World War II, Hopkins operated a small airport in California and flew for the Mexican Federal Police. He died in 1977. "They made a great fuss over getting me down," he once mused, "when the real feat was landing on Devils Tower."

CONCLUSION

Many visitors pose the inevitable question, "How many have lost their lives climbing the Tower?" The answer at the time of this writing is only one, although there have been many injuries. All things considered, it is thought to be a relatively safe climb.

But to the Tower itself, such hubris as Hopkins' would no doubt seem as inconsequential as so many snowflakes that manage to "land" on its summit. So, too, must climbers' efforts and conquests be tempered with a proper humility and regard. If George Hopkins had shown a certain respect for the nature of the Tower and its descent, perhaps he wouldn't have been stranded on its summit six days.

As a rule, climbers are exceptionally conscientious regarding their discipline. They bring to it a large measure of personal integrity and heart. At no time is life more precious than when it is in danger of being snuffed out. It concentrates the mind wonderfully, to paraphrase the poet Samuel Johnson.

However glib it may sound, simply because the Tower is just "there" may indeed answer the question, "why climb it?" Reasons often trivialize "The Reason."

So, may we "pause for a moment in reflection on this royal member of the world's prodigious marvels... and realize," as Nora Neeley of Gillette, Wyoming did as she wrote, "that it is more than a National Monument, as we view it resting in silent solemnity..."

It bespeaks volumes.

Opposite: Lightning on Devils Tower (Bob Kolbrener photo)

PART THREE

CLIMBER INFORMATION

1. For The Climber

The sport of rock climbing at Devils Tower is becoming increasingly popular. In the past several years, over 6,000 climbers have annually registered to climb here. With this popularity, regulations become essential in order to protect climbers, the general public, and our most important resource, the Tower itself. We ask that all climbers act responsibly and obey park regulations. Climbers are advised to check with monument personnel for updated regulations.

The goal of park management is to provide for your use while leaving this special resource unimpaired for generations to come.

2. Registration

All persons planning to climb or scramble above the boulder field are required to register at the Visitor Center or designated place. When registering there is a sample to assist you in filling out the registry card. When you finish your climb you must sign back in before leaving. A register board containing blank cards and a check-in-sheet is located outside after hours. Inquire about parking and special regulations when registering.

3. Devils Tower Climbing Regulations

A. Special regulations exist for use of drills, bolts, and pitons.
B. Leaving fixed ropes unattended on the Tower is prohibited. Pull your ropes when finished climbing for the day.
C. Overnight camping is prohibited on the Tower. Camping is permitted in the Belle Fourche Campground.
D. Chipping holds, gardening, gluing holds, and excessive route cleaning is prohibited. Leave the rock as you found it.
E. Pets are not permitted on any trail or in any undeveloped area of the park, which includes all climbing areas. Leaving a pet unattended and tied to an object, such as a vehicle is prohibited.
E. Observe seasonal climbing route closures posted at the visitor center.

Opposite: Beth Wald climbing on the first free ascent of "Let Me Go Wild," August 15, 1984

4. Tips for Minimum Impact Climbing

The top of the Tower is a fragile environment and is easily degraded by foot traffic. You can minimize your impact by stepping on rocks rather than the plants or soil at the top, not dragging ropes, and by watching where you set down and place your gear. Approach routes have been consolidated to minimize impacts. Check at the Visitor Center for the best approach to the climb you have chosen. You can help control erosion by staying on the switchbacks. There is no litter pickup on the Tower. Please pack out all litter.

If you are forced to leave webbing on the Tower, leave neutral colored webbing such as gray, brown, etc. Do not leave brightly colored webbing such as orange, red, pink, white, etc. Leave webbing that blends in with the rock, and will not be visible to visitors on the ground.

Minimize your use of chalk.

Practice minimum impact climbing. Leave no trace of your visit.

5. A Word of Caution

Rescue: The National Park Service does not maintain a rescue team at Devils Tower. Plan for self rescue or assistance from other climbers should an unexpected incident arise.

Available Park staff will assist to the limits of their ability. Response to an incident may be several hours or longer.

Injury: The closest medical facility that can treat significant trauma is 60 miles from the Tower. Caution should dictate your actions while climbing.

Weather: Storms come up quickly, posing a danger from slippery rock or lightning, as well as hypothermia. Carefully observe weather conditions and obtain forecast information before climbing. During dry weather dehydration is common; carry plenty of water.

Rappelling: Accidents and "epics" at Devils Tower are often associated with rappelling. The National Park Service does not maintain bolts installed by climbers; inspect all anchors and back them up if you feel they are inadequate.

Make sure you know where your rappel route is located. Devils Tower eats ropes: Always rappel over the nose of a column and take extreme care when pulling the rope, not to jam it into a crack. Avoid knocking off loose rock when pulling ropes.

Other Hazards: Be prepared for snakes, spiny plants, falcon attacks, wasps, and falling rocks while climbing on the Tower. Significant hazards should be reported to a Ranger so future climbers can be warned of the situation.

Safety: Due to danger of rockfall on many routes and rappels, helmets are recommended. In addition, carry a small flashlight. Many climbers have become stranded on the Tower due to darkness.

GENERAL INFORMATION

Climbers need to plan on adequate time (four to nine hours for most routes) in order to avoid being caught by nightfall. Plenty of water should be carried for the party (1 to 2 quarts per person) as well as rain gear in the summer months.

Weather should always be considered as an element in climbing at Devils Tower. Occasionally, violent thundershowers, lightning, hail, or high winds may be encountered. Afternoon showers are common and even a short shower can make the rock slick because lichen growing on the rock absorbs the water. This can instantly add one or two grades to the climbing difficulty.

Most locals consider late spring through early November to be the best times to climb. July and August are often very hot and unpleasant for long climbs. Mild winters in some years have found climbers making ascents in all months, although January and February are usually too cold.

The rock at Devils Tower is phonolite porphory. It is solid and could be compared in hardness to Teton or Yosemite granite. Although some loose rock may be found in the upper sections, holds are generally secure and only occasionally break off. Care should be taken when working on column tops where loose rock and debris accumulate. Rockfall from above also poses a danger at any time and helmets are recommended. Some of the approaches to the routes are high and exposed and climbers may wish to use ropes as needed.

Climbing Devils Tower entails risks that every climber must be aware of and respect. The fact that a route is described in this book is not an assurance that it will be safe for you. All routes are potentially dangerous.

You can minimize your risks by being knowledgeable, prepared and alert. There are a number of good books and public courses on climbing to increase your knowledge and experience. You should always be aware of your own limitations and the existing conditions. If conditions are unfavorable, or if you are not prepared to safely deal with them, change your plans! It is better to have wasted a few hours or days than to be the subject of a bad fall or rescue. Large numbers of people do climb Devils Tower each year with much joy and no injuries, however climbers have been seriously injured here and as of this writing there has been one climbing fatality. If you do climb, please exercise common sense and good judgement.

There are climbing guide services licensed to operate in the monument. You may get information on them from rangers or write the monument.

In rating each climb, the free rating is used in place of any aid rating that may have previously existed. The difficulty ratings of climbs at Devils Tower are usually the result of a consensus by expert climbers and seem to be fairly consistent. For example, one route rated 5.9 should be close in difficulty to another 5.9 route. In some cases, minor disagreement over a particular rating was present among local climbers and in these few cases the higher rating is given in the interest of safety. It is recommended that climbers new to the area start out conservatively.

Some climbers come to Devils Tower to work on their aid climbing techniques, and several good routes exist for this. In order to preserve the nature of the route and the rock, do not drive pitons into aid routes that have been climbed free. Use nuts, RPs, etc. that will not scar the rock. Pitons are rarely used at the Tower as they may cause damage to the rock. The National Park Service has sixteen-by-twenty-inch black and white photos with free- and aid-climbing routes shown on them at the visitor center. Contact a ranger if you have any questions.

A poison ivy crop grows in cracks and on several of the larger ledges, notably beneath The Window and on the northeast and northwest Buttress Approaches. Avoid dragging ropes and other equipment through these areas. Rattlesnakes are commonly found on the talus slopes near the base of the Tower.

The following information may be helpful to the reader. The routes are numbered from left to right on the photographs in a counterclockwise circle around the Tower. The identifying number for each route has generally been placed to the left of the route or directly on the route line where feasible. From photograph to photograph there is an overlap generally of one or more routes to make it easier to aid in the location of climbs.

Due to the crumbly nature of the rock near the summit, the original final pitch to a handful of routes may be unclear or a route may have more than one final pitch. Where possible the original or most popular final pitch has been given.

The terms route, pitch, and climb are used loosely in this book. The description of any route may vary from the first ascent, as other climbers add their descriptions. The National Park Service updates the route descriptions periodically, as more accurate information is received. Anyone with additional information or corrections regarding routes at Devils Tower is asked to submit written comments to: Devils Tower National Monument, P.O. Box 10, Devils Tower, WY 82714. You may also write to this address for information or call (307) 467-5283.

RATINGS OF ROUTES

Ratings of climbs represent a consensus of the climbers who have climbed the route. External factors such as weather can change that rating dramatically. The Roman numeral grading represents the approximate time element involved in a climb. The categories are:

    Grade I—a short climb of less than two hours.
    Grade II—a slightly longer climb of two to four hours.
    Grade III—a climb of four to eight hours.
    Grade IV—a long climb requiring eight to twelve hours.
    Grade V—a two day climb requiring an overnight stay.
    Grade VI—a multi-day climb.

The free routes at Devils Tower are rated by the Yosemite Decimal System. The numbers of that system represent the degree of difficulty presented by the terrain. The six classes are as follows:

    Class 1— walking on level ground.
    Class 2— off-trail walking with some uphill and light scrambling.
    Class 3— scrambling that includes the use of the hands for support and balance.
    Class 4— Scrambling that demands a rope for protection against exposure, but intermediate points of protection are not used.
    Class 5— technical rock climbing using ropes and intermediate protection.
    Class 6— direct aid climbing in which the leader uses the pieces of protection for support and advancement.

Climbers familiar with the Yosemite Decimal System will have little trouble interpreting the ratings for whole climbs or individual pitches. Others, who come from areas using other rating systems may find the following conversion scale helpful in interpreting a difficulty rating for fifth class climbs.

DECIMAL	UIAA	ENGLISH	FRENCH	AUSTRALIAN
5.0	III	MODERATE		4
5.1	III+	DIFFICULT		5
5.2	IV-	HARD DIFFICULT		6
5.3	IV	VERY DIFFICULT		7
5.4	IV+	HARD, VERY DIFFICULT		8, 9
5.5	V-	MILD SEVERE		10, 11
5.6	V	4a	4c	12, 13
5.7	V+	4b	5a	14, 15
5.8	VI-	4c	5b	16
5.9	VI	5a	5c	17
5.10a	VI+	5b	6a	18
5.10b	VII-	5b	6a	19
5.10c	VII	5c	6b	20
5.10d		5c	6b	21
	VII+			
5.11a		6a	6c	22
5.11b		6a	6c	23
	VIII-			
5.11c		6b	7a	24
	VIII			
5.11d		6b	7a	25
	VIII+			
5.12a		6c	7b	26
	IX-			
5.12b		6c	7b	27
	IX			
5.12c		7a	7c	28
	IX+			
5.12d		7a	7c	29
	X-			
5.13a		7b	7c	30
	X			
5.13b		7b	8a	31
	X+			
5.13c			8a	
5.13d			8a	
5.14a			8b	33
5.14b			8c	
5.14c			8c+	
5.14d				

Climbers must be reminded that ratings are subjective. At best, ratings are an approximation of difficulty, but they are influenced by many factors. For example, the routes at Devils Tower are mostly crack climbs. A climber who has trained in other crack-climbing areas might find a given route very easy and straightforward, while a climber from a face-climbing region might find the same route an impossible task.

Each route is generally given a rating by the first ascent party at the time of the first ascent. The Yosemite Decimal System has not been a static one. When it was designed, 5.9 was intended to be the hardest climb humanly possible. Eventually there were climbs rated 5.9 that were much harder than others rated 5.9; and 5.10 and other classifications were created. Thus, routes that were originally rated 5.9 (because there was no alternative) may be 5.10 or harder by today's standards.

As the Yosemite Decimal System developed, finer gradations than the numerical values developed and merit mention here. While the limit of technical rock climbing remained at 5.9, many climbers added a plus/minus rating. In this book there are examples of routes rated 5.8+ or 5.9-. This should be interpreted to mean that a route overall deserved a given rating, but certain factors colored the tone of that rating. A 5.8+ route should be seen as a difficult 5.8 route that may have a move or two that might be interpreted as 5.9.

As the system developed through 5.10, 5.11, 5.12, 5.13, and now 5.14, the plus/minus system seemed to fade out and another method emerged. Climbers wishing to distinguish between 5.10 climbs attached an additional a, b, c, or d rating following the 5.10. For example, a 5.10a climb would be the easiest climb that could still be rated 5.10. A 5.10d climb would be the hardest rated 5.10 and might, by a different climber, receive a 5.11 rating.

Direct aid climbing routes are rated on a scale of A1 to A5 with the easiest aid climb being A1 and the hardest being A5. The most difficult aid rating at Devils Tower is A4, The Window route. Most aid routes on the Tower are a combination of aid climbing and free climbing and thus will have two ratings (for example, 5.7, A2) in addition to the Roman numeral grades. There are several systems of rating/grading climbs in local areas and around the world that have not been noted in this book.

As with records and standards in any sport, the rating system for technical climbing may continue to expand, reflecting the quality of the participants and the ever-increasing difficulty of the routes they complete.

CLIMBING STATISTICS

Devils Tower is unique in that all climbing is done in one area and the Park Service has been able to record historical data with a high degree of accuracy. Monument records contain information about most ascents since Weissner in 1937. A quick look at such information is interesting and shows the growth of climbing as a sport and of the popularity of Devils Tower as a climber's destination. All the numbers below reflect climbs to the summit by year.

YEAR	YEARLY PARTIES	YEARLY CLIMBERS	ALL-TIME PARTIES	ALL-TIME CLIMBERS
1937	1	3	1	3
1938	1	2	2	5
1939	0	0	2	5
1940	0	0	2	5
1941	2	10	4	15
1942	0	0	4	15
1943	0	0	4	15
1944	0	0	4	15

YEAR	YEARLY PARTIES	YEARLY CLIMBERS	ALL-TIME PARTIES	ALL-TIME CLIMBERS
1945	0	0	4	15
1946	1	2	5	17
1947	1	2	6	19
1948	2	18	8	37
1949	3	20	11	57
1950	1	2	12	59
1951	5	13	17	72
1952	7	19	24	91
1953	8	27	32	118
1954	12	42	44	160
1955	5	17	49	177
1956	53	158	102	335
1957	11	46	113	381
1958	42	143	155	524
1959	32	119	187	643
1960	42	104	229	747
1961	50	123	279	870
1962	55	128	334	998
1963	36	92	370	1090
1964	75	187	445	1277
1965	48	119	493	1396
1966	33	100	526	1496
1967	51	134	577	1630
1968	53	136	630	1766
1969	71	184	701	1950
1970	82	216	783	2166
1971	103	297	886	2463
1972	138	357	1024	2820
1973	121	312	1145	3132
1974	164	424	1309	3556
1975	183	494	1492	4050
1976	308	774	1800	4824
1977	445	1098	2245	5922
1978	657	1638	2902	7560
1979	805	1969	3707	9529
1980	701	1754	4408	11283
1981	667	1624	5075	12907
1982	428	1277	5503	14184
1983	617	1621	6120	15805
1984	629	1266	6749	17071
1985	648	1591	7397	18662
1986	618	1477	8015	20139
1987	627	1569	8642	21708
1988	671	1675	9313	23383
1989	751	1879	10064	25262
1990	682	1688	10746	26950
1991	786	1694	11532	28644
1992	813	2017	12345	30661
1993		2192		32853
1994		2108		34961

Only in 1974 did the National Park Service start keeping records of non-summit climbers and climbs.

YEAR	NON-SUMMIT CLIMBERS	TOTAL CLIMBERS
1974	88	88
1975	117	205
1976	168	373
1977	183	556
1978	532	1088
1979	659	1747
1980	1053	2800
1981	1700	4500
1982	1753	6253
1983	1995	8248
1984	1870	10118
1985	2625	12743
1986	3301	16044
1987	3303	19347
1988	4334	23681
1989	4283	27964
1990	3694	31658
1991	3727	35385
1992	4097	39482
1993	3900	43382
1994	3927	47311

From June 1937, through August 1992, the following number of registered climbers have climbed these popular routes:

ROUTE NAME	TOTAL CLIMBERS
Durrance	16,810
Soler	4,435
Tad	3,507
Walt Bailey	3,246
New Wave	2,175
El Matador	2,051
Hollywood and Vine	1,930
Assembly Line	1,924
El Cracko Diablo	1,892
Bon Homme	1,656
Tulgey Wood	1,582
Bon Homme Variation	1,121
Belle Fourche Buttress	1,120
McCarthy West Face	1,111
One-way Sunset	1,094

NOTE: The park's figures are probably off for Bon Homme and the Bon Homme Variation. This is because most climbers just sign in for Bon Homme when they do the Horning Variation and this is by far the most popular of the two climbs. Very few climbers do the original route today (Guilmette).

APPROACHES TO THE ROUTES

All approaches leave from the visitor center parking lot.

1. **Durrance Approach**—Take the right fork of the Tower Trail heading east to the end of the first boulder field by the pine trees on your left. Climb the talus angling to the left of the obvious slab to the base of the Tower below the McCarthy West Face Route. From there scramble up and right to a large broken column which leads to the southwest shoulder. Traverse this shoulder to the right staying near the outer edge all the way around. At the end of the shoulder scramble up to the base of the Leaning Column. Several parts of this approach are quite exposed (traversing below the southwest buttress and also the friction slab below the leaning column) and some climbers choose to rope up for parts of it.

2. **South Face Approach**—Turn right at the fork in the Tower Trail and go east, circling around the Tower until you are directly below the Wiessner Route in

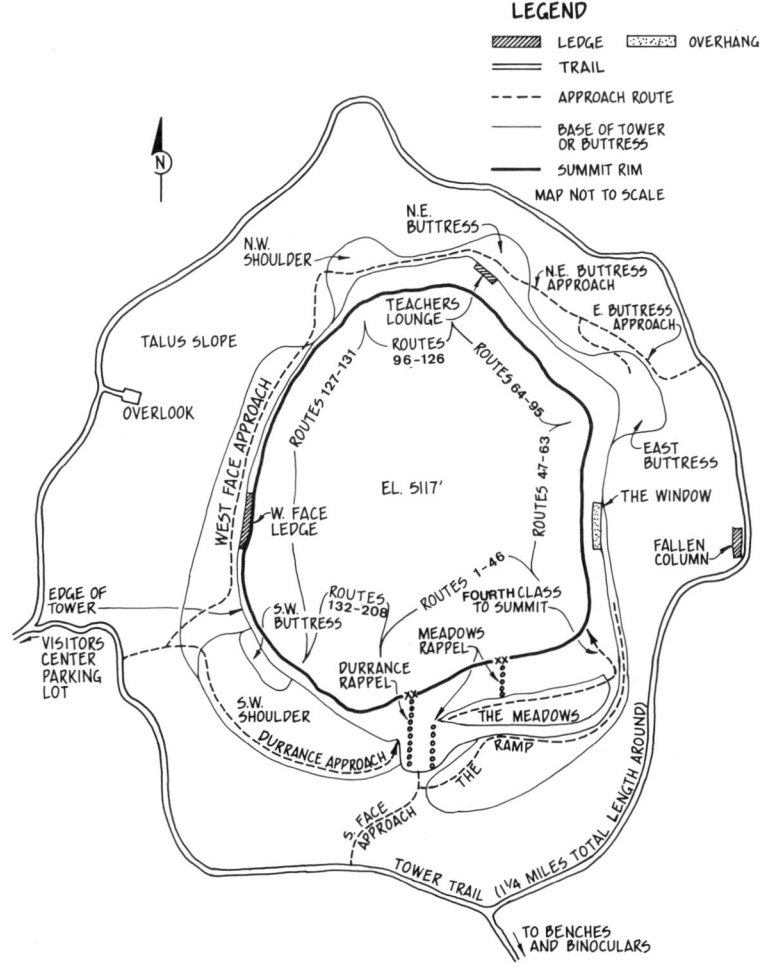

the main indentation (Bowling Alley) on the South Face. At this point you will be just short of the trail junction to the binoculars. Leave the trail at the sighting tube for the historic stake ladder and follow the climbers trail up to the rock. From here climb up to the base of the Meadows Rappel. Beware of rockfall. Helmets are recommended.

3. **The Ramp**—At the top of the South Face Approach, look slightly up and right and see a long ledge leading east. Follow this ledge for 100 feet where, just after a large flake, there is an obvious corner junction. Climbing up and left of this corner leads to Bon Homme and the stake ladder area. To continue up the Ramp, drop 8 feet and pass the corner. Just beyond the corner the angle of the Ramp steepens for 120 feet until you climb over a large flake. From there drop down and around the corner to the ledge beneath Soler, TAD, and El Cracko Diablo. The narrow ledge continues descending around one more corner where it becomes the large shelf beneath Beelzebub and The Window.

4. **East Buttress Approach**—Take the right fork of the Tower Trail and continue past The Window to a large fallen column beside the trail. Go 150 feet past the column to a faint trail on the left that starts up a shallow gully where you will be directly beneath the East Buttress. Stay on the trail which improves and climb up the right side of the shallow gully to the base of the buttresses. From this constriction traverse up and left to the top of the Buttress. Poison ivy thrives above the constriction.

5. **Northeast Buttress Approach**—Follow the East Buttress Approach to the constriction and traverse up and right until you reach the top of the Northeast Buttress below the Teacher's Lounge Ledge. The buttress may be followed west to the Northwest Buttress beneath the Northwest Corner Route.

6. **West Face Approach**—Leave the Tower Trail the same as for the Durrance Approach. At the top of the talus slope where it meets the trees, traverse up and left to the sloping shoulder which may be followed all the way to the northwest corner of the tower.

STANDARD MEADOWS FINISH

Once you reach the Meadows you will be able to pick up a well-worn trail on the upper edge of the Meadows that runs east and west. Follow the trail to the right (east) to a point where it narrows and enters a small notch formed by the cliff face and a boulder. Downclimb five feet through the notch, traverse right a few feet and then climb up over large chockstones. An obvious chimney leads up 140 feet to a face just below the summit. Climb up and right across this face to where you can easily walk up to the summit. A short walk leads to the actual summit cairn where a register is located in a metal container.

Though the climb is not difficult, exposure is encountered, and it is recommended that you fourth class (use a rope) this section as a fall here could be very serious or fatal.

RAPPEL ROUTES

Summit Rappels

There are three standard routes of descent from the summit of Devils Tower. All three routes are marked by cairns on the south side of the summit dome.

While you are looking south from the top center of the Tower, the cairn on your right (southwest) marks a set of rappel bolts which may be reached by downclimbing 15 feet to a ledge. From the bolts, look down and note that you can throw your rope well to the left or down right. By throwing your ropes (need two) left (as you face out) it is possible to rappel down to the west end of the Meadows beside the Jump Traverse and above the Meadows Rappel bolts. By throwing your ropes (need two) straight down or right, you will land at the bolts on the ledge above Pitch 5 (chockstone) of the Durrance route (separated from the Meadows by the Jump Traverse). It is possible to rappel from here down to the ground on the Durrance route with a single rope, but this is strongly discouraged because there is often a party of climbers on the Durrance route with the resultant danger of rockfall to them.

A second method of leaving the summit is from the middle cairn. Rappel bolts are found several feet below this cairn and a rappel from here (with two ropes) will place you in the middle of the Meadows.

The third method of descent is marked by the left or easternmost cairn (as you look from the summit). This is the top of the Standard Meadows Finish and climbers sometimes downclimb to the Meadows (third or fourth class, very exposed).

Meadows Rappel

From the Meadows, two rappel routes have become standard. The first is found at the west end of the Meadows on a ledge some 25 feet below the spot where a fallen column forms a tunnel. If you climb the Durrance route, stop on the top of Pitch 5 (chockstone). Looking across the Jump Traverse and slightly down and to your right, you will see the bolts for descent. This route requires two ropes as the rappels average 140 feet.

Throw your ropes directly out over the nose of a large ledge below these bolts and be sure to place your rope on a flat section about two feet wide as you rappel down the nose. Many rescues come about because rappel ropes slide into the left or right crack and the knot gets stuck there when the ropes are being pulled down and the climbers are unable or unwilling to climb to the top to free the rope. With the ropes on the flat of the nose this should not happen. The next bolts are directly below you on the shorter of the two column tops.

Rappel straight down the column and the next bolts will be found on a ledge just above a large tree and about 30 feet below where the column turns into the blocky base of the Tower.

One more rappel leads to the base of the vertical and the South Face Approach may be used in reverse to return to the Tower Trail and Visitor Center.

It is advisable to wear helmets on this rappel as anything dropped or knocked loose from above funnels down this chute and could be very dangerous.

Bon Homme Rappel

The other rappel route from the Meadows is on the Bon Homme route. Four rappel stations exist so a two-pitch rappel on two ropes or a four-pitch rappel on one rope may be used.

To locate the top of this rappel, follow the trail in the Meadows to the west to a point where it climbs steeply up to the column forming the tunnel. Instead of climbing up, stay level and approach a large boulder. Downclimb from here to find the bolts. There can be some difficulty and exposure here so you may want to use a rope to reach the bolts which are just above the vertical cliff.

Rappel straight off the ledge (go off the nose as these cracks snag ropes) and note a column top below you. For a single rope, stop at the bolts at the column top. For a double rope, rappel down the right side of this column (facing in) and land on a boxed-in column top below. Stand on the left (west side) of the column top. Pull the rope down (because pulling from the right side often causes the rope to slide into the right crack which snags as many ropes as it releases). Also be sure the rope is over the nose above, and not off to the left or right, before you start to pull.

As you rappel from this boxed-in column top, leave your ropes on the left (west) side as far as possible. For a single rope, stop at the hanging belay bolts halfway down the face and just above a pointed flake affectionately known as the Rope Eater. Rappel to the bottom and pull your rope from a tree at the left (west) end of the ledge. If using double ropes, make sure your ropes will reach and be extra **careful not to go off the end of your rappel ropes as you end up on some steep rock.**

Meadows rappel route (Dick Guilmette)

Downclimb (not recommended if wet) third or fourth class for about 50 feet to meet The Ramp. You could also set up a rappel on your own gear to rappel to The Ramp. Traverse west and down to the base of the Meadows Rappel, and again reverse the South Face Approach to reach the Tower Trail.

NOTE: Though these rappel routes are frequently used, they are not to be considered safe. All climbers are responsible for their own safety and should examine, but not strike, rappel anchors. If climbers do not like an anchor, they should place their own protection and not use anything with which they are not fully satisfied.

POPULAR AND RECOMMENDED CLIMBS

RATING	ROUTE, CLIMB, OR PITCH
5.7	Durrance
	New Wave (Pitch 1)
	Roach Addition
	Tad
5.8.	Bon Homme (Horning Variation)
	El Cracko Diablo
	El Matador (Pitch 1)
	Everlasting (Pitch 1)
	McCarthy North Face (Pitch 1)
5.9	Assembly Line
	McCarthy West Face (Pitch 1)
	Soler
	Walt Bailey Memorial
5.10a	Carol's Crack (Pitch 1)
	Klondike
	New Wave
	Tulgey Wood
5.10b	Belle Fourche Buttress
	Burning Daylight
	Jerry's Kids
	McCarthy West Face (Free Variation)
5.10c	Dusk In Dogtown
	Everlasting
	Hollywood And Vine
	One Way Sunset
5.10d	Back To Montana
	Casper College
	El Matador
	Soaring
	Spank The Monkey
5.11a	Carol's Crack
	McCarthy North Face
	Mr. Clean
	No Holds For Bonzo
	Way Layed
5.11b	Black Jones Direct
	California Dreaming
	Dedicated To The Game
	Direct Southwest
	Solar Eclipse

5.11c	McCarthy West Face
	McCarthy West Face (Hong Variation)
	Refractal
	Spiney Norman
5.11d	Avalon
	Bloodguard
	Deli Express
	Digital Extraction
	Direct Southeast
	Maid In The Shaid
5.12a	Adrenalin Surfer
	Brokedown Palace
5.12b	Let Me Go Wild
	Tunnel Vision
5.12c	Space Challenger
	Surfer Girl
5.12d	Good Holds For Godzilla
5.13	Mystery Express
A1	Zephyr
A2	Misty Morning Melody
A3	Blade City
	Centennial
A4	The Window

First ascent of Potatoes Alien (Route 102), 1985, with Mateo Pee Pee leading and Barney Fisher belaying (Dick Guilmette photo)

54

ROUTE DESCRIPTIONS

NORTHEAST CORNER: III, 5.7, A3

FIRST ASCENT: June 2, 1984, by Dean Moore and Paul Stettner.
APPROACH: Take the Northeast Buttress Approach until you are below the Teacher's Lounge Ledge.
EXPLANATION: There is more than a little confusion as to the exact location of this aid route. Park Service records and recent contact with one of the original party could not nail the route down definitely. Contact with knowledgeable climbers has not helped either. The description by Rypkema and Haire in their book "A Climbers Guide to Devils Tower National Monument" is as good as can be expected under the circumstances but could be off by one crack left or right. From the belay point above Teacher's Lounge, Rypkema and Haire indicate on their route photo, page 42, that the route goes up and right. Their description on their pitch #4 page 58 and park records and phone conversations with one of the original climbers indicates they went left. The following route list comes from the park records and is the same as the Rypkema and Haire description.
PITCH 1: Climb, bushwhack and climb about 120 feet up a feasible crack to a good belay ledge. This is past a large flake (120 feet, 5.4). **PITCH 2:** From your belay, traverse left about three feet to a parallel crack, avoiding bushes and climb straight up to a belay ledge just below and to the right of an overhang (75 feet, 5.3).
PITCH 3: Move into the crack on your right and climb about 85 feet on aid until the crack gets bad. Then move into the next crack left and set up a hanging belay (95 feet, A3). **PITCH 4:** Continue up this crack on aid until you reach a good ledge just below an overhang on your left. Move across this ledge and the column next to it and belay from the top of a protruding column (80 feet, 5.6, A2). **PITCH 5:** A scramble leads to the summit (150 feet, 5.6).
SUGGESTED EQUIPMENT: A wide selection including many blades, small and standard angles, and a few bongs.

M&CWTC: #5: (Old Army Aid Route)

FIRST ASCENT: July 16, 1956 (Exact army climber unknown).
EXPLANATION; Monument records show a drawing of this route and date but the sketch is not accurate enough to be absolutely certain of the route's location. It looks like they first went up one crack left of the Wiessner Column to the column top that ends the first pitch of Wiessner (Route 7). From here it shows a pendulum (one or more) across several columns to the right. This includes traversing right one crack past what is shown as "MTC 1" (probably M&CWTC #1) then climbing up to a belay above. From here the sketch shows them climbing up a short distance and then traversing right one column and climbing up to the Meadows from here. This last portion maybe the present "Path of Dissent" (Route 12).
NOTE: The unnumbered routes in this book are included for historical accuracy and completeness. Evidence of each climb exists, and each route is included in topographical order, but a number is not assigned since not enough detail is available to include the route on a photograph or in a written description.
NOTE: M&CWTC #7 was most likely done earlier on part or much of this route. Both of these routes are not shown on our photo plots due to uncertainty. Most feel the route is two cracks west or right of Assembly Line (Route 91) which is the free climb Surfer Girl (Route 92).

M&CWTC #3 AND #4.

FIRST ASCENT: July 12, 1956, by Cecil M. Ouellette and Charles Kness (M&CWTC #3).

FIRST ASCENT: July 14, 1956, by Marcus Russi and John Callahan (M&CWTC #4).
EXPLANATION: These routes are/were located in the Durrance (Route 1) - Sundance (Route 5) area and the Path of Dissent (Route 12) area. Very little is known about the exact route locations, therefore they are not described or located on photos. The M&CWTC stands for the "Mountain and Cold Weather Training Command". These climbs were done as part of a public demonstration by the military out of Colorado.
NOTE: The unnumbered routes in this book are included for historical accuracy and completeness. Evidence of each climb exists, and each route is included in topographical order, but a number is not assigned since not enough detail is available to include the route on a photograph or in a written description.

1. DURRANCE: II, 5.7

FIRST ASCENT: September 8, 1938, by Jack Durrance and Harrison Butterworth. Approach: Take the Durrance Approach.
PITCH 1: Leaning Column. Climb the face and obvious crack until you can get behind the left side of the column where it breaks. From here work up behind the column or stem up the side. There are fixed pins in this section (80 feet, 5.6).
PITCH 2: Durrance Crack. Jam the right crack while stemming over to the left crack most of the time and moving over into the right crack near the top. Nuts can be secured in the left crack. There is a good chock stone partway up the right side (72 feet, 5.7). **PITCH 3:** Cussing Crack. Climb up the outside of the crack a few feet and you will find a good spot for two #4 wired stoppers on the left. Then finish the chimney to a good narrow ledge that can be traversed around to the right. Climb up a few feet to the bolts via a good crack (30 feet, 5.5). **PITCH 4:** Flake Crack. Climb the corner crack and face to the top of the pitch onto a large ledge. (40 feet, 5.5) You can take the Conn Traverse from here by a long step onto the face of the right column, down a crack 12 feet onto a platform and up the other side to the Meadows and finish on the Standard Meadows Finish. **PITCH 5:** Chockstone Crack. Chimney up the large crack, passing a chockstone and overhang near the top (40 feet, 5.4). **PITCH 6:** Jump Traverse. Move out to the right on the down sloping slab beneath the overhang, swing left around the corner then step across to the other side. Jumping is not recommended. An old piton around the corner and a small horizontal finger crack facilitate the crossing (15 feet, 5.6 if you hold onto the piton and 5.8 if free climbed).
FINISH: Standard Meadows Finish.
SUGGESTED EQUIPMENT: Medium to large Hexcentrics, Stoppers, Friends and runners.
NOTE: Historically this has been given a 5.6 rating of difficulty but due to the sustained nature of the climb is rated 5.7. There are heavy duty eye bolts at each belay. Pitch 1 and 2 can be combined as can Pitch 3 and 4, but most climbers belay at each column top. If you free the Jump Traverse, the rating of this climb is 5.8. This is a three star classic route.

2. PIGEON ENGLISH: II, 5.9-

FIRST ASCENT: April 14, 1984, by Paul Piana and Bill Hatcher.
APPROACH: Complete the Durrance Approach to the base of the Leaning Column. The route starts at the break of the Leaning Column and is two cracks left of the belay bolts at the top of the leaning column.
PITCH 1: Climb Pitch 1 of Durrance (Route 1) to the bolts at its top (80 feet, 5.6).
PITCH 2: Step down and left into the Pigeon English crack. Hand jamming fol-

lowed by fist and then some off-width leads to the extreme end of the crack, which is the hardest part of the route. (A thin flake continues up and right.) At this point traverse left at the base of what appears to be a huge loose block. When a chimney (Manifest Destiny Route 208) is reached, follow it to large ledges where a belay may be set (160 feet, 5.9-).
FINISH: Rappel off or move left into Manifest Destiny to climb to the top.
SUGGESTED EQUIPMENT: Take a standard rack, medium to large pieces from 3/4 to 5 inches and a few runners.
NOTE: Use care on the traverse and notify the rangers if the block above it moves or appears to be especially dangerous. Problems with rope drag may occur if protection is placed beyond the apex of the Pigeon English crack. The original climbers placed no protection in the Manifest Destiny portion of pitch 2 and found no moves harder than 5.5 but reported it as a long runout.

3. PERSISTENCE: II, 5.9

FIRST ASCENT: May 17, 1980, by Steve Gardiner and Frank Sanders.
APPROACH: Take the Durrance Approach to just past the Leaning Column. Scramble up and right on blocks to the base of the Durrance Column. The route goes up its right side.
PITCH 1: Gotcha. Climb this off-width crack using jamming and face holds to the right. Belay from the bolts on top of the Durrance Column (150 feet, 5.8). **PITCH 2:** Hang in there. Cross the column top and take a long, traversing step to the left to reach the crack which leads up to the obvious roof 25 feet above. Climb this off-width crack through the roof and a smaller one just beyond. Continue to a large ledge where this route meets Manifest Destiny (Route 208) (145 feet, 5.9).
FINISH: Last pitch of Manifest Destiny (150 feet, 5.6).
SUGGESTED EQUIPMENT: Standard rack of Stoppers and Hexcentrics plus extra large Hexcentrics and some tube chocks for protecting of the off-width. Large Friends would help.
NOTE: A no star climb.

4. BAILEY DIRECT: II, 5.6 (One pitch variation of Durrance)

FIRST ASCENT: February 2, 1958, by Walt Bailey, Raymond Jacquot, Jim Kothel, Richard Williams, and Kenneth Johnson.
APPROACH: Take the Durrance Approach and Durrance (Route 1) to the top of the Chockstone Pitch (Jump Traverse bolts).
PITCH 6: At the top of the Chockstone Pitch (Jump Traverse bolts), climb up and left on moderate fifth class climbing to the top. Belay at the Durrance Rappel Route bolts just below the summit (150 feet, 5.6).
SUGGESTED EQUIPMENT: Medium to large Hexcentrics, Stoppers or Friends and runners.
NOTE: A variation of this is to go an extra crack left from the top of the Chockstone Pitch and climb straight up until you merge with the Baily Direct Route halfway up. Continue to the summit.

5. SUNDANCE: II, 5.7 (Starts on Wiessner and ends on Durrance)

FIRST ASCENT: August 17, 1985, by Bob Kamps, Dave Rearick, and Verena Frymann.
APPROACH: Take the Durrance Approach then traverse right to the Durrance rappel bolts. Third or fourth class up and right to the lower Meadows rappel bolts.
PITCH 1: Wiessner (Route 7). Climb up right and then left to the base of the two broken columns which stairstep up to the right. Climb the left side of the lower of

two broken columns that stairstep up to the right until it becomes possible to traverse left onto a column top with a bush growing just below its top. Belay here to start Sundance (120 feet, 5.6). **PITCH 2:** Climb the jam crack which runs up the face directly above you until you reach the ledge which marks the top of the Flake Crack on Durrance (Route 1) and belay from the eyebolts there (155 feet, 5.7). FINISH: You have several options here. The recommended routes would be the Conn Traverse, Durrance (Jump Traverse), or Bailey Direct (Route 4) to the summit.

SUGGESTED EQUIPMENT: A few small pieces with the rest medium to large Hexcentrics, Stoppers, and tubes. Large Friends are helpful.

NOTE: Pitch 2 can be done in two pitches by traversing to the top of the Cussing Crack on the Durrance route, about 95 feet to belay from the bolts there before continuing on. A one to two star route.

6. MATEO TEPEE: II, 5.7, A3

FIRST ASCENT: July 2, 1984, by Steve Gardiner and Joe Sears.
APPROACH: Take the Durrance Approach to the base of the Leaning Column and continue on ledges down, right, and up to the lower Meadows Rappel Bolts.
PITCH 1: Traverse right and up on a sloping ledge until it meets with another similar ledge leading to the left. Follow this ledge up and around the Wiessner Column and belay from a large horn (50 feet, 5.4). **PITCH 2:** Extended Wiessner (Route 9). Stem the wide crack behind the column by using the narrow crack on the left. Climb up the first column, onto a large ledge, and continue up a similar stemming crack system to the top of the Wiessner Column (70 feet, 5.8). Pitch 1 and 2 are normally done in one pitch now. **PITCH 3:** Mateo Tepee. Climb the shallow crack on the left of Pseudo-Wiessner on aid. Use a Lost Arrow in a horizontal crack to reach the main crack and climb on thin aid using RURPs, tied-off knifeblades, and skyhooks for 25 feet. At this point the crack flares. Another horizontal crack on the left face provides the first solid protection on the pitch. Above here the crack is filled with loose rock, dirt, and bushes. It may be climbed by using nuts and larger pitons to a large bush where free climbing takes one to the Conn Traverse and up to the Meadows. Belay from the upper rappel bolts (150 feet, 5.7, A3).
FINISH: Standard Meadows Finish.
SUGGESTED EQUIPMENT: Standard rack for the first two pitches. For Pitch 3, bring a collection of RURPs, skyhooks, knifeblades, bugaboos and tie-off loops.
NOTE: A no star pitch.

7. WIESSNER: II, 5.7

FIRST ASCENT: June 28, 1937, by Fritz Wiessner, William House, and Lawrence Covney.
APPROACH: Take the Durrance Approach to the base of the Leaning Column. Then traverse right and down to the first set of rappel bolts which are the bottom bolts of the Durrance Rappel.
PITCH 1: Climb directly up to the base of the two broken columns which stairstep up to the right. These are located just below and to the left of the Wiessner Crack. Climb the left side of the columns and belay from the top of the upper column. An easier way, commonly used today, is to climb up to the right past the first bolts to a second set at the base of the Meadows Rappel. Then climb up and traverse back to the left to the base of the two broken columns and climb up to the belay bolts (120 feet, 5.6). **PITCH 2:** Wiessner Crack. From the top of the highest of the two columns climb down three or four feet to the right and make the long stretch

across to the right-hand crack that is off width and jam your way to the top of the Wiessner Column. The lower portion is hard to protect. A long runner can be used to tie off a large chockstone three-quarters of the way up the crack (65 feet, 5.7).
PITCH 3: Climb straight up above the Wiessner Column until you reach the large platform at the lower left-hand corner of the Meadows and which is part of the Conn Traverse. Climb the right corner crack to a large ledge and belay from the Meadows Rappel bolts (55 feet, 5.4).
FINISH: Standard Meadows Finish.
SUGGESTED EQUIPMENT: #5 to #8-1/2 Stoppers, #6 to #9 Hexcentrics, tube chocks, and runners.
NOTE: This was the first climbing route put up on the Tower. A two star route.

8. PSEUDO WIESSNER: II, 5.8

FIRST ASCENT: August 10, 1954, by Ray Northcutt and Harvey T. Carter.
APPROACH: Take the Durrance Approach until you reach the base of the Leaning Column. Then traverse right and down to the last rappel bolts for the Durrance Rappel Route and start from there.
PITCH 1: Climb up right, and then back left, from the eyebolts to the base of the two broken columns which stairstep up to the right. These are located just below and to the left of the Wiessner (Route 7) Crack. Climb to, and belay from, the top of the higher of these two columns (120 feet, 5,7). **PITCH 2:** Climb the crack which runs directly up from the column you are belaying from, passing two currant bushes, until you reach a good belay ledge. This is a hand/fist crack with some off-width (90 feet, 5.8). **PITCH 3:** Climb straight up until you reach the west end of the Meadows by the Jump Traverse. Many people now climb up the right crack past the Meadows rappel bolts.
FINISH: Standard Meadows Finish.
SUGGESTED EQUIPMENT: Medium to large Hexcentrics, tube chocks, extra #4 Friends, and extra #10 to #11 Hexcentrics, and runners.
NOTE: A two star route.

9. EXTENDED WIESSNER: I, 5.8

FIRST ASCENT: June 25, 1977, by unknown climbers.
APPROACH: Take the Durrance Approach to the lower Durrance Rappel bolts and belay there.
PITCH 1: Climb up and right to the lower Meadows Rappel bolts. From here proceed up a few more feet until you can traverse back left and work up to the base of the Wiessner (Route 7) crack itself. You are now boxed in between two broken off columns on your left and the Wiessner Column on your right. Most climbers utilize both the left and right cracks by stemming back and forth between them while concentrating on the left crack. Climb up any way you wish to the topmost broken column on your left and belay here. This is the top of Wiessner Pitch 1 (120 feet, 5.8).
FINISH: You can rappel off from here or continue up on Wiessner or Pseudo-Wiessner (Route 8).
SUGGESTED HARDWARE: Same as Wiessner.
NOTE: Off-width. A one star pitch.

60

10. DEVILS DELIGHT - DIRECT: I, 5.7
FIRST ASCENT: September 8, 1974 by Dennis Horning, Judd Jennerjahn and Rob Wheeler. **APPROACH:** Take the Durrance Approach to the Meadows Rappel Bolts. This route follows the right side of the Wiessner Column.
PITCH 1: From the bolts, climb up and into the jam crack which starts on the right side of the bottom of the Wiessner Column. Instead of climbing up 30 feet and traversing right stay in the initial crack all the way up to the Meadows Rappel bolts. This chimney takes large pieces (135 feet, 5.7).
FINISH: Rappel off or continue up Devils Delight (Route 11) and Wiessner (Route 7) to your left or take the harder Path of Dissent (Route 12) which is the crack on your right.
SUGGESTED EQUIPMENT: Standard rack, medium to large nuts, and six to seven inch tubes, and whatever equipment the other routes above call for.
NOTE: This route is not often done because of the need for tubes etc. (off-width) A one star route.

11. DEVILS DELIGHT: (M&CWTC #1) II, 5.8+
FIRST ASCENT: July 9, 1956 by Cecil Ouellette and Charles Kness (II, Aid).
FIRST FREE ASCENT: July 2, 1962, by John Evans and Dennis Becker.
APPROACH: Take the Durrance Approach to the base of the Leaning Column then traverse down to the right past the lowest Durrance Rappel bolts and up to the bottom Meadows Rappel bolts. This route essentially follows the Aid Route M&CWTC #1, though the exact location of some portions of the aid route are disputed.
PITCH 1: From the bolts, climb up and into the jam crack which starts on the right side of the bottom of the Wiessner Column. Climb about 30 feet until it becomes possible to traverse right to the next crack. Climb 15 - 20 feet up this crack and traverse right to the next crack. Climb this crack 20 - 25 feet and traverse right one crack. Now climb this short, widening jam crack past a currant bush in the crack to a ledge formed by two column tops. Traverse left across three columns and climb 25 feet up to the top of the column where you will find the middle set of Meadows Rappel bolts (125 feet, 5.8+). **PITCH 2:** Climb to the top of the Wiessner Column on your left. From here to the Meadows is Pitch 3 of Wiessner (Route 7). Climb the cracks which run straight up from the top of the Wiessner Column to a small platform at the west end of the Meadows. (100 feet, 5.5)
FINISH: Standard Meadows Finish.
SUGGESTED EQUIPMENT: Standard rack, #5 to #8-1/2 Stoppers, #6 to #10 Hexcentrics, tube chocks, and runners.
NOTE: A no star route.

12. PATH OF DISSENT: II, 5.9
FIRST ASCENT: July 30, 1979, by Mark Smedley, Jim Black and Rich Jaskiewiez.
APPROACH: Take the Durrance Approach then traverse right past the Durrance Rappel bolts to the bottom Meadows Rappel bolts and belay here. You may wish to fourth class the last part. **PITCH 1:** Traverse right up ramps until you are one crack left of Sunfighter (Route 13). Proceed up this crack and belay on the column top to your left (140 feet, 5.9). **PITCH 2:** Climb the dirty crack that leads up the left side of the Meadows Rappel overhanging block at the top of the pitch. There is loose rock on this pitch (155 feet, 5.8).
FINISH: Standard Meadows Finish
SUGGESTED EQUIPMENT: #1 to #8 Hexcentrics, #3 to #12 Stoppers, a 4-inch piece, and extra medium to large Hexcentrics.
NOTE: A no star route.

13. SUNFIGHTER: II, 5.9

FIRST ASCENT: August 31, 1975, by Dennis Horning and Jim Slichter.
APPROACH: Take the Durrance Approach then move down to the lower Durrance rappel bolts. Third or fourth class up and right to the lower Meadows rappel bolts to belay. This crack is one crack left of The Best Crack in Minnesota (Route 14) and five cracks right of Wiessner (Route 7).
PITCH 1: Traverse right from the bolts to a large ledge at the start of the crack. The crux of the pitch is to reach a ledge left of the crack a short distance up. This can be laybacked. The hanging belay is about even with the rappel bolts, about 8 feet below the last bush in the crack (150 feet, 5.9) **PITCH 2:** Chimney up the crack to the Meadows Rappel bolts (135 feet, 5.6).
FINISH: Standard Meadows Finish.
SUGGESTED EQUIPMENT: #1 to #8 Hexcentrics, #2 to #12 Stoppers, five 2- to 5-inch pieces, and slings to tie off the chockstone.
NOTE: A one star climb.

14. THE BEST CRACK IN MINNESOTA: I, 5.9

FIRST ASCENT: July 20, 1984, by Paul Piana, Bob Cowan, Todd Skinner and Beth Wald.
APPROACH: Take the Durrance Approach to the base of the Leaning Column then traverse right past Wiessner (Route 7) until you are at the start of Sunfighter (Route 13).
PITCH 1: Begin with the initial moves of Sunfighter and a short distance above the ledge, move right into what certainly would be The Best Crack in Minnesota, if the poor souls at Taylor Falls were lucky enough to have it. This is a pitch of good hand jamming right to the top of the crack. From here, step right to an anchor (around the arete) and contemplate the interesting problem below (100 feet, 5.9).
FINISH: Rappel off from a two bolt (chained) anchor.
SUGGESTED EQUIPMENT: #2 and #3 Friends and medium Stoppers.
NOTE: Two star route.

15. JOURNEY TO IXTLAN: II, 5.10b

FIRST ASCENT: June 9, 1976, by Dennis Horning and Perry Ohlsen.
APPROACH: Take the Durrance Approach, then traverse right until you reach the crack well past the rappel bolts. This route lies between Sunfighter (Route 13) and Danse Macabre (Route 16). The route is marked by two large bushes, with two smaller bushes on each side of the larger ones.
PITCH 1: Climb to the first small bush doing very hard stemming. Two fixed pins protect these moves. The crux (flared crack) is getting from the higher smaller bush to the lower larger bush. A #5-1/2 Stopper is a good quick-draw piece for the crux. Continue climbing to a good belay ledge on your right (140 feet, 5.10b). **PITCH 2:** Continue climbing the now wide crack to the top of the column, and finish at the Meadows Rappel bolts (130 feet, 5.7).
FINISH: Scramble up to the right to the Meadows and take the Standard Meadows Finish to the summit.
SUGGESTED EQUIPMENT: Standard rack, medium to large Stoppers, and two to five inch nuts.
NOTE: A no star route.

16. DANSE MACABRE: II, 5.10d

FIRST ASCENT: August 19, 1964, by Royal Robbins and Peter Robinson.

APPROACH: Take the Durrance Approach until you reach the Meadows Rappel Bolts. Traverse right to the route about 10 cracks right of the Meadows Rappel. Start on top of a flake or pinnacle, between Journey to Ixtlan (Route 15) and My Unsung Hero (Route 17).
PITCH 1: Traverse to the right crack on a difficult move. Jam the crack with fingers and hands until you are about 30 feet below a roof overhead. Traverse left to a crack above a bush and follow that crack to a ledge on your left. Belay here (160 feet, 5.10d). **PITCH 2:** Climb the large crack through the roof to a belay ledge on your left at the Meadows (80 feet, 5.9).
FINISH: Standard Meadows Finish.
SUGGESTED EQUIPMENT: Standard rack, #1 to #8 Hexcentrics, #3 to #12 Stoppers, 4" pieces, and extra large Hexcentrics.
NOTE: The original party did not finish on the Standard Meadows Finish but climbed straight up and slightly left to the summit from the end of Pitch #2. This is not used anymore. A variation at 5.10c is to start at the base of the crack just right of the original start. A two star route.

17. MY UNSUNG HERO: II, 5.10c

FIRST ASCENT: June 6, 1989, by Dennis Horning and Frank Ducel.
APPROACH: Take the South Face Approach then traverse right on The Ramp. Climb up as for Bon Homme (Route 25) but traverse up and left to Bittersweet (Route 18). This climb starts 65 feet up Bittersweet.
PITCH 1: Climb 65 feet up Bittersweet to a bolt (65 feet, 5.10b). **PITCH 2:** Traverse left one crack. Face climb up until you reach Pitch 2 of Bittersweet and belay at a bolt (75 feet, 5.10c).
FINISH: Climb Pitch 2 of Bittersweet and take the Standard Meadows Finish to the summit.
SUGGESTED EQUIPMENT: Standard rack, RPs, Rocks and Friends to #3.
NOTE: Protection is good. A one star route.

18. BITTERSWEET: II, 5.10c

FIRST ASCENT: September 25, 1977, by Dennis Horning and Frank Sanders.
APPROACH: Follow the South Face Approach then traverse right on The Ramp to the first corner. Climb up as for Bon Homme (Route 25) but then turn left and work your way up and back to the start of the route. This route lies two cracks to the right of the Danse Macabre (Route 16) and two cracks to the left of Delta I (Route 20).
PITCH 1: Climb the crack almost to it's end. There are two difficult sections. One is encountered 20 feet off the ground and is poorly protected by nuts. The second hard section is some 30 feet higher just above a horizontal ledge that affords good protection. There are several fixed pins in the first hard section. Set up a hanging belay (145 feet, 5.10c). **PITCH 2:** Do a delicate traverse left to the next crack. Continue up the increasingly easy crack until you reach the Meadows for a belay (130 feet, 5.6).
FINISH: Standard Meadows Finish.
SUGGESTED EQUIPMENT: A standard rack, RPs, full set of Stoppers, Hexcentrics, and runners for pitons and chockstones. Also extra Stoppers, #9 and #10 Hexcentrics and #2-3 Friends.
NOTE: A two star route.

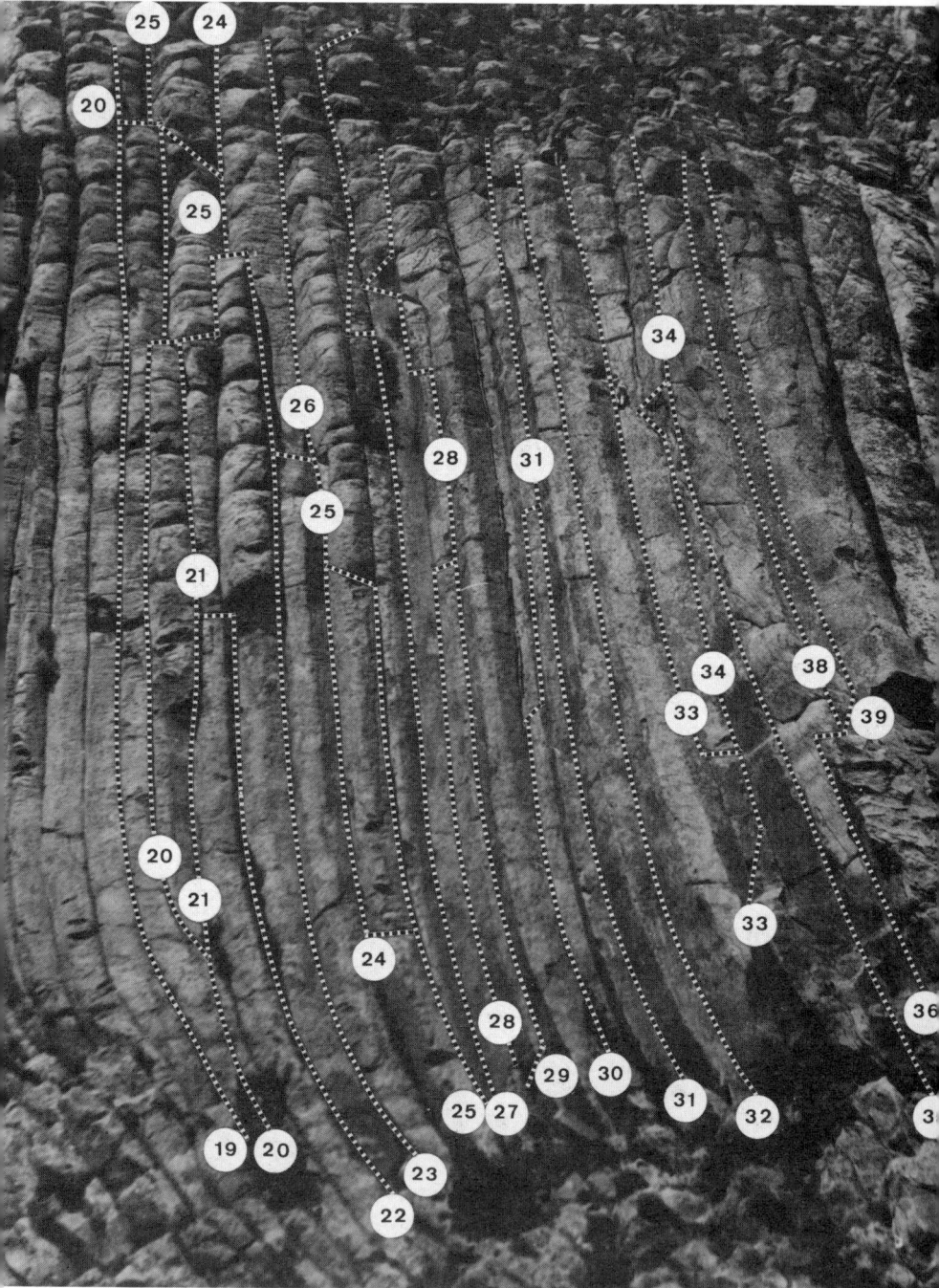

19. MORCHELLA ESCULENTA: II, 5.11c

FIRST ASCENT: June 1, 1979, by Larry Wydra and Tom Ptacek (II, 5.7, A3).
FIRST FREE ASCENT: September 6, 1980, by Dennis Horning and Mark Smedley.
APPROACH: Take the South Face Approach and traverse right on The Ramp until you come to the first corner. From here climb straight up under the Bon Homme rappel to the large tree on the left. The route is the crack left of this tree. It is one crack right of Bittersweet (Route 18) and one crack left of Delta I (Route 20).
PITCH 1: Climb up this left-curving, overhanging finger crack through a roof to the belay bolts on your right (150 feet, 5.11c). **PITCH 2:** Follow the wide crack above you through some bushes and past a column top on your right to the Meadows (150 feet, 5.7).
FINISH: Standard Meadows finish.
SUGGESTED EQUIPMENT: Take #1 to #8 Hexcentrics, #3 to #12 Stoppers, and extra small to medium Stoppers, Hexcentrics, and Friends.
NOTE: The last few feet of Pitch 2 are on Delta I. A one to two star route.

20. DELTA I: II, 5.9-

FIRST ASCENT: October 31, 1964, by Bob Schlichting and Bill Heatley (II, 5.8, A2).
FIRST FREE ASCENT: September 15, 1976, by Dennis Horning and Frank Sanders.
APPROACH: Take the South Face Approach and traverse right on The Ramp until you are below the large roof. Climb up to the route. This route lies three cracks left of the largest roof on the south face or one crack left of Waterfall (Route 21). Belay from the highest Juniper tree. **PITCH 1:** Stem and climb the Waterfall crack to the top of the bushes. Then move into the Delta I crack and continue to a good flake on the left. Place some good chocks. The next section, 35 feet, offers excellent hand and toe jamming with little opportunity for further protection placement. Belay at the bolts (125 feet, 5.9-). **PITCH 2:** Climb and stem a Durrance-like crack to the top of the column on your right (60 feet, 5.7). **PITCH 3:** (Variation of Delta I Aid Route) Traverse right to the next crack and climb up for about 40 feet, then cross a face to your left on friction and continue up the crack to the Meadows. The original free-route 3rd pitch was done this way. You can also climb up the 5.5 crack directly above (120 feet, 5.5).
FINISH: Standard Meadows Finish.
SUGGESTED EQUIPMENT: A full set of Hexcentrics and larger Stoppers. Also several 3 to 4 inch pieces.
NOTE: The old Aid Route Delta 1 finish is favored and can be done in one pitch. From the bolts at the top of pitch #1, climb and stem to the column top on your right and then continue up the crack above you where you can belay from a column top on your left (155 feet, 5.5). Take the scramble up the left crack to the Meadows. A one star route.

21. WATERFALL: II, 5.9

FIRST ASCENT: May 31, 1976, by Dennis Horning, Skip Fossen, and Mark Santangelo.
APPROACH: Take the South Face Approach and traverse right on The Ramp until you are below the large roof. Climb up to the start on Delta 1 (Route 20) and belay from the highest juniper tree. This crack lies one crack left of B.O. Plenty (Route 22) on the South Face.
PITCH 1: Start up on Delta 1 and where it moves left continue up. Climb the crack through the roof, past a large (loose?) flake, to a height equal to that of the roof on B.O. Plenty. This belay stance is much improved by the use of a seat (140 feet, 5.9).
PITCH 2: Continue up the crack on your left to the top of the column on your left.

The upper portion is a difficult off-width crack (70 feet, 5.8). **PITCH 3:** Climb to the Meadows via the crack which bisects the belay column (100 feet, 5.5).
FINISH: Standard Meadows Finish.
SUGGESTED EQUIPMENT: #4 to #8 Stoppers, #5 to #11 Hexcentrics and three or more four-inch pieces.
NOTE: Pitch 2 and 3 can be combined where you would belay on a left column top just short of the Meadows and then scramble up the left crack from there. A zero to one star route.

22. B.O. PLENTY: II, 5.8+

FIRST ASCENT: October 18, 1970, by Charles Bare and Jim Olson (III, A2).
FIRST FREE ASCENT: September 16, 1976, by Frank Sanders and Dennis Horning.
APPROACH: Take the South Face Approach then traverse right on The Ramp to the first corner and up to the base of the Bon Homme Rappel. You should be at the crack now which is one crack right of the large juniper tree and one crack left of Seamstress (Route 23).
PITCH 1: Belay from some large flakes at the base of the crack. These flakes are about the same height as the highest juniper tree. About 15 feet up a few thin moves gets one to easier climbing. Finish the last 12 feet below the roof with a gentle but committing layback. To the left of the roof is a small belay ledge (130 feet, 5.8+). **PITCH 2:** From the belay, stem and jam the crack on the left to the top of the left column. From here continue straight up an easy chimney and belay from the large ledge on your left (155 feet, 5.8).
FINISH: Standard Meadows Finish.
SUGGESTED EQUIPMENT: Standard rack, #1-8 Hexcentrics, #3-12 Stoppers, extra large Hexcentrics and some 4" pieces.
NOTE: A one star route.

23. SEAMSTRESS: II, 5.12a

FIRST ASCENT: March 13, 1982, by Chris Engle and Dave Johnson (II, A2).
FIRST FREE ASCENT: June, 1982, by Steve Hong and Karin Budding.
APPROACH: Take the South Face Approach and The Ramp then up to Bon Homme (Route 25). This route is two cracks left of the start of Bon Homme and one crack right of B.O. Plenty (Route 22).
PITCH 1: Belay high and climb up this long, hard pitch using finger locks, stemming, and face holds. It is 5.11 near the first two bolts and the crux is climbing from the last bolt to the roof. The roof is easy 5.10. This pitch ends at the Bon Homme ledge bolts (150 feet, 5.12c).
FINISH: Rappel off, or continue up to the Meadows on Bon Homme or Second Thought (Route 26) and then take the Standard Meadows Finish to the summit.
SUGGESTED EQUIPMENT: #1 and #2 Friends and 25 small nuts with a few quick draws. If you go to the top, take equipment for Bon Homme or Second Thought.
NOTE: The protection on the crux is difficult to place but okay once you have it. The bolts are drilled out too far so watch for rope drag. A one star route.

24. BON HOMME, HORNING VARIATION: II, 5.8

FIRST ASCENT: November 5, 1972, by Dennis Horning and Howard Hauck.
APPROACH: Take the South Face Approach. Same as Bon Homme (Route 25). Belay on a high ledge above the dead tree.
PITCH 1: Climb the Bon Homme crack past the chockstone. Traverse left across the column below the small roofs (crux) on the face and above a small bush in the

crack to the left. Continue on up the double crack to a good ledge (155 feet, 5.8).
PITCH 2: Climb the left crack. This is the second pitch of Bon Homme (150 feet, 5.5).
FINISH: Standard Meadows Finish or rappel off.
SUGGESTED EQUIPMENT: Standard rack, medium to large Hexcentrics, and Stoppers, plus small wired Stoppers for the traverse. Friends help.
NOTE: A three star route.

25. BON HOMME: II,5.8+

FIRST ASCENT: August 20, 1958, by Bob Kamps and Donald Yestness.
APPROACH: Take the South Face Approach to the base of the Meadows Rappel. Traverse The Ramp to the right 100 feet to a corner junction. Climb third class up to the base of the columns. This route starts four cracks left of the old Stake Ladder (Carpenter's Caper Route 30). Belay on a high ledge above the dead tree.
PITCH 1: Climb about 100 feet in this large crack, six to eight inches wide, and traverse left around the column below a small roof on the face of the column. Climb the double crack in the left-facing dihedral to a great belay ledge on a column top. A more popular variation of this pitch is the Horning Variation (Route 24) (155 feet, 5.8+). **PITCH 2:** Climb the left crack to the column top on your left. Continue straight up from here past a bush to the Meadows and belay at the bolts (150 feet, 5.7). Some climbers belay at the left column top and then climb to the Meadows.
FINISH: Standard Meadows Finish.
SUGGESTED EQUIPMENT: Standard rack, few small wired Stoppers, tubes, and medium to large Hexcentrics and Stoppers.
NOTE: A two star route

26. SECOND THOUGHT: II, 5.7 (last pitch variation of Bon Homme)

FIRST ASCENT: September 28, 1977, by Dennis Horning and Howard Hauck.
APPROACH: Same as Bon Homme (Route 25).
PITCH 1: Climb Bon Homme Horning Variation (Route 24) to the bolts at the column top. PITCH **2:** Second Thought. Climb the sustained right hand crack to the Meadows (140 feet, 5.7).
FINISH: Standard Meadows Finish.
SUGGESTED EQUIPMENT: Same as Bon Homme.

27. UNCLE REMUS DIRTY VEGETABLE GARDEN: II, 5.4, A2

FIRST ASCENT: September 14, 1972, by Mike Brown and Frank Sanders.
APPROACH: Take the South Face Approach then go right on The Ramp. As you reach the southeast corner, climb up to the first crack right of Bon Homme (Route 25) and left of Double Indemnity (Route 28).
PITCH 1: Nail up this dirty crack using bugaboos, two-inch angles, Lost Arrows and small tied-off angles. Continue up on small bongs as the crack widens through small trees, and set up a hanging belay in the crack on your right (160 feet, A2).
PITCH 2: Continue up this widening crack to the top of a very large, very loose flake then step across, as the crack flares, to a narrower crack (standard angles) on your left. Use three or four solid aid pins, then go free; traversing up and right and finish on top of a column (35 feet, 5.4, A2).
FINISH: Standard Meadows Finish.
SUGGESTED EQUIPMENT: Three bugaboos, 10 or more Lost Arrows, six baby angles, 5 standard and five 7/8-inch angles, four 1-inch angles, five bongs up to 4 inches, large Chouinard chocks (#7 to #10) would go well in the top crack. A belay seat helps.
NOTE: Pitch 2 follows Double Indemnity. Not recommended. A no star climb.

28. DOUBLE INDEMNITY: II, 5.11a

FIRST ASCENT: May 24, 1980, by Steve Hong, Karen Budding, and Mark Smedley.
APPROACH: Take the South Face Approach then right on The Ramp. At the first corner junction of The Ramp, climb up to the start of the route. The route is two cracks left of the old Stake Ladder (Carpenter's Caper Route 30) and two cracks right of Bon Homme (Route 25).
PITCH 1: Climb this crack about 90 feet stemming left one crack much of the time. Traverse right one crack on a large hold when the crack becomes too small to continue, but do not cross to early. Follow this crack (Speedway) for 15 feet and hang the belay on a small ledge with double bolts (130 feet, 5.11a). **PITCH 2:** Speedway. Follow this flaring hand crack for 35 feet. Traverse left one crack from a large hold on the left. Follow this crack to the Meadows (135 feet, 5.10d). This pitch is quite poor.
SUGGESTED EQUIPMENT: Standard rack, many small and medium Stoppers, #1 and #2 Friends, one small RP for crux, and numerous slings (20 pieces).
NOTE: Steve Hong rates this a one star route while others give it three stars? On 06-22-1992, Stuart Ritchie and Ed Ash made a variation by traversing from a point sixty feet up Pitch 1 to English Beat, one crack to the right, and then up. The traverse was rated 5.11c. Some climbers say this traverse has been previously done.

29. ENGLISH BEAT: II, 5.12b

FIRST ASCENT: May 14, 1978, by Terry Rypkema and Steve Gardiner as the aid route Speedway (II, A3).
FIRST FREE ASCENT, July 22,1984, by Todd Skinner, Paul Piana, Bob Cowan, Frank Hill and Kevin Lindorff with belaying/encouragement by Beth Wald.
APPROACH: Take the South Face Approach and traverse right on The Ramp until you are just short of the corner. Climb up and right to the route from here. This route lies one crack left of the old Stake Ladder (Carpenter's Caper Route 30).
PITCH 1: Move into the crack from blocks between Double Indemnity (Route 28) and the target climb by utilizing a diagonal fracture that enables one to reach the leaning fingerlocks that only suggest the difficulty of the crux above. The crux is a series of wild, out-of-control, heinously jingus lieback moves to a flared crack that is comparatively easy but still 5.11. This is a test-piece climb with intellectual moves, desperate protection for the crux, and a need for an up-tempo rock-and-roll approach to solving the moves. It is desperate until it joins Double Indemnity. Belay at the bolts on your right (110 feet, 5.12b). **PITCH 2:** This is pitch 2 of Double Indemnity. The crux is a short distance above the belay bolts. Shortly above the crux and before the crack ends, traverse left one crack. Climb up this crack until you are nearly level with the top of the crack on your right. Traverse up left and back up to the right at a bush. Belay at the bolts on your right just above a bush (135 feet, 5.10d).
FINISH: Scramble to the Meadows and take the Standard Meadows Finish to the summit.
SUGGESTED EQUIPMENT: Standard rack, many small and medium Stoppers, a set of Hexcentrics, RPs, #1 and #2 Friends and runners.
NOTE: English Beat is one pitch and you can rappel off from the bolts if you do not want to go to the summit or Meadows. A one star route. On 6-22-92, Stuart Ritchie and Ed Ash made a variation by starting on Double Indemnity and traversed approximately sixty feet up to English Beat just above the crux to make an easier ascent. They called this 5.11c traverse Double Time.

30. CARPENTER'S CAPER: II, 5.7, A2

FIRST ASCENT: July 10, 1972, by Terry Rypkema, Roger Holtorf and Bruce Bright.

NOTE: USE OF THIS ROUTE IS PROHIBITED DUE TO ITS PROXIMITY TO THE STAKE LADDER WHICH IS A HISTORICAL OBJECT AND MUST NOT BE DISTURBED, DAMAGED OR REMOVED. THIS ROUTE WAS ESTABLISHED BY RANGERS IN THE PROCESS OF MAKING APPROVED REPAIRS TO THE STAKE LADDER. The following is for historical purposes only.
APPROACH: Take the South Face Approach to the base of the Meadows Rappel Route. Go right and follow The Ramp to the corner junction and scramble up to the base of the Stake Ladder.
PITCH 1: Climb the blocks at the base of the Stake Ladder crack. Now free climb that crack and the one just to the right of it until you reach the base of the Stake Ladder itself. Move over into the right-hand crack and climb on direct aid about 50 feet where you can set up a hanging belay (140 feet, 5.7, A2). **PITCH 2:** Continue up about 60 feet until you reach a point where a horizontal crack in the column on your right makes it possible for you to traverse around that column and continue up the next crack on your right. This is the Afternoon Delight aid crack that has now been climbed free as The Power That Preserves and is rated (5.12a). Aid up this crack until you can free climb (110 feet, 5.5, A2).
FINISH: Standard Meadows Finish.

31. THE POWER THAT PRESERVES: II, 5.12a
FIRST ASCENT: April 2, 1978, by Terry Rypkema and Frank Sanders as Afternoon Delight (II, A2).
FIRST FREE ASCENT: July 12, 1983, By Todd Skinner and Moana Roberts, who jumarred and belayed.
APPROACH: Take the South Face Approach and The Ramp. The Route is the first crack left of Direct Southeast (Route 32) and two cracks right of the Stake Ladder (Carpenter's Caper Route 30). This route follows the Afternoon Delight aid crack.
PITCH 1: Depressingly thin tips crack that has stemming and fair protection. The crux is approximately 90 feet up and sustained. Set up a hanging belay from the bolts at the horizontal crack (155 feet, 5.12a). **PITCH 2:** Continue up the enjoyable finger and hand crack to the Meadows (70 feet, 5.10).
FINISH: Standard Meadows Finish.
SUGGESTED EQUIPMENT: Pitch 1 - Many RPs, #2 to #3 Stoppers and sliders, and #1 Friends. Pitch 2 - Small Stoppers and #2 to #2-1/2 Friends for the top section. A cleaning tool is helpful.
NOTE: There is a loose flake about 2 feet square, right at the top that must be avoided. A one to two star route.

32. DIRECT SOUTHEAST: II, 5.11d
FIRST ASCENT: May 1, 1965, by Peter Oslund and John Horn (5.5, A2).
FIRST FREE ASCENT: August 24, 1978, by Steve Hong, Mark Smedley and Karin Budding.
APPROACH: South Face Approach to the base of the Meadows Rappel, then traverse right on The Ramp until you can third or fourth class up to the base of the climb. The route is three cracks right of the old Stake Ladder Carpenter's Caper Route 30).
PITCH 1: Belay at the base of the thin crack. This is a variable finger crack with occasional natural finger pockets and one hands down rest. Climb up on continuous, thin moves getting progressively harder until you reach a stance belay on fixed pins that are located in a horizontal crack to the left (160 feet, 5.11d). **PITCH 2:** Continue up this crack until you reach the Meadows (50 feet, 5.7).
FINISH: Standard Meadows Finish.
SUGGESTED EQUIPMENT: Three sets of RPs, many #1 to #8 Stoppers, one #1 Friend and two #2 Friends.
NOTE: Steve Hong rates this climb a three star classic.

33. WALT BAILEY MEMORIAL: II, 5.9
FIRST ASCENT: July 26, 1959, by Gary Cole, Raymond Jacquot, and Charles Blackmon (5.8, A2).
FIRST FREE ASCENT: May 27, 1974, by Jeff Overton and Scott Woodruff.
APPROACH: Take the South Face Approach to the base of the Meadows Rappel. Traverse right on The Ramp until you are just below some large blocks at the southeast corner of the Tower. The route starts on top of these blocks and is four cracks right of the old Stake Ladder (Carpenter's Caper Route 30). Climb to the start of the route, three cracks left of Hollywood and Vine (Route 39). This is third or fourth class climbing. Some parties prefer to rope up on this very exposed area.
PITCH 1: Climb left and immediately traverse up and right to the top of the flake. Climb the left finger and hand crack to the Meadows. The belayer may have to climb a few feet so the leader can reach the Meadows belay ledge (165+ feet, 5.9).
FINISH: Standard Meadows Finish.
SUGGESTED EQUIPMENT: #1 to #9 Hexcentrics, two sets small to medium Friends, #2 to #12 Stoppers, and extra #4 to #12 Stoppers.
NOTE: Many climbers consider this route one of the finest 5.9 pitches on the Tower. A three star climb.

34. PHILLIP'S RETREAT: I, 5.9+
FIRST ASCENT: July 22, 1978, by Dennis Horning with a belay by Phillip Chandler.
APPROACH: Take the South Face Approach to the base of the Meadows Rappel. Traverse right on The Ramp until you are just below some large blocks at the southeast corner of the Tower. The route starts on top of these blocks and is one crack right of Walt Bailey Memorial (Route 33) and two cracks left of Hollywood And Vine (Route 39). Third or fourth class up to the start of the route. This is very exposed and many rope up here.
PITCH 1: This route follows the first 20 feet of Walt Bailey Memorial and then continues up the right finger crack from the top of the flake. Follow the finger crack a ways and then move right into a leaning dihedral for a short distance before moving back left for a short distance. Now traverse up to the right to the next crack (a left leaning dihedral), climb this a few feet and set up a belay (160 feet, 5.9+). **PITCH 2:** Climb the same crack to the Meadows (30 feet, 5.4).
FINISH: Standard Meadows Finish.
SUGGESTED EQUIPMENT: Standard rack, small to medium Hexcentrics, small to large Stoppers, and extra medium to large Stoppers.
NOTE: Pitch 2 is on the DOM (Route 35) (Dirty Old Man), an old aid route. One to two stars.

35. THE D.O.M.: II, A2 or A3
FIRST ASCENT: September 4, 1967, by Ron Howe, Terry O'Donnell and Evans Winner.
APPROACH: Take the South Face Approach to the base of the Meadows Rappel. Traverse right on The Ramp until you are just below some large blocks at the southeast corner of the Tower. Climb up to the start which is one crack left of Hollywood And Vine (Route 39), and two cracks right of Walt Bailey Memorial (Route 33).
EXPLANATION: Park records indicate a first and second ascent of The D.O.M. but no route description was given. This is the route Rypkema and Haire marked on their photo, in their book, under route 17, page 24, South Face photo. Because of this and tradition we are marking the same crack for government records.
PITCH 1 2: Nothing is definitely known about this crack except that two pitches will get you to the Meadows.
FINISH: Standard Meadows Finish.

SUGGESTED EQUIPMENT: No suggestion given by first ascent climbers.
NOTE: Rypkema and Haire "A Climbers Guide to Devils Tower" indicate Pete Ostlund and Ralph Farrar made the first ascent. Park records show this was the second ascent with the first ascent being made by the three climbers listed above. The leader of the climb is unknown and The D.O.M. stands for The Dirty Old Man.

36. A PIECE OF THE ACTION: I, 5.10d
FIRST ASCENT: May 28, 1987, by Jim Swenson and Scott Flesner.
APPROACH: Take the South Face Approach to the base of the Meadows Rappel. Traverse right on The Ramp until you get to some large blocks at the southeast corner of the tower. The route is the west crack between the broken column on Hollywood and Vine (Route 39) and the wall.
PITCH 1: Climb the flaring hand crack up to the top of the column. Half way up, the crack widens into a comfortable chimney rest. It narrows down to a hand crack for the last 10 feet. Protection is good but strenuous because it is leaning to one side and is over-hanging (35 feet, 5.10d).
FINISH: Climb Hollywood and Vine or rappel off.
SUGGESTED EQUIPMENT: Friends through #3 and #1 to #12 Stoppers. A large Hexcentric works well to protect the first few moves.
NOTE: Needs cleaning. A no star pitch.

37. ROACH ADDITION: I, 5.7
FIRST ASCENT: Est. 1991, by Steve Roach
APPROACH: Take the South Face Approach and The Ramp until you are below Hollywood And Vine (Route 39). The pitch is on the face of a large block that's right of A Piece Of The Action (Route 36) and Left of the Hollywood And Vine approach pitch which is where you start.
PITCH 1: Climb up and left passing a few bolts until you are at the belay on top of the block (5.7)
FINISH: Rappel off or continue up Hollywood And Vine.
SUGGESTED EQUIPMENT: Quickdraws for the bolts.
NOTE: The first ascent party did not submit a description to the National Park Service for it's files. Two stars.

38. ROCKSUCKERS: II, 5.11c
FIRST ASCENT: Est. 1992, by unknown climbers.
APPROACH: Take the South Face Approach and The Ramp to the southeast corner. The route is on the face left of Hollywood And Vine (Route 39) and starts at the Hollywood And Vine belay bolts. The start can be reached by climbing Roach Addition (Route 37) (5.7) or the Hollywood And Vine approach pitch (5.5).
NOTE: The first ascent party did not submit a route description for National Park Service files. Anyone with information on this route should contact the Park Service.

39. HOLLYWOOD AND VINE: II, 5.10c
FIRST ASCENT: May 8, 1960, by Gary Cole and Raymond Jacquot (III, 5.5, A1).
FIRST FREE ASCENT: May 26, 1974, by Jeff Overton and Scott Woodruff.
APPROACH: Take the South Face Approach. Traverse right on The Ramp toward the southeast corner of the Tower. The route starts on the right side of the highest broken column on the southeast corner. There is quite a bit of poison ivy on this section of the shoulder, but it can be easily avoided.
PITCH 1: Climb the chimney on the right side of the broken column and belay from the bolts on top of the column (75 feet, 5.5). **PITCH 2:** Using fingerlocks and stemming, climb up the old aid crack in the center of the shallow dihedral to a

ledge at the top of the crack. The crux, fingertip liebacking on pin scars, is halfway up this pitch (160 feet, 5.10c). **PITCH 3:** A short pitch of easy free climbing brings one to the Meadows (40 feet, 5.4).
FINISH: Standard Meadows Finish.
SUGGESTED EQUIPMENT: #1 Hexcentrics, lots of #1 to #12 Stoppers and runners.
NOTE: A 165 foot rope is necessary for pitch two, in order to stretch this lead to a ledge at the top of the crack. A three star classic route.

40. SOLAR ECLIPSE: II, 5.11b
FIRST ASCENT: Est. 1991, by Eric Fazio-Rhicard, Dennis Horning, and Brent Kertzman.
APPROACH: Take the South Face Approach and The Ramp to the southeast corner. The route is on the column face right of the Hollywood And Vine approach and left of Soler (Route 41).
PITCH 1: Climb up on the right side of the face (arete), along a line of bolts, through the roof crux then up and left to the bolted belay (5.11b). **PITCH 2:** Follow the line of bolts up the left side of the face to the Meadows and belay bolts (5.10a).
FINISH: Rappel off or take the Standard Meadows Finish to the top.
SUGGESTED EQUIPMENT: Quickdraws for the bolts. If you go higher check for equipment on that route.
NOTE: A three star route.

41. SOLER: II, 5.9-
FIRST ASCENT: August 30, 1951, by Tony Soler, Art Lembeck, Herb Conn, Ray Moore, and Chris Scordus. This was the first tension climb on Devils Tower.
FIRST FREE ASCENT: May 2, 1959, by Layton Kor, and Raymond Jacquot.
APPROACH: Take the South Face Approach to the base of the Meadows Rappel. Traverse The Ramp to the right until you just turn the southeast corner below Hollywood and Vine (Route 39) to the next crack which is Soler. The crack is in a right-facing dihedral.
PITCH 1: From a high but small belay ledge begin the climb and continue up the crack. A comfortable hanging belay can be set up above the chockstones at bolts (150 feet, 5.8+). **PITCH 2:** Continue up the crack to its finish at the Meadows (110 feet, 5.9-).
FINISH: Standard Meadows Finish.
SUGGESTED EQUIPMENT: Standard rack, some Friends, and medium to large Stoppers.
NOTE: There is no crux, as such - simply two pitches of well protected and continuous fingers, hand jams, and laybacks. The original aid party did not finish in the same crack. They worked their way out onto the left face about 30 feet below the Meadows for an easy finish. This is not used much now as climbers prefer the straight line. A three star climb.

42. TODTMOOS: II, 5.9-
FIRST ASCENT: May 1, 1976, by Dennis Horning and Jim Slichter.
APPROACH: Take the South Face Approach and go right on The Ramp past the southeast corner. The climb lies in the crack between Soler (Route 41) and TAD (Route 43).
PITCH 1: Climb up to, through, and above the bushes to a hanging belay at a horizontal crack on the right. The crux is just below the first bush (125 feet, 5.9-).
PITCH 2: Continue up the crack to a belay at the Meadows. The upper parts of the pitch are hard to protect because of dirt and moss in the crack (145 feet, 5.8+).
FINISH: Standard Meadows Finish.
SUGGESTED EQUIPMENT: Cleaning tool, #1 to #8 Hexcentrics, #3 to #12 Stoppers with extra small Stoppers, and a belay seat helps.
NOTE: Dirt and bush climb; infrequently done. A no star route.

43. TAD: II, 5.7 (M&CWTC #2)
FIRST ASCENT: July 10, 1956, by Dave Gallagher and Jack Morehead. (Aid)
FIRST FREE ASCENT: July 3, 1973, by Dan Burgette and Charles Bare.
APPROACH: Take the South Face Approach to the base of the Meadows Rappel. Traverse The Ramp to the right until you turn the southeast corner. The crack you

want is two cracks right of Soler (Route 41) which is the right facing dihedral. Originally this was done in three pitches.
PITCH 1: Climb the crack to a small slanting ledge, just below where the crack begins to narrow, and set up a semi-hanging belay (120 feet, 5.7). **PITCH 2:** Climb straight up on hand and fist jams to the Meadows. The crack flares for a short distance just below the Meadows. (150 feet, 5.7)
FINISH: Standard Meadows Finish.
SUGGESTED EQUIPMENT: Friends, assorted small nuts, medium to large Stoppers and Hexcentrics with extra large pieces.
NOTE: A letter in park files by Jack Morehead shows that the name of this route comes from the exclusive Playful TAD Climbing Club, which is composed of only four people, two of which are the first ascent climbers listed above. Others have thought it represented Third Armored Division or Tactical Army Demonstration Team. A three star climb.

44. EL CRACKO DIABLO: II, 5.8
FIRST ASCENT: October 21, 1973, by Rod Johnson and Pat Padden.
APPROACH: Take the South Face Approach and traverse The Ramp all the way around until you are one crack right of TAD (Route 43) and one crack left of Exit-US (Route 45).
PITCH 1: Climb a short face just left of the crack for a few feet, then step into the jam crack. Climb this hand crack and off width until you reach a narrow ledge system which leads to the hanging belay bolts well out on the right face (120 feet, 5.7). **PITCH 2:** Climb this crack on foot and hand jams while utilizing small face holds on the right face. The crux is about 40 feet up at a bulge where some off width is encountered. Belay at the bolts on the right block (150 feet, 5.8).
FINISH: Standard Meadows Finish or rappel down.
SUGGESTED EQUIPMENT: Standard rack, #4 to #11 Hexcentrics, large Stoppers and extra medium to large pieces. Large Friends are helpful.
NOTE: There is a problem with loose rock and dirt at the upper belay. This is a three star route.

45. EXIT US: II, 5.9
FIRST ASCENT: July 6, 1968, by Dave Ingalls and Roy Kligfield (II, 5.5, A2).
FIRST FREE ASCENT: September 27, 1976, by Frank Sanders and Dennis Horning.
APPROACH: Take the South Face Approach and go right on The Ramp until you are past El Cracko Diablo (Route 44) at the belay for Cave (Route 47). Use this same belay. We recommend that you fourth class up to the belay ledge. The route is one crack left of Cave.
PITCH 1: Take the left crack from the belay ledge. Climb the crack up the corner and through a dihedral, surmounting a bulge. Continue using crack and face holds until you come to a hanging belay position at the bolts on the left face (140 feet, 5.9). **PITCH 2:** From the belay, traverse right up sloping ramps to the next crack, which is Cave. Climb the second pitch of Cave to the Meadows and belay there (155 feet, 5.9).
FINISH: Take the Standard Meadows Finish to the summit.
SUGGESTED EQUIPMENT: A standard rack, #3 to #9 Hexcentrics, many #1 to #12 Stoppers.
NOTE: Some climbers think that Exit US is derived from "Exodus". Park records do not give any information on this. This route is very dirty and not climbed much. A no star route.

46. EXTENSION: II, 5.11a
FIRST ASCENT: July 21, 1985, by Dennis Horning and Jim Schlinkmann.

APPROACH: Take the South Face Approach and go right on The Ramp until you reach the start of El Cracko Diablo. The route lies one crack right of the second pitch of El Cracko Diablo (Route 44). The route follows the EXIT US crack above the bolts. (The EXIT US route traverses right above the bolts, whereas Extension follows the crack straight up.)
PITCH 1: Climb El Cracko Diablo Pitch 1. Belay at the bolts well out on the right face. **PITCH 2:** Climb up the right crack to bolts on the Meadows ledge. The climbing is very delicate, with lots of face moves and weird crack climbing. The crux is encountered about half way up the pitch, where the crack thins out. Protection is not abundant, but there are some creative placements in the shallow crack. Three bolts help protect the second half of the pitch (140 feet, 5.11a).
SUGGESTED EQUIPMENT: Standard rack, full set of Stoppers, RPs, Friends to #2, small to medium Hexcentrics; sliders and quickdraws are very helpful.
NOTE: A one star pitch.

47. CAVE: II, 5.9
FIRST ASCENT: August 26, 1965, by Pete Oslund and Dave Ingalls (II, 5.5, A2).
FIRST FREE ASCENT: September 20, 1976, by Dennis Horning and Frank Sanders.
APPROACH: Take the South Face Approach, then traverse right on The Ramp until you are just past TAD (Route 43). Look up and see the Cave hole. Climb exposed fourth or fifth class up to a high belay ledge on the face between Exit-US (Route 45) and Cave. The Cave route is three cracks right of TAD.
PITCH 1: Belay high up on a good ledge to the left of the dihedral below the roof. Climb up the dihedral onto a friction slab and then turn the roof on the left. Rope snag can be a problem here. Continue about 25 feet past the roof to a horizontal crack that makes for a good standing belay. There are some fixed pins in the lower dihedral. This pitch affords poor small Stopper protection (150 feet, 5.9). **PITCH 2:** Continue up the hand jam crack to its end at the base of the Meadows finish. Ample protection is afforded by Stoppers (145 feet, 5.8).
FINISH: Standard Meadows Finish:
SUGGESTED EQUIPMENT: Standard rack, Hexcentrics through #9, #2 to #8-1/2 Stoppers, and RPs. Extra #9 Hexcentrics and small and large Stoppers.
NOTE: A two star route.

48. LAST COWGIRL CAMP: II, 5.11b
FIRST ASCENT: October 6, 1968, by Pete Oslund and John Chuta as Second Cave (II, 5.7, A2).
FIRST FREE ASCENT: August 27,1979, by Dennis Horning and Jay Smith.
APPROACH: Take the South Face Approach and The Ramp until you are below Cave (Route 47). This route starts five cracks right of the prominent dihedral which is Soler (Route 41) on the southeast corner of the Tower.
PITCH 1: Belay high up from an adequate ledge at the start of EXIT-US. From here traverse right to the next crack which is Cave. Ascend the dihedral turning the roof of the cave on the right and continue to a small belay stance 25 feet above the roof on your left (140 feet, 5.9). **PITCH 2:** Continue up the right-facing dihedral stemming, laybacking and crack climbing to the base of the Meadows (140 feet, 5.11b).
FINISH: Standard Meadows Finish.
SUGGESTED EQUIPMENT: Standard rack, RPs, #3 to #9 Hexcentrics, #1 to #2 Friends and extra #1 to #12 Stoppers.
NOTE: This free climb is believed to be on the old aid route Second Cave. Some consider the aid route Second Cave to have been climbed one crack right of Last Cowgirl Camp or in the crack Troglodytes Trauma (Route 50) starts in. Piton placements and pin scars were found in the Last Cowgirl Camp crack, but none have been reported in the crack to the right. A two star route.

49. LIFE DURING WARTIME: II, 5.10d
FIRST ASCENT: March 30, 1986, by Mike Friedrichs and Dennis Horning.
APPROACH: Take the South Face approach to the Base of the Meadows Rappel, then traverse right or East on The Ramp around the Southeast Corner past Cave (Route 47). The pitch is one crack right of Last Cowgirl Camp (Route 48) and one crack left of Troglodytes Trauma (Route 50). Climb up to a bolt that is 15 feet above to set up your belay.
PITCH 1: After moderate stemming for about 60 feet, one encounters a couple of 5.10 moves. Easy stemming then leads to a roof. The crux is climbing over the roof and about 12 feet to a bolt. Fifteen or twenty more feet of face climbing takes one to a three-bolt hanging belay (165 feet, 5.10d).
FINISH: Rappel off.
SUGGESTED EQUIPMENT: Stoppers (all sizes), RPs, small Friends and extra runners.
NOTE: Two 165 foot ropes are needed for the rappel. You may be a few feet off the ground at the end of the rappel. Be sure to use your runners to keep the rope straight. The belayer may have to tandem climb a few feet so the leader can make the rappel bolts. A one to two star route.

50. TROGLODYTES TRAUMA: II, 5.11c
FIRST ASCENT: April 22, 1971, by Ian Wade, Barbara Euser, and Walter Fricke (II, A3).
FIRST FREE ASCENT: June 14, 1979, by Jim Beyer and Dennis Horning.
APPROACH: Take the South Face Approach and The Ramp until you are between TAD (Route 43) and The Window. The route starts at the base of the Life During Wartime (Route 49) crack and three cracks left of Aerial Boundaries (Route 51).
PITCH 1: Traverse up and right to the next crack then climb up and traverse right under a roof to the next crack. Pass the roof on the right and belay above it (150 feet, 5.10d). **PITCH 2:** Continue up the crack until you can belay among some bushes (150 feet, 5.11c). **PITCH 3:** Climb up to a roof and pass it on the left. Continue up to the summit (160 feet, 5.9+). Or you can belay above the roof at a good spot and scramble up to the summit from there.
SUGGESTED EQUIPMENT: A full set of Hexcentrics and Stoppers with extra Stoppers of all sizes.
NOTE: The aid route started one crack right of the start of the free route. The rock is dirty and not solid. A no star route.

51. AERIAL BOUNDARIES: II, 5.11d
FIRST ASCENT: May 21, 1989, by Layne Kopischka and Dennis Horning.
APPROACH: Take the South Face Approach and traverse right on The Ramp to The Window. This climb starts one crack left of Beelzebub (Route 52) and two cracks right of Troglodytes Trauma (Route 50). Third class up about ten feet from the approach ledge to a small tree on right side of the crack. Belay from two bolts across from the tree.
PITCH 1: Climb up the face on the column to the left of the bush
and poison ivy filled crack and then through five protection bolts. From the last bolt, traverse right to the crack and follow it up through the pitch's crux and through a small roof. The belay is at a small awkward stance with two bolts (130 feet, 5.10b). **PITCH 2:** Continue up the crack through some thin moves. The first half of pitch is the crux. Continue up and follow the right branch of the crack to the Beelzebub belay ledge (70 feet, 5.10d). **PITCH 3:** This pitch is the crux of the climb. Climb back down the branch crack until you can stem left into the main crack and proceed. The crack becomes imaginary below a major bulge which is protected by four bolts on the right face. Move up to the fifth and last bolt and traverse right to

the crack formed by a section of column jammed between two other columns. If you are tall enough, stem right at the bottom of this plug. If not, move up to the higher holds and then over to the crack. Follow this easier crack fifteen feet to the top of the wedged column. Belay from three bolts (110 feet, 5.11d). **PITCH 4:** Rappel from here or continue up the left crack or up the right crack (Beelzebub) to a belay with two bolts. Up and to the left join with the Standard Meadows Finish to the top (100 feet, 5.9).
FINISH: Standard Meadows Finish.
SUGGESTED EQUIPMENT: Two to three sets of #1-8 Rocks, two sets of #0-2 1/2 Friends, two small RPs, Set of steel nuts, small HBs and Quick Draws for Bolts.
NOTE: If you are looking for some interesting climbing that "Ain't Duck Soup", this climb is for you. Beware of the loose flake on Pitch 3. Two stars.

52. BEELZEBUB: II, 5.10b
FIRST ASCENT: September 24, 1976, by Dennis Horning and Frank Sanders.
APPROACH: Take the South Face Approach then traverse right on The Ramp until you reach The Window. This route passes through the first roof left of the group of roofs on the east side of the Tower and is between Aerial Boundaries (Route 51) and Dusk In Dogtown (Route 53).
PITCH 1: Flake. Begin below a prominent flake just right of the base of the crack. After a few face moves follow a hand-jam crack to the top of the flake. Belay at the bolts (55 feet, 5.8). **PITCH 2:** Dihedral. From the top of the flake, step left into the crack and continue through the dihedral. Above the first dihedral traverse left into a smaller dihedral for a few moves, then back into the crack and up to a good belay ledge. There are some fixed pins in this pitch. Belay at the bolts on the left ledge (140 feet, 5.8). **PITCH 3:** Roof. Continue up the crack. The crux is about 12 feet below the roof. An irremovable pin is at the bottom of the roof. After the roof is negotiated on the right face, climb above a bush and belay at the bolts on the left ledge (110 feet, 5.10b). **PITCH 4:** Meadows. Follow the most prominent line. After a large ledge one can pick up the fourth class Standard Meadows Finish by going 25 feet left (125 feet, 5.9).
FINISH: Standard Meadows Finish.
SUGGESTED EQUIPMENT: Standard rack, #1-9 Hexcentrics, #2-12 Stoppers and extra small Stoppers.
NOTE: A no star route.

53. DUSK IN DOGTOWN: I, 5.10c
FIRST ASCENT: October 21, 1978, by Steve Gardiner, Terry Rypkema, and Frank Sanders as Tower Classic (Route 55) (III, 5.7, A2).
FIRST FREE ASCENT: September 20, 1980, by Mark Smedley and Jim Black
APPROACH: Take the South Face Approach and go right on The Ramp to The Window. The pitch is in the first right-facing dihedral left of The Window and just right of Beelzebub (Route 52).
PITCH 1: Climb up this delightful combination of hand crack, perfect liebacking, face climbing, and thin fingers pitch that includes a few good rests. Hang a belay at the pins above a horizontal crack (140 feet, 5.10c).
FINISH: Rappel down or continue up on Let Me Go Wild (Route 54) and Tower Classic to the top.
SUGGESTED EQUIPMENT: Small to medium Stoppers, RPs, and #1 Friends.
NOTE: This is a three star classic all the way.

54. LET ME GO WILD: II, 5.12b
FIRST ASCENT: October 21, 1978, by Steve Gardiner, Terry Rypkema and Frank Sanders as the aid route Tower Classic (Route 55) (III, 5.7, A2).

FIRST FREE ASCENT: Of Pitch 1 as Dusk In Dogtown (Route 53) - September 20, 1980, by Mark Smedley and Jim Black. Of Pitch 2 - August 15, 1984, by Todd Skinner and Beth Wald.
APPROACH: Take the South Face Approach and The Ramp until you reach The Window. This route is in the first beautiful, right-facing dihedral to the left of The Window roofs.
PITCH 1: Dusk In Dogtown. Climb up this delightful combination pitch (handcrack, perfect liebacking, face climbing and thin fingers) which includes a few good rests. Hang a belay at the pins above a horizontal crack (140 feet, 5.10c). **PITCH 2:** Let Me Go Wild. Continue up on absolutely incredible, thin stemming, face climbing and liebacking with a great deal of 5.11 leading up to a stemming crux. This is aesthetic climbing with four fixed pins and superb stopper placements for the entire length. Belay at a cluster of pins below some loose blocks (90 feet, 5.12d).
FINISH: Todd recommends rappelling off, or you can easily climb up the same crack to the summit on Pitch 3 of Tower Classic (165 feet, 5.7).
SUGGESTED EQUIPMENT: Pitch 1 - small and medium Stoppers and #1 Friends. Pitch 2 - many small stoppers, quick draws and RPs. Take larger pieces to go to the top.
NOTE: Todd Skinner says, "One of the most classic corners of this grade in America." A three star route.

55. TOWER CLASSIC: III, 5.7, A2
FIRST ASCENT: October 21, 1978, by Steve Gardiner, Terry Rypkema, and Frank Sanders.
FIRST FREE ASCENT: Pitch 1 as Dusk In Dogtown (Route 53) - September 20, 1980, by Mark Smedley and Jim Black. Pitch 2 as Let Me Go Wild (Route 54) - August 15, 1984, by Todd Skinner and Beth Wald.
APPROACH: Take the South Face Approach and The Ramp to The Window. The route is in the first right facing dihedral left of The Window Roofs.
PITCH 1: This has now been climbed free as Dusk In Dogtown (140 feet, 5.10c)
PITCH 2: This has now been climbed free as Let Me Go Wild (90 feet, 5.12b).
PITCH 3: Tower Classic. Continue straight up the crack to a belay at the end of your rope (165 feet, 5.7).
FINISH: Walk to the top.
SUGGESTED EQUIPMENT: Standard rack with many small to medium Stoppers, #1 Friends, Quickdraws, and RPs. The larger pieces are for the top.
NOTE: Please do not use pitons to aid, but use nuts etc. instead to protect this climb. A three star climb.

56. ANIMAL CRACKER LAND: I, 5.12b
FIRST ASCENT: August 1, 1984, by Todd Skinner and Beth Wald.
APPROACH: Take the South Face Approach and The Ramp until you have traversed around to The Window. Start one crack right of Beelzebub (Route 52) which is Dusk In Dogtown (Route 53) (Pitch 1, free) of the old Tower Classic (Route 55) aid route. On the left edge of The Window is a striking, finger size fracture crack on an overhanging column face. This is the route.
PITCH 1: Climb up a short distance on Dusk In Dogtown to the start of the route on your right. Enter this thin crack on lieback edges after a blind Friend placement. Continue on sustained, strenuous locks and stems to a chockstone with a ring angle. Don't clip into the pin as it exists only to help keep the chockstone in place. Continue until you come to the end of the finger crack and then make a move left into a right leaning hand crack. Continue up to the hanging belay with two chained bolts (155 feet, 5.12b).
FINISH: Rappel off.

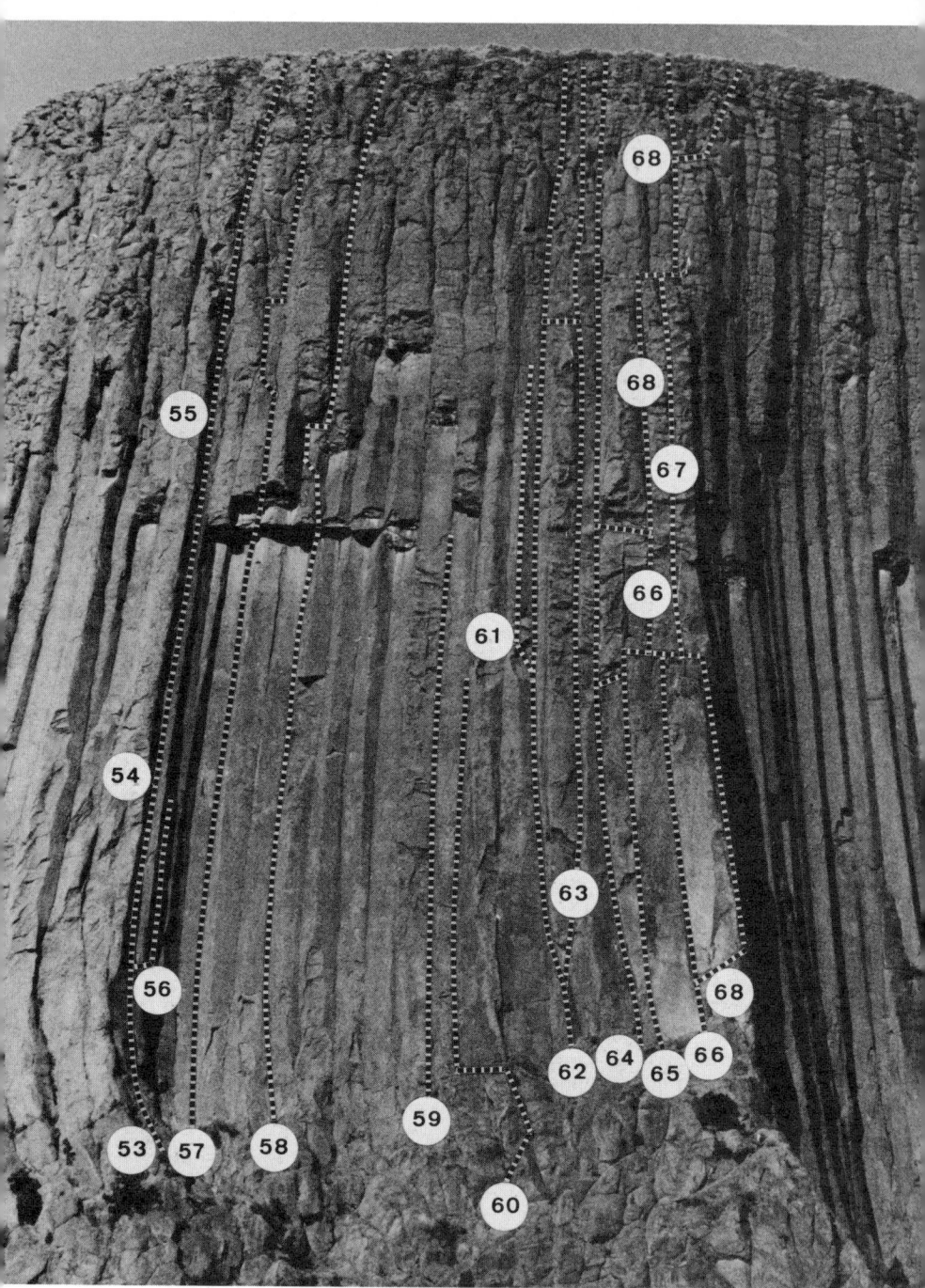

SUGGESTED EQUIPMENT: Many small and medium stoppers, RPs, and also #1, #1 1/2 and #2 Friends.
NOTE: This crack is wild and very unlike any of the other cracks at the Tower according to Todd Skinner. Two stars.

57. THE WINDOW: IV, 5.6, A4
FIRST ASCENT: August 20, 1964, by Royal Robbins and Peter Robinson. This climb took 10 hours and 60 pitons the first time it was done.
APPROACH: Take the South Face Approach to the base of the Meadows Rappel and traverse The Ramp to the right all the way around to the base of The Window. Plan for a long day.
PITCH 1: Take the first crack right of the inner most right-facing dihedral on the left side of The Window. Climb up on easy placements. The belay is in slings suspended from good pitons. Bring a good selection of smaller nuts as much of this section can be done clean (140 feet, A2). **PITCH 2:** This pitch gets progressively more difficult until the first ceiling is reached. Here one can get in some solid pins. Passing the two roofs is the crux of the climb. The roof is now almost completely fixed. Pins lead over the second roof to a belay in slings 25 feet higher. Bring small nuts and RPs for use in pin scars. Bring some Friends (#1 to #3) for the crack past the roofs, as rope drag makes free climbing this stretch difficult (150 feet, A4).
FINISH: Traverse left one crack and climb 25 feet before returning to the original crack which is followed to the summit (150 feet, 5.6).
SUGGESTED EQUIPMENT: A good selection of blades, including Lost Arrows, short thicks and short thins, small to medium knifeblades, Leepers, SMCs, baby and long angles, and lots of tie-off loops and carabiners. Also, small nuts, RPs, and Friends.
NOTE: This is a major test piece on the Tower for aid climbing but seldom done.

58. THE SKUNK: IV, 5.6, A3
FIRST ASCENT: September 8, 1986, by Igor Jamnikar and Matjaz Ravhekar.
APPROACH: Take the South Face Approach and The Ramp to The Window. The route is in the second crack right of The Window (Route 57).
PITCH 1: Take the third crack right of the innermost right facing dihedral on the left side of The Window. There is one old piton with a sling halfway up the pitch. The last 17 feet is the hardest. Belay from two bolts, of which only the sleeves remain. It will be necessary to supply 8mm by 15mm bolts at this belay. (175 feet, A2) **PITCH 2:** Difficult climbing over the crux of the climb leads to the ceiling. There is a nut left 50 feet up the pitch. Also a piton left under the roof. Take care of a large loose block immediately above the roof which moves easily and is potentially dangerous for the climber below. Immediately above the roof, follow the lower, outer corner of the column to the left for twenty feet then move upward a short distance into the crack on your left, climbing up to a roof. Traverse around the roof to a crack on the right. Belay 20 feet above from Friends and nuts (165 feet, A3).
FINISH: Free climb to the summit following the same crack. Use small RPs and Friends (165 feet, 5.6).
SUGGESTED EQUIPMENT: Full set of Friends (#1 to #4), small nuts, small RPs, and knifeblade pitons.
NOTE: The crux of this climb is the last 15 feet of Pitch 1 and from the belay to the roof on Pitch 2. First ascent party would like to be notified when route is first free climbed.

Igor Jamnikar
Vandotova 5
610000 Ljubljana
Jugoslavija

Matjaz Ravheka
Koroska 8
64280 Kranjskar Gora
Jugoslavija

59. LUCIFER'S LEDGES: III, A3
First Ascent: October 29, 1978, by Frank Sanders, Steve Gardiner, Terry Rypkema, and Mark Brackin.
APPROACH: Take the South Face Approach and The Ramp to below the Window. Continue past the start of The Window (Route 57) to a point below the right most roof of The Window series. The next column face is broken badly and leads to a roof higher than The Window roof. The route lies in the right-hand crack of this broken face.
PITCH 1: Climb on varying aid to an established hanging belay (155 feet, A2+).
PITCH 2: Continue in the same crack on more difficult placements through some sections of very loose and unappealing rock to a standing ledge where a nut and pin anchor is found (120 feet, A3). **PITCH 3:** Climb on questionable placements to a point where the crack ends and a large, blank wall is above (50 feet, A3).
SUGGESTED EQUIPMENT: A full rack of Stoppers and Hexcentrics, with pitons ranging from RURPs to bongs.
NOTE: This route is not recommended. No stars.

60. SATAN'S STAIRWAY: III, 5.8, A3
FIRST ASCENT: July 4, 1984, by Steve Gardiner, Joe Sears, Chris Engle, and Dave Johnson.
APPROACH: Take the South Face Approach and go right on the Ramp to The Window. At the right edge of The Window roofs you will see a higher roof, then another roof to the right at the same level as The Window overhangs. The right-hand crack below this roof is in a dihedral and is the route. It is one crack right of Lucifer's Ledges (Route 59) and three cracks left of Witchie (Route 62).
PITCH 1: Scramble on the blocks just to the right of the actual route to a point where a six-inch ledge traverses into the crack. From there, climb on mixed free and aid to a fixed hanging belay on pins and nuts. The crux is a small roof about 120 feet up. Turn this roof on a sky hook (145 feet, 5.8, A2+). **PITCH 2:** Continue on sustained thin aid (using several tie-offs) up the same crack to a fixed hanging belay (140 feet, A3).
FINISH: Rappel off.
SUGGESTED EQUIPMENT: A full rack of Stoppers, Hexcentrics, and pitons, including many knifeblades, tie-offs, RURPS, and at least one sky hook.
NOTE: The first ascent party chose to rappel from here because the crack dies out.

61. ADRENALIN SURFER: III, 5.12a
FIRST ASCENT: May 27, 1989, by Nathan (Nate) B. Postma, Dan Meyer with assist by Dan Feda.
APPROACH: Take the South Face Approach then traverse right on The Ramp past The Window to the base of Witchie (Route 62). The route starts part way up Witchie.
PITCH 1: Witchie pitch #1. **PITCH 2:** Climb the first half of Witchie pitch #2 then move left to a chain belay anchor. **PITCH 3:** Step left and move up under the roof onto the nose of the arete. Follow the bolts up the arete using mostly face climbing and edging to a double bolt belay. The crux is approximately 40 to 45 feet up from the belay and about eight feet long. Two bolts protect it well (110 feet, 5.12a).
FINISH: Rappel down using two 165 foot ropes to reach the top of the first pitch of Witchie or continue up on Witchie to the summit.
SUGGESTED EQUIPMENT: Standard rack, many Stoppers, #0-1/2 Friend, for the crack on the left face after bolt #8, and eleven quick draws.
NOTE: Protection is good with good rests and the roof pulls are fun. First ascent party gives it three stars.

62. WITCHIE: III, 5.10b
FIRST ASCENT: August 31, 1975, by Geoffrey Conley and John Pearson.
APPROACH: Take the East Buttress Approach to the top of the buttress and traverse left of Casper College (Route 64) two cracks. This is Witchie and also the start of Crocodile (Route 63).
PITCH 1: After climbing 30 feet to a roof, work left around the corner to a hand and fist crack. A couple of bushes make the crux of the first pitch. Belay at the bolts on the left side (80 feet, 5.9). **PITCH 2:** Follow this open-book, left-leaning crack with jams from finger to hand size (160 feet, 5.10b). **PITCH 3:** Jam and stem until the crack becomes a chimney which you climb to a column top on your right (90 feet, 5.7).
FINISH: Step left to a shallow chimney and climb to the summit (70 feet, 5.5).
SUGGESTED EQUIPMENT: #2 to #12 Stoppers with extra #3 to #12s, and a full set of Hexcentrics.
NOTE: A two star route.

63. CROCODILE: III, 5.10d
FIRST ASCENT: July 2, 1976, by Dennis Horning and Curt Haire.
APPROACH: Take the East Buttress Approach to the top of the East Buttress. Continue to the far side (left) until you are at the start of Witchie (Route 62) which is two cracks left of Casper College (Route 64).
PITCH 1: Climb up the start of Witchie, an easy dihedral about 30 feet, to the nose of the Crocodile (Route 63). Turn the overhang on the right (crux) and continue up the thin crack (there's a fixed Leeper here) which widens to a chimney, then narrows to a hand jam up to a bush. Belay at the bolts (75 feet, 5.10d). **PITCH 2:** Jam the crack directly up from the belay to a good belay stance atop the right-hand column (155 feet, 5.7). **PITCH 3:** Climb the leftmost crack (off-width but not too difficult) from the ledge to the top of the left-hand column (about 90 feet). Traverse right to another crack, and continue up it for another 50 feet to a belay on a good ledge (150 feet, 5.7).
FINISH: Third class to the summit.
SUGGESTED EQUIPMENT: Standard rack, #1 to #11 Hexcentrics with extra #7s to #9's, and #3 to #12 Stoppers with extra #7s and 8's.
NOTE: A one star route.

64. CASPER COLLEGE: III, 5.10d
FIRST ASCENT: June 7, 1956, by Dud McReynolds, Walt Bailey, David Sturdevant and Bruce Smith (III, 5.7, A2).
FIRST FREE ASCENT: June 1, 1979, by Jim Beyer and Dennis Horning.
APPROACH: Take the East Buttress Approach until you reach a large platform on top of the East Buttress. Look up from here and you will see a large crack with two gooseberry bushes growing out of it, running up between the faces to two yellow columns. This is Gooseberry Jam (Route 66). The Casper College Route starts two cracks left of it and has a few fixed pins in it.
PITCH 1: Climb this crack until you reach a good belay ledge and belay from the bolts on the right. The crux of the climb is about 70 feet up where the crack thins and the face bulges (150 feet, 5.10d). **PITCH 2:** Continue up the same gradually widening crack and pass an overhang on your right about 50 feet up. From here on, the column and crack to the right make the free climbing easier. Stop and belay from a good ledge just left of the crack (145 feet, 5.7).
FINISH: Climb and scramble easily to the summit (85 feet, 5.3).
SUGGESTED EQUIPMENT: Standard rack, #1 to #8 Hexcentrics, several #3 to #12, Stoppers, and runners.
NOTE: A three star route.

65. BURNING DAYLIGHT: II, 5.10b
FIRST ASCENT: October 30, 1977, by Dennis Horning and Mike Todd.
APPROACH: Take the East Buttress Approach to the top of the East Buttress. This route lies one crack left of Gooseberry Jam (Route 66) and one crack right of Casper College (Route 64).
PITCH 1: Ascend the left facing dihedral, moving past a crackless overhanging section to a strenuous finger, jam crack leading through a roof. Above the roof, the going is somewhat easier. Belay at the platform on top of the columns (160 feet, 5.10b). **PITCH 2:** Above the platform are four roofs. Climb the second from the left crack to a column top on the left side of the crack. The crux is going through the roofs. This is pitch three of Belle Fourche Buttress (Route 68) (155 feet, 5.8). **PITCH 3:** Work up and to the right for an easy finish (100 feet, 5.4).
SUGGESTED EQUIPMENT: Standard rack, #1 to #8 Hexcentrics, #3 to #12 Stoppers with extra #8 to #12 Stoppers.
NOTE: A three star route.

66. GOOSEBERRY JAM: III, 5.9-
FIRST ASCENT: July 23, 1959, by Bob Kamps and Don Yestness.
APPROACH: Standard East Buttress Approach to the top of the East Buttress. Look up and you will see a large crack with two gooseberry bushes growing out of it, running up between the faces of the two yellow columns. This is the route and also two cracks right of Casper College (Route 64).
PITCH 1: Climb onto the flakes at the base, or lieback up a large slab for about 20 feet. Proceed up the off-width jam crack, climbing up a large flake and passing the first bush. Lieback or jam up and past the second bush where the steepness eases a little and the crack begins to widen so that climbing is a little easier. Continue up to large belay ledge (150 feet, 5.9-). **PITCH 2:** Continue straight up on easy climbing about 30 feet where you will be on a ledge under some roofs. Traverse left two cracks under the roofs. Climb past the roof to a good belay ledge on your left (50 feet, 5.4). **PITCH 3:** Casper College, Pitch 2. Climb the gradually widening crack and stop and belay from either the top of the column on your right or on a ledge to your left about 10 to 15 feet higher (125 feet, 5.7).
FINISH: Same as Casper College finish (80 feet, 5.3).
SUGGESTED EQUIPMENT: Standard rack, set each of Hexcentrics and Stoppers. Friends help. Take several 3 to 4 inch pieces.
NOTE: A two star route.

67. GOOSEBERRY JAM - PETERSON VARIATION: III, 5.10a
FIRST ASCENT: May 7, 1978, by Don Peterson.
Approach: Take the East Buttress Approach to the top of the East Buttress and climb Gooseberry Jam (Route 66) to the large ledge below the main roofs.
PITCH 1: Gooseberry Jam, Pitch 1 (150 feet, 5.9-).
Pitch 1: Climb the right crack above you. This is one crack right of Belle Fourche Buttress (Route 68). Climb up through some bushes and the bulges above. Belay at a large column-top ledge (150 feet, 5.10a).
FINISH: You can climb and scramble straight up or traverse right and up easily to the summit.
SUGGESTED EQUIPMENT: Same as Gooseberry Jam.
NOTE: Don Peterson was belayed from below while he climbed this Peterson Variation.

68. BELLE FOURCHE BUTTRESS: III, 5.10b
FIRST ASCENT: May 28, 1961, by Don Ryan and Gary Cole (III, 5.8, A3).
FIRST FREE ASCENT: October 16, 1977, by Dennis Horning and Dave Rasmussen.

APPROACH: Take the East Buttress Approach to the top of the buttress and the base of Gooseberry Jam (Route 66).
PITCH 1: Start up Gooseberry Jam then traverse right and belay from two bolts on top of a large block. The route follows the first crack on the north side of the buttress. The original aid climb started at the very base of the crack (30 feet, 5.6).
PITCH 2: Traverse right to a hand and finger crack and follow it to the top of the buttress. The crux comes after 10 feet of handjams where the crack constricts to 20 feet of finger size jams leading to a rest. Strenuous hand jams complete this pitch (155 feet, 5.10b). **PITCH 3:** Climb two cracks left above you (two cracks right of Casper College). Climb easily to the roofs and continue up the crack to a belay on a column top (150 feet, 5.8).
FINISH: Easy fourth class climbing and scrambling to the summit directly up or up and right.
SUGGESTED EQUIPMENT: Standard rack, #1-8 Hexcentrics, #3-12 Stoppers, extra #8- 12 Stoppers, and #1/2-3 Friends help.
NOTE: Small fingers make it harder. A three star route.

69. TWO LEFT SHOES: III, 5.8, A1
FIRST ASCENT: July 27, 1978, by Jim Beyer (solo).
APPROACH: Take the East Buttress Approach until you are almost on top of the Buttress. The route is located one crack to the right of Belle Fourche Buttress (Route 68) and left of Marriage Was My First Mistake (Route 71). Scramble up to the belay below a short vertical wall.
PITCH 1: Climb the short wall and step left. Climb up the right-facing dihedral to the top of the flakes. Climb the hand crack above to get a high nut in, then drop down and face climb to the right and belay above the traverse (5.8). **PITCH 2:** Continue up the crack and bear right into the Groove. Free climb as high as possible then traverse on aid from the groove to the crack on the left face then left to the face crack outside the groove. About 5 points of aid, mostly horizontal pitons. (5.8, A1) **PITCH 3:** Aid up to a belay just right of a roof (75 feet, 5.6, A1). **PITCH 4:** Mixed free and aid leads to an easy chimney. Belay on top of the pedestal on your left (5.8+, A1).
FINISH: Class IV to the top.
SUGGESTED EQUIPMENT: A big blade, 6 horizontals, 2 or 3 of each angle up to 1", a set of Stoppers and a set of Hexcentrics.
NOTE: Some of this has been climbed free as Dump Watt (Route 70). Jim Beyer said, "The route is named for a mistake I had to live with."

70. DUMP WATT: II, 5.10b
FIRST ASCENT: August 29, 1981, by Mark Smedley, Eric Rhicard and Dave Larsen.
APPROACH: Take the East Buttress Approach. This route is one crack right of Belle Fourche Buttress (Route 68) and starts on the old aid route Two Left Shoes (Route 69).
PITCH 1: Belay fairly high. Start on Two Left Shoes until it goes left then climb straight up the finger and hand crack which again becomes Two Left Shoes. Continue up to the bolts for a belay at the bottom of an acute dihedral (150 feet, 5.9+).
PITCH 2: Continue up on Two Left Shoes until it traverses left and you go straight up the acute dihedral to a horizontal ledge leading left. Hand traverse left to good ledges, then climb the finger and hand crack (crux) to a small bush that is below and left of the big overhang that tops the acute dihedral. Hang a belay here (135 feet, 5.10b). **PITCH 3:** Climb the crack up through a chimney to the top of a pillar on your left (150 feet, 5.9).
FINISH: Two Left Shoes finish.

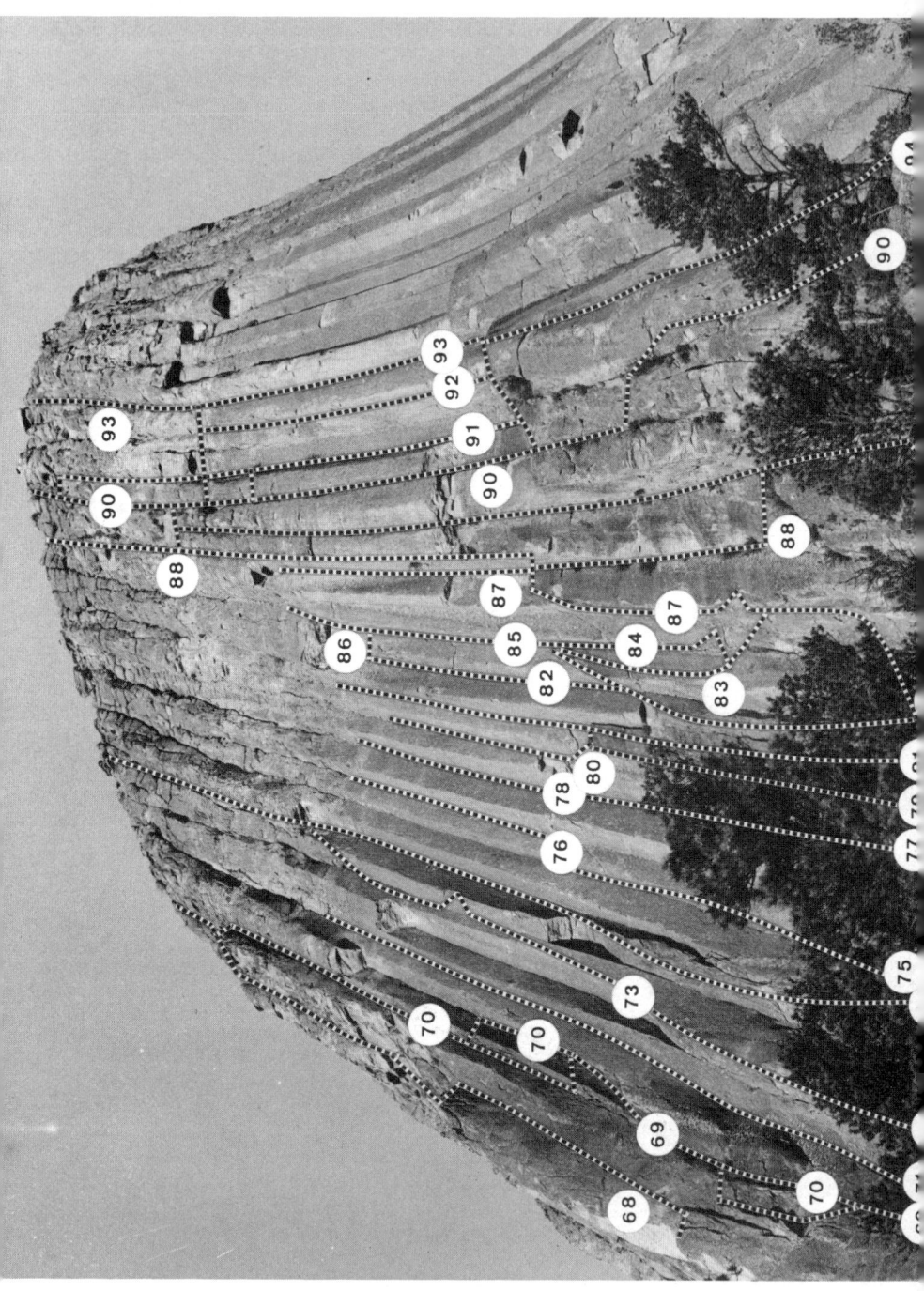

SUGGESTED EQUIPMENT: Standard rack, #1 to #8 Hexcentrics with extra #9's and #10's, and #3 to #12 Stoppers with extra small to medium sizes.
NOTE: A two star route.

71. MARRIAGE WAS MY FIRST MISTAKE: II, 5.7, A3
FIRST ASCENT: July, 1989, by Frank Sanders, solo.
APPROACH: Take the East Buttress Approach. This route follows the crack just right of Dump Watt (Route 70).
PITCH 1: Climb to a three bolt belay. (140 feet, 5.7, A2). **PITCH 2:** Continue climbing to another three bolt belay. (140 feet, A3).
FINISH: Rappel off after Pitch 2.
SUGGESTED EQUIPMENT: Standard aid rack.

72. BUCKSPECK: II, 5.10c
FIRST ASCENT: Summer 1991, Dennis Horning and Hollis Marriott.
APPROACH: Take the Northeast Buttress Approach and climb up to the area between Marriage Was My First Mistake (Route 71) and Calculus Affair (Route 74).
PITCH 1: Follow the line of bolts on this exposed arete with an exiting slab for the finish at the bolted belay that starts Stepping Out Of Flatland (Route 73) (170 feet, 5.10c).
FINISH: Rappel off or continue up on Stepping Out Of Flatland (5.11b).
SUGGESTED EQUIPMENT: Eighteen assorted length quickdraws.
COMMENTS: No description of this route has been submitted for National Park Service records by the first ascent party. Contact the first ascent party for more details.

73. STEPPING OUT OF FLATLAND: 5.11b
FIRST ASCENT: Est. 1991, by undisclosed climbers.
APPROACH: Take the East Buttress Approach and move right of Dump Watt (Route 70) and Marriage Was My First Mistake (Route 71) and before Calculus Affair (Route 74) to Buckspeck (Route 72) where you start.
PITCH 1: Climb Buckspeck (5.10c) **PITCH 2:** Follow the bolts up and right to the crack then straight up until you can move onto the right face a short distance. Climb up and left past the crack and up to the belay at the bolts (5.11a). **PITCH 3:** Climb and stem up past a line of bolts to the belay bolts under a roof (5.11b)
FINISH: Rappel down.
NOTE: The first ascent party did not leave a route description with the Park Service for its files. If you have more information on this route contact the Park Service.

74. CALCULUS AFFAIR: III, 5.10d, A0
FIRST ASCENT: June, August and September 1990, by "Tintin" Ziebell, "Scooter" Metcalf (Pitch 1), and "Batman" Stevens.
APPROACH: Take the East Buttress Approach and climb up from the Hourglass until you are two cracks left of Old Guys In Lycra (Route 77). This is the start of Skinny Puppy (Route 75) where you start.
PITCH 1: From the start of Skinny Puppy, traverse left to the thin crack on the arete with a pin in it. Climb left of the crack, past the pin, and up the left side of the arete, clipping four bolts. The crux is at the second bolt. Belay at the three bolt chained anchor (155 feet, 5.9+). **PITCH 2:** From the belay, step right into the corner and up. A pin and six bolts protect this strenuous and sustained pitch. Protection is marginal and the crack seems to attract dirt and grass. Belay at the three bolt chained anchor (160 feet, 5.10d, A0). **PITCH 3:** Climb up to the roof (5.10d). Traverse left and up dirt filled, rotten cracks and a gnarly face to the two bolt anchor (150 feet, 5.10d).

FINISH: Scramble to the summit or rappel the route with double ropes.
SUGGESTED EQUIPMENT: Standard rack plus extra, medium Stoppers.
COMMENTS: This route has marginal protection. After four days of cleaning, the first ascent party to completely ascend the route (Ziebell/Stevens) had high expectations of the line. Their hopes were dashed, however after the exhausting ascent of Pitch 2 which involved falling, hanging, and plenty of stark fear. They rated Pitch 2 as 5.11b but a subsequent party rated it 5.11d/512a and reportedly backed off for lack of protection. Pitch 2 has yet to see a "clean" free ascent. Pitch 2, by some climbers, is not considered valid due to much falling and hanging. Another guidebook only lists Pitch 1. The area above Pitch 1 is not recommended because of poor protection. A no star route.

75. SKINNY PUPPY: I, 5.10d
FIRST ASCENT: July 24, 1987, by David Thomas, Seth Pierce and Mike Robinson.
APPROACH: Take the East Buttress Approach then up and right to the base of the route. The route begins two cracks left of Old Guys in Lycra (Route 77) and at the start of Calculus Affair (Route 74).
PITCH 1: Climb up the right column (face holds and stemming) approximately 70 feet, to a hollow flake. A bolt on the left side of the crack protects the climb directly up over the flake. Continue up to a small bulge, then right on the column face for fifteen feet to a bolt. Clip it, then make a 5.10c move left to a pocket mantle. Clip another bolt, then move up on 5.10c holds to a stance just right of the now widening crack. Follow this finger crack eight feet to the two bolt hanging belay (105 feet, 5.10c).
FINISH: Rappel off.
SUGGESTED EQUIPMENT: Two sets of RPs #2-#4, medium Stoppers, TCU's and four quick draws.
NOTE: This is a one star route.

76. SUICIDAL TENDENCIES   III, 5.10c, A3+ (a midface pitch)
FIRST ASCENT: July 24, 1987, by David Thomas and Seth Pierce.
APPROACH: Take the East Buttress Approach to the start of Skinny Puppy (Route 75) which starts just above the start of Calculus Affair (Route 74) and is two cracks left of Old Guys In Lycra (Route 77).
PITCH 1: Climb Skinny Puppy to the belay bolts (105 feet, 5.10c). **PITCH 2:** From the Skinny Puppy belay, pendulum one crack to the right. This is Suicidal Tendencies. Aid up this crack using a variety of equipment from hooks, RPs, knife blades, and Lost Arrows. The crux is 115 feet up where tied off blades, copperheads and hooks are required for ten feet (160 feet, A3+).
FINISH: Rappel from the belay bolts to the Skinny Puppy bolts and down from there to the start of the climb.
SUGGESTED EQUIPMENT: Four sets of RPs, small Stoppers, TCUs, knifeblades, Lost Arrows, Copperheads, three quickdraws for the bolts, and several hooks.
NOTE: The crack is very shallow and rotten in places, but the abundance of face holds indicates that with much cleaning and bolting this pitch would go free. This climb is rated one star out of a possible three stars.

77. OLD GUYS IN LYCRA: I, 5.10d
FIRST ASCENT: May 25, 1986, by Carl Coy and Bill Pelander.
APPROACH: Take the Northeast Buttress Approach half way. From here climb up to the base of the climb directly above you and between the buttresses. The pitch is the second crack to the left of The Chute (Route 79) and is a corner crack.
PITCH 1: Climb this sustained crack using fingers and stemming. The crux of the climb is a stemming problem at the very end. Set up a hanging belay from the

bolts on the right side of the crack and just below a small double roof on your right (160 feet, 5.10d).
FINISH: Rappel off.
SUGGESTED EQUIPMENT: RPs, small to medium Stoppers, #1 to #3 Friends.
NOTE: Poison Ivy can be found on the approach. A two star route.

78. YOUNG MAN BLUES: II, 5.12b
FIRST ASCENT: September 28, 1989, by Keith Pike.
APPROACH: Northeast Buttress Approach. This pitch starts on top of Old Guys In Lycra (Route 77) which is just left of The Chute (Route 79).
PITCH 1: Old Guys In Lycra (160 feet, 5.10d). **PITCH 2:** Climb up on high angle stemming along a seam (no crack), through three stemming cruxes to the belay bolts at the end of the pitch. There is one hands down rest in the middle of the pitch (155 feet, 5.12b).
FINISH: Rappel off.
SUGGESTED EQUIPMENT: Ten or so small to large wires, RPs, a #2-1/2 Friend (for the second roof), and ten quickdraws.
NOTE: The rappel bolts are just over a small bulge and just below the upper broken section with a large crack. There are ten bolts on the route. A two star route.

79. THE CHUTE: I, 5.10d
FIRST ASCENT: July 11, 1982, by Dennis Horning and Hollis Marriott.
APPROACH: Take the Northeast Buttress Approach until you reach the constriction (Hourglass) between the East Buttress and the Northeast Buttress. From here climb up to the base of the climb above you between the buttresses. The route is on the left side of a long leaning column in the crack just left of Nitro Express (Route 81).
PITCH 1: Climb up the left side of The Chute Column using finger and hand jams, stemming and face climbing. The first 20 feet is loose. Finish climbing the top off-width to the belay bolts at the column top. A 5.9 off-width move at the top can be protected with a #4 friend. Belay at the bolts on the column top (160 feet, 5.10d).
FINISH: Rappel from here or continue up on another route.
SUGGESTED EQUIPMENT: #1 to #8 Hexcentrics, #3 to #12 Stoppers, a #4 friend and many extra small to medium pieces.
NOTE: A one or two star route.

80. SEE YOU IN SOHO: II, 5.12b
FIRST ASCENT: August 14, 1985 by Todd Skinner and Beth Wald.
APPROACH: Take the Northeast Buttress Approach until you are directly below The Chute (Route 79). Climb up to the start of The Chute which gets you to the pitch above. The route starts one crack left of the top of The Chute Column.
PITCH 1: The Chute. Climb up this crack to the bolts on top of the column (160 feet, 5.10d). **PITCH 2:** From the top of The Chute Column, step left one crack and climb through a roof to a thin finger crack. Follow this narrowing crack to a two-pin hanging belay at the base of the broken rock (130 feet, 5.12b).
FINISH: Rappel off.
SUGGESTED EQUIPMENT: Many #2 to #5 RPs, cleaning tool, small to medium Stoppers, and one quick draw for a fixed pin.
NOTE: A one star climb.

81. NITRO EXPRESS: II, 5.12a
FIRST ASCENT: Pitch 2 - August 1, 1985, by Steve Petro, Beth Wald and Todd Skinner. Pitch 1 and Pitch 3 - September 11, 1986, by Steve Petro and Paul Piana.

APPROACH: Follow the Northeast Buttress Approach half way until you are directly below The Chute Column. The route starts one crack right of The Chute (Route 79).
PITCH 1: Work up the thin crack before moving left to a bolt. Continue up 30 feet to a piton, then up to off-width where a bolt protects the face so you can stay out of the off-width. Belay at the bolts on top of The Chute (165 feet, 5.9). **PITCH 2:** From the top of The Chute Column, climb up the finger crack above you. This is an interesting pitch with intricate face climbing, some stems, and very thin finger-tip cracks. A thin face move 40 feet up is the crux for the pitch. Continue up to a hanging belay at the bolts (80 feet, 5.11c). **PITCH 3:** Stem and layback 20 to 40 feet. Continue up the finger crack. Near the end of the pitch, it opens up to a hand crack. Belay from two bolts (85 feet, 5.12a).
FINISH: Rappel from two bolts.
SUGGESTED EQUIPMENT: Three sets RPs #2 to #5, #1 to #5 Rocks (three sets of #1 to #3), #1-1/2 to #3 Friends and small to medium Stoppers.
NOTE: Good protection on Pitch 2 and 3. Most climbers like to start by doing The Chute (5.10d) which has good protection. A two star climb.

82. STRONGBACK: II, 5.11d
FIRST ASCENT: July, 1990, by Dennis Horning, Steve Olson, and Steve Babbits.
APPROACH: Take the Northeast Buttress Approach until you are between Nitro Express (Route 81) and Kama Sutra (Route 88).
NOTE: The first ascent party did not submit information on this route for inclusion in Park Service records.

83. ANTS ON ANGEL FOOD: II, 5.11d
FIRST ASCENT: June 2, 1990, by Dennis Horning and Steve Babbits.
APPROACH: Take the East Buttress Approach and climb up until you are just right of The Chute Column and Nitro Express (Route 81).
COMMENTS: No description of this route has been submitted for NPS records. This short pitch is not a crack climb. It is a pitch that is protected by bolts. Contact the first ascent party for details.

84. NATURAL PERVERSITY: I, 5.11a
FIRST ASCENT: Summer 1990, by Dennis Horning and Hollis Marriott.
APPROACH: Take the Northeast Buttress Approach half way then back up until you are just right of Nitro Express (Route 81). The climb starts at the start of Strongback (Route 82).
PITCH 1: Move right three cracks as you climb, and up that crack to the point at a bolt where All American Ecstasy Boy (Route 87) goes straight up and this route goes left and up past two cracks to the bolted belay (130 feet, 5.10b).
PITCH 2: Climb up to a bolt right of the right crack then up and left back into the crack and follow the crack up to the belay bolts on a ledge to your left (5.11a).
FINISH: Rappel off, or continue up on Soaring (5.10d) or Strongback (5.11d).
SUGGESTED EQUIPMENT: Standard rack, quickdraws, RPs, and a set of Rocks for this route only.
EXPLANATION: The first ascent party did not submit information on this route for the National Park Service files. Contact the first ascent party for details. If you have further information contact the National Park Service.

85. SOARING: II, 5.10d
FIRST ASCENT: Summer, 1990, by Dennis Horning and Danny Rosen.

APPROACH: Take the Northeast Buttress Approach and make your way just to the right of Nitro Express (Route 81). The pitch is mid-face two cracks right of Nitro Express Pitch 2 and is a stemming pitch.

NOTE: The first ascent party did not give the National Park Service a description of this climb for their files. Contact the first ascent party for details.

86. FOUR WINZE: III, 5.10c

FIRST ASCENT: Summer 1990, by Dennis Horning and Robin Jones.

APPROACH: Take the Northeast Buttress Approach and climb back up until you are just right of Nitro Express (Route 81). Four Winze starts at the top of Strongback (Route 82) and Soaring (Route 85).

PITCH #1 to 3: Your choice; Strongback (5.11d), Soaring (5.10d), or Natural Perversity (Route 84) (5.11a). **PITCH 3 or 4:** Four Winze. Climb the crack right of the bolts to the roof. Pass the roof on the right side in the hand crack and climb up until you can set up a belay (5.10c).

FINISH: There is no information on this so you take your own chances or contact the first ascent party for details.

COMMENTS: The first ascent party did not submit information regarding this route for inclusion in National Park Service files. Some information has been received from other climbers. If you can fill in any information, contact the National Park Service.

87. ALL AMERICAN ECSTASY BOY: II, 5.11

FIRST ASCENT: August or September 1991, by Dennis Horning, Danny Rosen, and Scott Brachtmann.

APPROACH: Take the East Buttress Approach and climb up until you are just right of Nitro Express (Route 81). Start two cracks right of The Chute (Route 79) on Natural Perversity (Route 84).

PITCH 1: Climb right and up on Natural Perversity until you have moved three cracks to your right. Climb this thin crack to where Natural Perversity goes left. Continue up now on All American Ecstasy Boy then slightly right to reach the belay bolts (5.10d). **PITCH 2:** Climb the left crack (stemming and thin fingers) until you are at the column top belay at the bolts (5.11). **PITCH 3:** Climb the crack above you which is just left of Kama Sutra (Route 88), to a two bolt belay (5.11a). **PITCH 4:** Continue up this thin crack with stemming to the belay under a roof (5.11).

SUGGESTED EQUIPMENT: Standard rack, quickdraws for the bolts, small pieces, and RPs.

COMMENTS: No description of this route has been submitted for National Park Service records by the first ascent party. Other climbers have given this description and if you have more information (length of pitches etc.) notify the National Park Service. You can contact the first ascent party for more details. This route may be named after Danny Rosen.

88. KAMA SUTRA: III, 5.10a

FIRST ASCENT: September 28, 1976, by Dennis Horning, Cody Paulson and Frank Sanders.

APPROACH: Take the Northeast Buttress Approach and start at the base of Suchness (Route 89). Most of the route lies one crack left of Suchness. The first climb started further left but that is not used now.

PITCH 1: Begin left of the crack just below two weathered tree stumps. Climb up on Suchness through a bush and belay where this route starts left of Suchness (70 feet, 5.5). **PITCH 2:** Traverse left above this ledge using small holds and friction

and ascend the bushy crack to a comfortable belay stance on a broken column on the left (130 feet, 5.7). **PITCH 3:** Climb down several feet and traverse right into a crack. The first 70 feet of this crack is hand jamming. About 15 feet above the bush is a fixed bong where a good hanging belay anchor can be set (100 feet, 5.10a).
PITCH 4: The next section of crack passing the horizontal crack on the right is fist jamming; the crack above widens to a squeeze chimney leading to a belay ledge on top of the column (110 feet, 5.9).
FINISH: Continue up the same crack to the top. You can also take the right crack to the summit (150 feet, 5.6).
SUGGESTED EQUIPMENT: Standard rack, #1 to #8 Hexcentrics and a set of #3 to #12 Stoppers. Also a five inch tube chock or equivalent and five 2 to 3-1/2 inch pieces.
NOTE: Kama Sutra is the route of a hundred and one positions, each one harder than the last. A one star route.

89. SUCHNESS: III, 5.10b

FIRST ASCENT: June 2, 1974, by Dennis Horning and Paul Piana (III, 5.8, A1).
FIRST FREE ASCENT: September 7, 1976, by Dennis Horning and Frank Sanders
APPROACH: Take the Northeast Buttress Approach. This crack is one crack left of Patent Pending (Route 90) at the mid-face level and is in the crack that goes between the two mid-face roofs.
PITCH 1: The pitch begins left of the crack just below two weathered tree stumps. Climb up through a bush and belay where Kama Sutra (Route 88) starts left. Watch for poison ivy (70 feet, 5.5). **PITCH 2:** Continue up the crack. About two-thirds of the way up there is a tricky bulge. Just below the roof traverse left to a thin sitting belay ledge. The belay anchor takes some rigging (150 feet, 5.8). **PITCH 3:** Climb over the four foot roof which is the crux and protect with 2- to 3-inch pieces. The crack above the roof remains quite hard for about 12 feet. Continue up the crack protecting with tube chocks and large hex nuts. Continue up past some natural rocks and belay at a good belay ledge on top a large chock rock near the North Face Tunnel (155 feet, 5.10b). **PITCH 4:** Chimney up to the top of a broken column, then traverse left to a crack and continue up the crack except for veering right around a bush (135 feet, 5.5). **PITCH 5:** Climb up to the summit in the crack above you (60 feet, 5.5).
SUGGESTED EQUIPMENT: Standard rack, a set each of Hexcentrics and Stoppers, extra medium to large pieces, and six 3- to 4 inch pieces. A couple of tube chocks and large Friends help; also extra runners.
NOTE: A one star route.

90. PATENT PENDING: III, 5.8+

FIRST ASCENT: May 8, 1971, by Charles Bare and Jim Olson (III, 5.7, A1 or A2).
FIRST FREE ASCENT: August 17, 1972, by Bruce K. Bright and Dennis Drayna.
APPROACH: Take the Northeast Buttress Approach until you are on top of the east end of the Northeast Buttress directly below three prominent roofs and Teacher's Lounge.
PITCH 1: Climb up face holds and the obvious crack through some bushes to a good belay ledge behind a large flake (120 feet, 5.5). If you belay high it is 80 feet. **PITCH 2:** From the belay traverse up and left a short distance, then climb straight up to the Teacher's Lounge belay ledge (160 feet, 5.4). **PITCH 3:** Climb one crack left of Assembly (Route 91) Line through the overhang which is the crux of the climb. Continue up this off-width crack and belay in the chimney below the tunnel (160 feet, 5.8+). **PITCH 4:** Continue up on easy climbing to the end of your rope and belay (160 feet, 5.6).
FINISH: Easy scramble to the summit.

SUGGESTED EQUIPMENT: Standard rack, #1 to #8 Hexcentrics, #3 to #12 Stoppers, and six 2-1/2 to 4-inches.
NOTE: Instead of traversing left after pitch one, the original route probably went straight up to Teacher's Lounge. A three star route if you like big cracks, Otherwise two stars.

91. ASSEMBLY LINE: III, 5.9-
FIRST ASCENT: May 18, 1975, by Dennis Horning and Judd Jennerjahn.
APPROACH: Take the Northeast Buttress Approach until you are on top of the east end of the buttress directly below three prominent midface roofs. Start on Patent Pending (Route 90).
PITCH 1: You can get to Teacher's Lounge, a large ledge below the overhangs, in one pitch if you tandem climb (180 feet if you start high). We recommend doing it in two pitches from the bottom. Climb up an easy crack to a good belay ledge behind a large standing flake (80 feet, 5.5) 120 feet if you start low. **PITCH 2:** Climb up and traverse left one crack with a wide step across. Take this crack to Teacher's Lounge (160 feet, 5.5). **PITCH 3:** Face climb and stem to start this crack which is the long hand crack on the right side of the three roofs. The fingercrux is near the bottom. Climb to the belay bolts on the left side of the crack (155 feet, 5.9-). **PITCH 4:** Continue up the crack to a belay right below a roof (140 feet, 5.8).
FINISH: Traverse left one crack and climb this easy crack to the summit.
SUGGESTED EQUIPMENT: A standard rack, full set of Hexcentrics, and larger wired Stoppers. Also runners. Be sure to take extra medium Hexcentrics and large Stoppers.
NOTE: Petzl eye bolts are at the belay. A three star route.

92. SURFER GIRL: II, 5.12c
FIRST ASCENT: See explanation under "Note" below.
FIRST FREE ASCENT: July 14, 1984, by Todd Skinner and Beth Wald.
APPROACH: Take the Northeast Buttress Approach. This route starts from Teacher's Lounge, a large ledge that is mid-face on the north side of the Tower. It is two cracks right from Assembly Line (Route 91) and one crack left from Maid in the Shaid (Route 93).
PITCH 1 2: Use the first two pitches of Patent Pending (Route 90) or any other route that will get you to the Teacher's Lounge ledge. **PITCH 3:** Surfer Girl. This is a clean, enjoyable finger, face, and stemming problem with extremely good protection for most of the route. There are some fixed pins. Climb one crack left of Maid In The Shaid with very desperate and sustained flaring fingers. The crux of the climb is about 90 feet up. After this crux, the climbing is easy up to a bolt belay on the right column face (155 feet, 5.12c).
FINISH: Rappel down or you can go up and left to reach the top via Assembly Line or Patent Pending; or you can go up to your right and finish on Maid in the Shaid.
SUGGESTED EQUIPMENT: Many small and medium Stoppers with a few #1 Friends and runners. Bring a few larger pieces for the first two pitches and whatever you might need if you go higher.
NOTE: Two earlier aid routes have been put up right of Assembly Line and a lot of confusion exists as to their location. Rypkema and Haire "A Climbers Guide to Devils Tower" show the aid route "Northeast Corner" going up two cracks right of Assembly Line. National Park Service information indicates that any of the three cracks right of Assembly Line could be this route. After contacting one of the original climbers no further information was obtained. Another M&CWTC aid route was put up in some part of the Surfer Girl crack. Todd Skinner did the crux of this route in the midst of a hail storm using "mad dog motivation." A one star route.

93. MAID IN THE SHAID: III, 5.11d
FIRST ASCENT: May 13, 1978, by Terry Rypkema, Steve Gardiner Frank Sanders, and Debbie Berglund (III, 5.8, A2).
FIRST FREE ASCENT: June 25, 1983, by Steve Hong, Andy Hong and Karin Budding.
APPROACH: Take the Northeast Buttress Approach. This route is three cracks right of Assembly Line (Route 91) and starts on the right side of Teacher's Lounge (rightmost crack).
PITCH 1 AND 2: Climb New Wave (Route 94) or Broken Tree (Route 95) to Teacher's Lounge (200 feet, 5.10a or 5.10b). **PITCH 3:** The start of the route is a classic, beautiful corner that is one of the purest stemming pitches at the Tower. The entire pitch is sustained with no real rests, but with good protection. Many small wired stoppers are needed for the first half and small hand size protection for the last half. Belay at two bolts on the left column face (165 feet, 5.11d). Many rappel from here which makes it grade II. **PITCH 4:** Chimney and jam to the end of your rope and belay on a large block (160 feet, 5.6).
FINISH: Scramble to the top.
SUGGESTED EQUIPMENT: Three sets of RPs, cleaning tool, many small to medium Stoppers and three or four #1 to #2 Friends (30 pieces in all).
NOTE: A three star route.

94. NEW WAVE: I, 5.10a
FIRST ASCENT: June 10, 1982, by Dave Larsen and Dennis Horning.
APPROACH: Take the Northeast Buttress Approach. This route starts under Teacher's Lounge ledge at the same point Broken Tree (Route 95) starts.
PITCH 1: Start up and traverse up and left two cracks. This is the New Wave route. Work up the jam crack and face until you come to the small belay ledge at the bolts on your right (100 feet, 5.7). **PITCH 2:** Continue up the crack to the crux of the climb that is protected by a bolt on the crack. Step up right on friction only and lay back left until you can get back in the crack, up and right. Finish on mixed climbing to the Teacher's Lounge bolts (140 feet, 5.10a)
FINISH: Rappel down the way you came or go to the summit via any of several routes above.
SUGGESTED EQUIPMENT: #1 to #7 Hexcentrics, #3 to #12 Stoppers and any other items you may need if you go to the summit.
NOTE: This is a good three star route.

95. BROKEN TREE: I, 5.10b
FIRST ASCENT: June 22,1982, by Dennis Horning and Dave Larsen.
APPROACH: Follow the Northeast Buttress Approach just around a corner past Assembly Line (Route 91). The start is the same as New Wave (Route 94) but follows the crack above the broken tree you have to step over. This is also just left of the Everlasting Column.
PITCH 1: Climb the crack, in a left-facing dihedral, that is the western most crack to achieve the Teacher's Lounge Ledge. There is easy climbing to a double bolt belay (80 feet, 5.7). **PITCH 2:** Climb this varied crack with thin stemming, some rotten rock and a crux which is a 15 foot finger crack at the top. Belay at the Teacher's Lounge bolts (140 feet, 5.10a).
FINISH: Rappel from here or climb any of several other routes above to the summit.
SUGGESTED EQUIPMENT: Use a variety of nuts but mostly small nuts and Stoppers.
NOTE: Petzl eye bolts will be found at the belays. This is a two star route.

96. THE MAIDEN: I, 5.10a
FIRST ASCENT: May 27, 1987, by Scott Flesner and Jim Swenson.
APPROACH: Take the Northeast Buttress Approach. The crack is one crack right of Broken Tree (Route 95) and has a V-shaped evergreen growing about 35 feet up in the crack.
PITCH 1: Free climb and stem up along the crack using the crack for protection. The crux (110') is thin face climbing up through the crack running through the green flakes. Traverse right around the corner to the Everlasting (Route 97) belay bolts (160 feet, 5.10a).
FINISH: Rappel from here or climb the second pitch of Everlasting or Back to Montana (Route 100).
SUGGESTED EQUIPMENT: Standard rack, #1 to #10 Stoppers, #1 to #5 RPs.
NOTE: Do not use the left side of the green flakes as the flake is very loose and dangerous. This is not a very aesthetic climb. Parts of this route have been done by Carl Coy and others. They think the complete pitch has been done before. This is a no star route.

97. EVERLASTING: I, 5.10c
FIRST ASCENT: August 13, 1983, by Dennis Horning and Dave Larsen.
APPROACH: Take the Northeast Buttress approach past New Wave (Route 94) to the base of the Everlasting Column. This route starts just right of The Maiden (Route 96) and start on Sympathy For The Devil (Route 99) (the crack) or just left of it for the Horning Variation which goes up and right a short distance to join Sympathy For The Devil.
PITCH 1: Sympathy For The Devil (free). Climb up this low-angle crack until the crack thins. Now traverse left and up until you can traverse back right to a small belay ledge at the belay bolts which starts Everlasting and Back To Montana (155 feet, 5.8+). **PITCH 2:** Everlasting. Climb left and up on a line of bolts until you get to the fifth bolt. Move onto the left face, up and back to the right on airy moves (If you stay direct without the left face move it becomes 5.11b). From here face climb the center of the column until you reach its top. Belay at the bolts (150 feet, 5.10c). Bolts protect this pitch.
FINISH: It is recommended that you rappel off here. You could attempt the difficult crack above which is Hollow Men (Route 98).
SUGGESTED EQUIPMENT: Standard rack, eleven quick draws, and medium Stoppers.
NOTE: A two or three star route.

98. HOLLOW MEN: II, 5.12c
FIRST ASCENT: September 5, 1981, by Frank Sanders and Chris Engle as Sympathy For The Devil (Route 99) (III, 5.9, A2).
FIRST FREE ASCENT, August 6, 1985, by Todd Skinner and Beth Wald.
APPROACH: Take the Northeast Buttress Approach traversing right to the base of the climb. The Hollow Men pitch starts from the top of the Everlasting Column.
PITCHES 1 and 2: You can reach the start of the pitch by climbing any route that gets you to the Teacher's Lounge ledge where a short pitch takes you to the base of Hollow Men; this was recommended by Todd Skinner. Or you can climb Everlasting (Route 97), Sympathy For The Devil (Route 99), and Back to Montana (Route 100) to get to the top of the Everlasting Column (310 feet). PITCH 3: Hollow Men. Climb up this desperate and sustained blank corner with a noticeable lack of fingerlocks. This is a stemming problem with numerous 5.12 sections. Belay at the bolts under the roof (140 feet, 5.12c).
FINISH: Rappel off or continue up on Sympathy For The Devil (140 feet, 5.9).

SUGGESTED EQUIPMENT: First ascent party had five #1 RPs, fourteen #2 RPs, and five each of #3 to #5 RPs; also a few small Stoppers and a #1 Friend.
NOTE: This is a one star route.

99. SYMPATHY FOR THE DEVIL: III, 5.9, A2 (5.12c free)
FIRST ASCENT: September 5, 1981, by Frank Sanders and Chris Engle.
FIRST FREE ASCENT: Pitch 2 as Back to Montana (Route 100) - June 27,1982, by Dennis Horning and Monte Cooper (5.10d). Pitch 3 as Hollow Men (Route 98) - August 6, 1985, by Todd Skinner and Beth Wald (5.12c).
APPROACH: Take the Northeast Buttress Approach until you are on the right side of the Everlasting Column. This route starts one crack left of Mystic And The Mulchers (Route 101). Belay at the tree, in the crack, that is two cracks right of the route.
PITCH 1: Climb the crack to where it pinches in, then mantle and climb the face on the left. Belay at the Back to Montana starting bolts (160 feet, 5.8). **PITCH 2:** This pitch has now been climbed free as Back to Montana. Belay at the bolts on the top of the Everlasting Column (150 feet, 5.10d). **PITCH 3:** This has now been climbed free as Hollow Men (140 feet, 5.12c). **PITCH 4:** Climb up and traverse left under the roof. Keep on until you can set a belay (140 feet, 5.9).
FINISH: Scramble to the top (40 feet, 5.4).
SUGGESTED EQUIPMENT: Hexcentrics, Stoppers, #1 Friend, and many Lost Arrows and angles. See the free-climb descriptions for equipment used on them.
NOTE: Pitch 2 and 3 were originally climbed "A2" but in following our policy of stressing free climbs we have now listed them under the free name. Two stars for the free portion.

100. BACK TO MONTANA: II, 5.10d
FIRST ASCENT: September 5, 1981, by Frank Sanders and Chris Engle as Sympathy For The Devil (Route 99) (III, 5.9, A2).
FIRST FREE ASCENT: June 27, 1982, by Dennis Horning and Monte Cooper.
APPROACH: Take the Northeast Buttress Approach and traverse west just pass Broken Tree (Route 95). You can reach the route by climbing pitch 1 of Everlasting (Route 97) or Sympathy For The Devil (155 feet, 5.8+) or (160 feet, 5.8, Belay at the bolts.
PITCH 2: Just above the bolts traverse right to a crack in a right facing dihedral. Climb this very thin crack with fingers where they fit, and stem where they don't, to the top of the broken column and belay at the bolts there (150 feet, 5.10d).
FINISH: Rappel from here or continue up on Hollow Men (Route 98) (II, 5.12c).
SUGGESTED EQUIPMENT: Standard rack, #1-8 Hexcentrics and #3-12 Stoppers. Also a #1 Friend, five to seven over-the-shoulder length slings, and RPs.
NOTE: A two or three star route.

101. MYSTIC AND THE MULCHERS: I, 5.8-
FIRST ASCENT: July 27, 1985, by Jim Schlinkmann, Richard Guilmette, "Barney" Fisher, and Mateo Pee Pee.
APPROACH: Take the Northeast Approach to McCarthy North Face (Route 105). The climb is three main cracks left of the first pitch of McCarthy North Face, and two cracks right of the Pitch 1 of Back to Montana (Route 100) or two cracks right of the start of Sympathy for the Devil (Route 99). The climb starts at a pine tree in the crack at the base of the climb.
PITCH 1: Climb the finger crack and face to a three bolt belay. The crux is near the end of the pitch and is protected by a bolt. (150 feet, 5.8-).
FINISH: Rappel from the bolts.

SUGGESTED EQUIPMENT: Many wired rocks, RPs, #2 to #5 Hexcentrics, #1 to #3 Friends, and sliders.
NOTE: This pitch has many good face holds and rests with good protection. A two star pitch.

102. NEVERLASTING: I, 5.9-
FIRST ASCENT: August 26, 1985, by David Kozak and Denny Hochwender.
APPROACH: Take the Northeast Approach until you are just short of McCarthy North Face (Route 105). The pitch begins in the shallow dihedral one crack right of Mystic and the Mulchers (Route 101) and one crack left of Leaping Lizards (Route 103).
PITCH 1: Climb the shallow dihedral and then the face above to a stance between Mystic and the Mulchers and Leaping Lizards. Traverse left from here to the single bolt on Mystic and the Mulchers (it is more difficult if you traverse higher) and climb to the bolts that finish Mystic and the Mulchers (150 feet, 5.9-).
FINISH: Rappel from here.
SUGGESTED EQUIPMENT: Take many small nuts, RPs, small Stoppers, and a #1-1/2 Friend. A one star route.

103. LEAPING LIZARDS: I, 5.10b
FIRST ASCENT: August 29, 1981, by Frank Sanders and Dale Chamberlain as Jumpin' Jack Flash (III, 5.7, A2).
FIRST FREE ASCENT: August 3, 1985, by Carl Coy and Mark Jacobs.
APPROACH: Take the Northeast Buttress Approach until you are below McCarthy North Face (Route 105). Belay high, just above a tree that is just a few feet left of the start of McCarthy North Face. The route is right of Neverlasting (Route 102) and left of McCarthy North Face.
PITCH 1: Follow the crack up on thin stemming moves. The crux is mid way up the pitch. Near the end traverse out to the left to belay at a small ledge from some bolts (130 feet, 5.10a). **PITCH 2:** Utilize thin crack climbing and face moves for this pitch. Climb up and right to the original crack and then traverse up and left over a series of three small ledges to the left crack. Follow this crack up past the McCarthy roof until you can traverse back right to a hanging belay at the Daredevil Index (Route 104) bolts (100 feet, 5.10b).
FINISH: Rappel off or climb Daredevil Index directly above (5.12a); you can go to the summit from there on McCarthy North Face.
SUGGESTED EQUIPMENT: RPs, wired Stoppers and a #1-1/2, #2-1/2, and #3 Friend.
NOTE: This is a two star route.

104. DAREDEVIL INDEX: III, 5.12a
FIRST ASCENT: August 29, 1981 by Frank Sanders and Dale Chamberlain as the aid route Jumpin' Jack Flash (III, 5.7, A2).
FIRST FREE ASCENT: June 18, 1985, by Paul Piana and Steve Petro.
APPROACH: Take the Northeast Buttress Approach and traverse right well past the Everlasting Column until you are under the North Face. Start at McCarthy North Face (Route 105) under a roof about 200 feet up. Third or fourth class up about 50 feet to a six inch diameter tree and belay from a small ledge up and right.
PITCH 1: Same as McCarthy North Face Pitch 1 (165 feet, 5.8+). **PITCH 2:** Traverse left, and utilize the next two cracks and the area between for climbing and protection. Climb this insecure and poorly protected pitch to the hanging belay at the bolts and one piton. There is as much face climbing on the pitch as there is finger-tip crack climbing. A #2 Friend halfway up the pitch is the only reliable piece (40 feet, 5.9+). **PITCH 3:** Continue up these desperate #1 to #3 RP size cracks where

protection is hard to place. There are no jams, so you have to climb on fingertips, palming, lay away moves and painful stemming. The crux is "enduro" technical-stemming three-quarters of the way up this pitch. Set up a hanging belay at the bolts under the roof (155 feet, 5.12a).
FINISH: Rappelling is recommended, but you can traverse right 10 feet to McCarthy North Face and go to the summit on that. At the belay/rappel you will find carabiners with their gates epoxied shut that you can use for belay/rappel anchors.
SUGGESTED EQUIPMENT: Standard rack, take at least four each of #1 to #3 RPs; two #0.5 Tri-cams; one #1 Tri-cam; one #1 Friend; one #10 Stopper; two #5 and #6 Stoppers and many #1 to #3 Stoppers. A #2 Friend for Pitch 2 and quickdraws for the bolts.
NOTE: There are six bolts and five fixed pitons in pitch #3. A one star route.

105. McCARTHY NORTH FACE: III, 5.11a
FIRST ASCENT: August 5, 1957, by Jim McCarthy and John Rupley (III, 5.7, A2).
FIRST FREE ASCENT: May 28, 1978, by Dennis Horning and Frank Sanders.
APPROACH: Take the Northeast Buttress Approach. When you get onto the buttress, continue west around a corner past Everlasting (Route 97) until you are 200 feet below a main roof. Third or fourth class up about 50 feet to a six inch diameter tree and belay from a small ledge to it's right, just below some friction.
PITCH 1: Climb the steep friction and right crack, passing two small bushes and a small bulge. Climb into a dihedral by making use of ledges on the left side, then get back into the crack. Climb past a small roof and over a loose block to a finger crack in the dihedral. Climb directly up the finger crack to a sloping belay ledge directly under the large roof. Belay at the bolts (165 feet, 5.8+). **PITCH 2:** Climb over the right side of the roof and continue up on the sustained finger crack (shallow) to a belay at the bolts (120 feet, 5.11a). **PITCH 3:** Continue up the thin hand-to-hand crack above to a small belay stance at some bolts (120 feet, 5.9). **PITCH 4:** Continue up through a chimney and to the end of your rope (140 feet, 5.6).
FINISH: Scramble to the top.
SUGGESTED EQUIPMENT: Standard rack, #1 to #8 Hexcentrics, lots of #3 to #12 Stoppers, Friends, and runners for the fixed pins on the first two pitches.
NOTE: Climbers are not recommending the bolts at the end of pitch 3, so you should set up your own belay a little lower or higher. A three star route.

106. McCARTHY'S BROTHER: II, 5.10a
FIRST ASCENT: June 15, 1985, by Dennis Horning and Jim Schlinkmann.
APPROACH: Take the Northeast Buttress approach and continue West onto the Northwest Buttress just past McCarthy North Face. The route is between McCarthy North Face (Route 105) and Emotional Rescue (Route 107).
PITCH 1: Start in the rightmost of two thin cracks on the arete. Belay low if you want. Work your way up the thin crack and gradually traverse left on face holds to the semihanging belay at the bolts (80 feet, 5.8). **PITCH 2:** Face climb on moderate 5.7 to 5.9 past five bolts. Climb the crux the last few feet on face holds to the bolts for a hanging belay (120 feet, 5.10a).
SUGGESTED EQUIPMENT: Pitch 1 - RPs, and small to medium Stoppers. Pitch 2 - Five quickdraws (for bolts), small to medium Stoppers and RPs.
FINISH: Rappel from the bolts.
NOTE: Protection is listed as fair. Beware of loose rock on Pitch 2, especially a large flake midway in the pitch. The route could use more cleaning. A one star route.

107. EMOTIONAL RESCUE: III, 5.7, A3+
FIRST ASCENT: May 21, 1981, by Frank Sanders and Chris Engle.

APPROACH: Take the Northeast Buttress Approach until you are two cracks right (west) of McCarthy North Face (Route 105), just left of Klondike (Route 110). The route goes up the obvious gully which has a chockstone in it.
PITCH 1: Free climb the crack, up and over the bulge where a secure belay can be set (140 feet, 5.7). You could also traverse right one crack (5.9) and belay at a set of bolts. **PITCH 2:** Aid up the same crack until it is feasible to traverse left one crack (a hook move or a very long reach). Continue up the left hand crack to a small tree and a horizontal crack. A belay can be set here or a better belay can be found in the crack to the right (120 feet, A2). **PITCH 3:** Continue up the crack on tied-off knife blades, thin pins and even a RURP just under the small roof. Over the roof at the rope's end, the crack widens and allows an excellent belay on larger angles (160 feet, 5.7, A3+). **PITCH 4:** Climb up a few feet, then traverse left into the McCarthy North Face chimney and climb that (130 feet, 5.7).
FINISH: Go to the top.
SUGGESTED EQUIPMENT: Standard aid rack and about 20 knifeblades, many tie-offs, 1 RURP and a couple hooks.
NOTE: This is one fine aid climb. It is composed of long pitches of thin nailing and connected by wonderfully secure belays that come as a knight in shining armor to your emotional rescue. Pitch 1, 4, 5, and part of Pitch 3 were climbed free.

108. GIMME SHELTER: III, 5.7, A3 (Variation of Emotional Rescue)
FIRST ASCENT: May 29, 1981, by Frank Sanders (solo).
APPROACH: Take the Northeast Buttress Approach and traverse right, under the northeast corner. Climb up to the start of Emotional Rescue (Route 107) which is right of McCarthy North Face (Route 105) and left of Klondike (Route 110).
PITCH 1: Emotional Rescue, Pitch 1 (140 feet, 5.7). **PITCH 2:** Aid up the same crack until feasible to traverse left. Gimme Shelter starts here and Emotional Rescue goes left. Aid up the same crack until level with a small tree on the left and a horizontal crack. The crux is a number of tied-off knife blades. Set a belay here (120 feet, A3). **PITCH 3:** Lost Arrows and small angles lead ever upwards. The aiding is easy and the view is just fine. Towards the end of the rope, as the crack withers, traverse left across the top of a small roof and belay on secure larger angles (160 feet, A1/A2). You are now back on Emotional Rescue. **PITCH 4:** Climb up a few feet then traverse left into the McCarthy North Face chimney and follow that (160 feet, 5.6)
FINISH: Climb and scramble to the summit.
SUGGESTED EQUIPMENT: Standard aid rack and about a dozen knifeblades, 24 Lost Arrows and some tie-offs.
NOTE: This is a highly enjoyable climb that is mostly secure nailing with a few thin spots for thrills.

109. TWO MOONS OVER HULETT: II, 5.11b
FIRST ASCENT: July 24, 1983, by Dennis Horning and Dave Larsen.
APPROACH: Take the Northeast Buttress Approach to the northwest corner. The route starts above Klondike (Route 110) which is one crack right of Emotional Rescue (Route 107) and left of Dr. Zen (Route 111).
PITCH 1: Klondike (150 feet, 5.10a). **PITCH 2:** Climb up the crack a short distance and then step out onto the left face and climb on the crack and face holds there until you can traverse back to the same crack. Just above you on your right you will find two bolts to belay from (85 feet, 5.11b). **PITCH 3:** Climb the crack upward and onward to the next set of bolts on your right and set up your belay (85 feet, 5.10d). **PITCH 4:** Traverse left two columns where you join Emotional Rescue. Climb up to the column top on your left where you take the left crack (McCarthy

North Face Route 105) and climb to the end of your rope. You should now be able to belay off a good ledge (160 feet, 5.7).
FINISH: Continue up the crack to the summit (40 feet, 5.6).
SUGGESTED EQUIPMENT: Standard rack, long runners, quickdraws, two sets of RPs, and Rocks.
NOTE: You can also start this route on Emotional Rescue (5.9) one crack left of your original start, but this is not recommended.

110. KLONDIKE: I, 5.10a
FIRST ASCENT: August 15, 1983, by Dave Larsen and Dennis Horning.
APPROACH: Take the Northeast Buttress Approach and traverse it west to the Northwest Shoulder just past McCarthy North Face (Route 105). This climb goes below the face of the second pitch of Two Moons Over Hulett (Route 109) and is one crack right of Emotional Rescue (Route 107). Scramble up to a belay ledge 20 feet to the right of a large chockstone.
PITCH 1: Climb up the face through a five-foot-long, shallow dihedral. Continue up traversing right at a small roof, then climb up the face following the fixed protection to the belay bolts (150 feet, 5.10a).
FINISH: Rappel from the bolts or continue up on Two Moons Over Hulett or Emotional Rescue.
SUGGESTED EQUIPMENT: Quick draws, long runners and small to medium Stoppers for use at the start.
NOTE: Harder if you are short. A three star route.

111. DR. ZEN: III, 5.11c
FIRST ASCENT: July 24, 1969, by David Lunn, John Luz and Bruce Morris as the aid route, The Route of All Evil (III, 5,8, A3).
FIRST FREE ASCENT: September 1, 1983, by Steve Mankenberg and Dave Larsen.
APPROACH: Take the Northeast Buttress Approach traversing west to the Northwest Corner. The route lies between Klondike (Route 110) and No Kiss For Dog Lips (Route 112). It follows The Route of All Evil aid route.
PITCH 1: Two prominent roofs at the base of the climb help identify the start. Climb up to the left roof and pass it on its right. Continue up to the bolts for a belay where the two cracks separate from each other (130 feet, 5.8). **PITCH 2:** Climb the right crack straight up and belay at the bolts at a prominent outward sloping edge (90 feet, 5.10). **PITCH 3:** Climb the crack and face above through three points of fixed protection. Traverse to the left crack and climb up to a stance where you can belay at the bolts (90 feet, 5.11c). **PITCH 4:** Climb the crack above until you come to a large ledge on your right where you can set up a belay (165 feet, 5.11a).
FINISH: Scramble up to the summit (50 feet, 5.6).
SUGGESTED EQUIPMENT: Standard rack, two sets of RPs, extra small to medium Stoppers, and #1 to #4 Friends.
NOTE: Two stars?

112. NO KISS FOR DOG LIPS II, 5.9
FIRST ASCENT: July 23, 1986, by Mateo Pee Pee, David Ek and Barney Fisher.
APPROACH: Go to the northwest corner of the Tower by the Northeast Buttress Approach. This route is between Dr. Zen (Route 111) and Psychic Turbulence (Route 113).
PITCH 1: Begin below the obvious overhang using thin hands through the overhang which is the crux. Climb the good finger crack to the belay bolts (140 feet, 5.8). **PITCH 2:** Continue up with a combination of face and crack climbing using thin fingertips (85 feet, 5.9).
FINISH: Rappel from the Dr. Zen anchors.

SUGGESTED EQUIPMENT: RPs, wired rocks, medium Stoppers, and a #1 Friend. Protection is excellent through crux sections but poor in the broken, loose sections.
NOTE: A one star route.

113. PSYCHIC TURBULENCE: I, 5.11a
FIRST ASCENT: August 15, 1984, by Todd Skinner, Daniel Rosen, and Beth Wald.
APPROACH: Take the Northeast Buttress Approach and traverse to the northwest corner. The route is one crack right of No Kiss For Dog Lips (Route 112) and one crack left of Four Play (Route 114).
PITCH 1: Climb up just left of Four Play a short distance and traverse left under the crack and set up a belay at the bolts. (45 feet, 5.7) **PITCH 2:** This crack is a remarkable stemming pitch similar to El Matador (Route 170) but with thinner cracks and not as wide. Crank in an endurance factor for the calves. Use two ropes or have long runners. Protection can be placed in both cracks and as one crack runs out you can protect in the other. Two bolts in the middle are not crucial but are welcome (155 feet, 5.11a).
FINISH: Rappel off or traverse right to Four Play (Route 114) and go to the summit on that.
SUGGESTED EQUIPMENT: Many small to medium nuts, RPs, two ropes or long runners and a rack for the top pitches if you go to the summit.
NOTE: A two star route.

114. FOUR PLAY: III, 5.11c
FIRST ASCENT: May 25, 1980 by Steve Hong, Karin Budding, Mark Smedley and Bill Feiges.
APPROACH: Take the Northeast Buttress Approach and traverse right to the northwest corner. Third or fourth class to the large flakes at a high stance at the start of Northwest Corner (Route 115).
PITCH 1: Climb the left side of the flake and the thin fingercrack above which is one crack left of Northwest Corner. Belay from bolts on the column top (160 feet, 5.11c). **PITCH 2:** Loose Flake. Climb the wide crack (right side) to a belay ledge. Several large Hexcentrics protect this dirty pitch (160 feet, 5.9).
FINISH: Climb easily straight up to the summit (20 feet, 5.4).
SUGGESTED EQUIPMENT: Standard rack, cleaning tool, three sets of medium RPs, three sets of small to medium Stoppers, 2 to 3 #1 Friends, and several large Hexcentrics.
NOTE: On a scale of 1 to 3 stars, Steve Hong gives this climb 2 stars.

115. NORTHWEST CORNER: III, 5.8+, A3
FIRST ASCENT: July 16, 1961, by Layton Kor and Herb Swedlund.
FIRST FREE ASCENT: Part of Pitch 2 - July 18, 1985 by Todd Skinner and Beth Wald as Spiney Norman (Route 117) (5.12a). Part of Pitch 2 and most of 3 - August 23, 1989, by Carl Coy and Rick Hays as Whine And Bruises (Route 116) (5.12b).
APPROACH: Take the West Face Approach and climb third class to the top of the Northwest Shoulder of the Tower. Belay from a small Juniper tree. Looking up past the broken rock above you, you can see a small sloping ledge formed by the top of a broken column. The route runs up the crack on the right side of this column.
PITCH 1: Easy free climbing leads to a belay at the top of the broken section (150 feet, 5.5). **PITCH 2:** Climb straight up the small dirt and moss filled crack to a belay at a bolt (145 feet, A3). **PITCH 3:** Continue up on aid until it becomes possible to free climb to a belay at the top of a broken column on your left (80 feet, 5.6, A2). **PITCH 4:** Climb straight up the awkward chimney on the right, to a belay ledge at the top of the right hand column (145 feet, 5.8+).

PITCH 5: Climb cautiously over loose terrain up and left to the summit (45 feet, 5.5).
SUGGESTED EQUIPMENT: Large numbers of knifeblades, short thick blades, and many hero loops. Four 1/2 inch angles, two 3/4 inch angles, two 1 inch angles, four #1 Stoppers, four #2 Stoppers, three #2-1//2 Stoppers, four #3 Stoppers, five #4 Stoppers, #6 to #9 Stoppers, #4 to #7 Hexcentrics, three #11 Hexcentrics, two 4 inch tube chocks, two 6 inch tube chocks, and gardening tools.
NOTE: If you have to aid Pitch 1 and 2, use nuts and small pieces to save the rock since it has been climbed free. Two stars for the free portion.

116. WHINE AND BRUISES: II, 5.12b
FIRST ASCENT: July 16, 1961, by Layton Kor and Herb Swedlund as Northwest Corner (Route 115) (III, 5.8+, A3).
FIRST FREE ASCENT: August 23, 1989, by Carl Coy and Rick Hays.
APPROACH: Take the Northeast Buttress Approach to the northwest corner. Third of fourth class up to the start of the pitch. The climb is one crack right of Four Play (Route 114) and one crack left of Spiney Norman (Route 117).
PITCH 1: Climb this finger crack around a small roof (crux) and up to a bolted belay at a ledge (130 feet, 5.8). **PITCH 2:** Climb this finger to nonexistent finger crack with thin edging and stems. You will climb past five bolts and a fixed pin to reach a bolted belay on a ledge to your left (160 feet, 5.12b).
FINISH: Rappel off.
SUGGESTED EQUIPMENT: Two sets of RPs, one set of TCUs from #0 to #1-1/2, two to three each of #1 and #2 Rocks, plus quickdraws for bolts and a fixed pin. See other routes for equipment if you go higher.
NOTE: A two star route.

117. SPINEY NORMAN: I, 5.11d
FIRST ASCENT: July 18, 1985, by Todd Skinner and Beth Wald.
APPROACH: Take the Northeast Buttress Approach and traverse to the northwest corner. The climb is one crack right of Whine And Bruises (Route 116) and one crack left of Carol's Crack (Route 118).
PITCH 1: Climb up this pitch which is basically a fingers and stemming problem. The crux is the last ten feet. Belay at the bolt and fixed nut (160 feet, 5.11d).
FINISH: Rappel from here.
SUGGESTED EQUIPMENT: Many small wired Stoppers, two sets of medium to large RPs, and Friends up to #2.
NOTE: A three star pitch.

118. CAROL'S CRACK: III, 5.11a
FIRST ASCENT: August 19, 1978, by Bob Yoho, Carol Black, Chick Holtkamp and Jeff Baird.
APPROACH: Take the West Face Approach to the northwest shoulder. Climb up to the start which is one crack left of Raindance (Route 119).
PITCH 1: Begin at the large right-facing corner three cracks to the left of the start of One-Way Sunset (Route 123). Climb the corner, following the finger crack up to the double bolt belay at the foothold on the right nose. The crux is just below the bolts (100 feet, 5.10a). **PITCH 2:** Follow the crack in the corner up to a hanging belay at the bolts. This pitch is strenuous finger locks and stemming with few rests (160 feet, 5.11a). **PITCH 3:** Follow the crack up to belay ledges on the right (60 feet, 5.7).
FINISH: Climb the chimney above through a small roof and follow the crack to the summit (150 feet, 5.7).

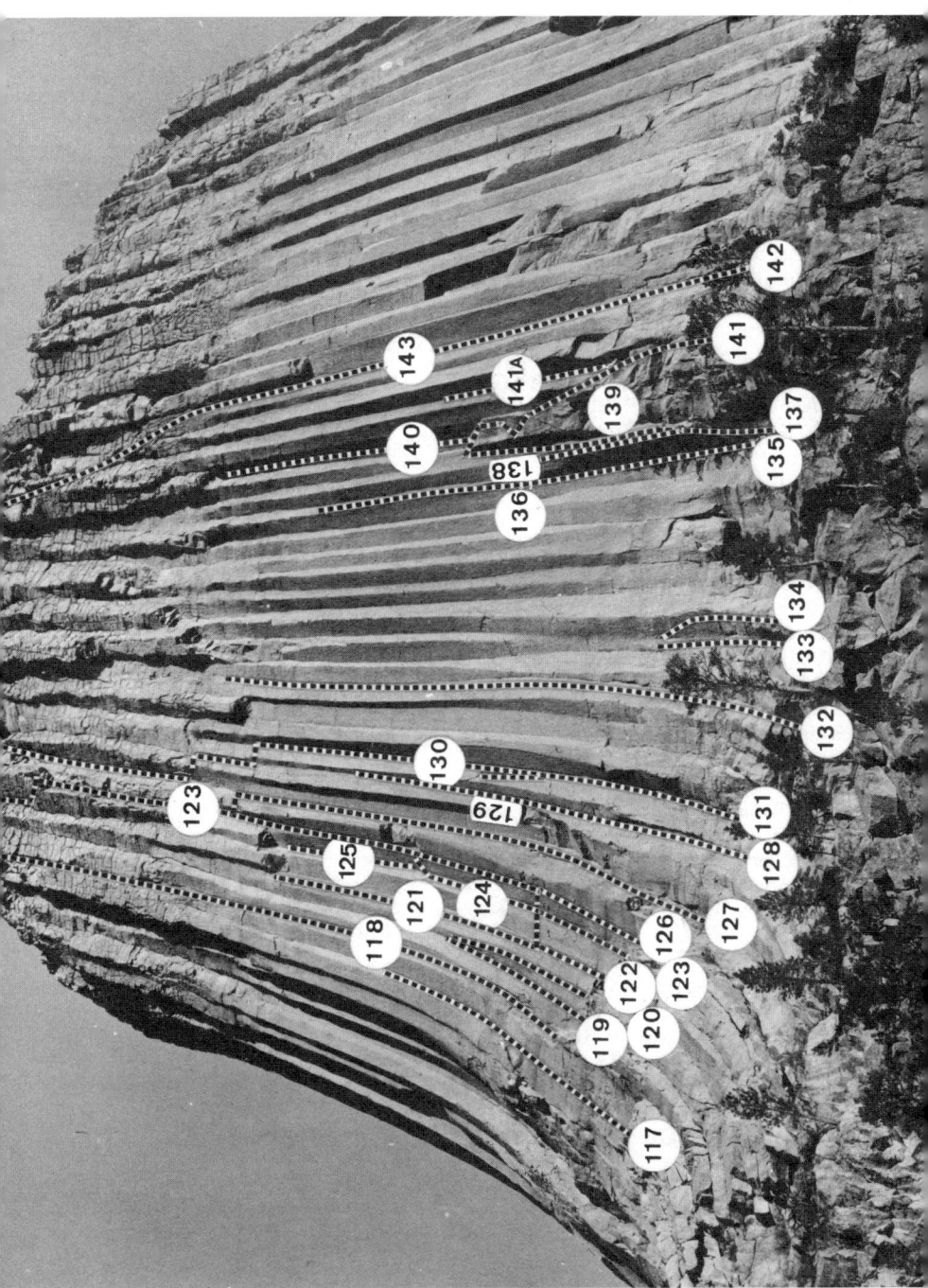

SUGGESTED EQUIPMENT: Many medium wired Stoppers around #7 and #8. Larger nuts are useful in the top two pitches (#8 to #10 Hexcentrics).
NOTE: Most climbers rappel off at the top of the Pitch 2. A three star route.

119. RAINDANCE: I, 5.10b
FIRST ASCENT: July 17, 1985, By Carl Coy and Beth Wald.
APPROACH: Take the Northeast Buttress Approach and traverse to the northwest corner of the Tower. Climb up to the base of Carol's Crack (Route 118). The route is one crack right of Carol's Crack.
PITCH 1: Follow the finger crack to a double bolt hanging belay. The finger crack is initially straight in, then becomes shallow in an obtuse dihedral. Climbing is mostly fingertips and face moves, with a few flared hand jams. The crux is midway in the pitch, but the last couple of moves are also difficult. Protection is fair, and tricky to place (100 feet, 5.10a).
FINISH: Rappel from the bolts.
SUGGESTED EQUIPMENT: RPs, small to medium stoppers, Friends up to #2.
NOTE: A one star route.

120. CARL'S FACE: I, 5.10c
FIRST ASCENT: September (?), 1990, by Danny Rosen and Dennis Horning.
APPROACH: Take the Northeast Buttress Approach and traverse right (west) to the northwest shoulder. Climb up to the start of Raindance (Route 119).
PITCH 1: Climb the face and arete right of Raindance, clipping bolts and placing protection in the small cracks to the two bolt anchor (120 feet, 5.10c).
FINISH: Rappel with two ropes.
SUGGESTED EQUIPMENT: Quickdraws, small Friend, Rocks, & RPs.
NOTE: The first ascent party did not submit information to the National Park Service about this route. For more information contact the first ascent party. A two star route.

121. APPROACHING LAVENDER: II, 5.11c
FIRST ASCENT: July 19, 1984, by Paul Piana, Bob Cowan, Todd Skinner, and Beth Wald.
APPROACH: Take the Northeast Buttress Approach and traverse around to the Northwest Shoulder. Climb up to the base of Carol's Crack (Route 118) then traverse down and right to the start of One Way Sunset (Route 123).
PITCH 1: Climb One Way Sunset for about 40 feet (about 10 feet below the poor pitons). Traverse left to the route. The crack is the one that leads up to the left side of the two prominent roofs above you. It is also two cracks right of Carol's Crack. Stem and climb this crack about 100 feet to a hanging belay (140 feet, 5.11c).
PITCH 2: Continue up with more painful stemming until you are below a roof. Step left to a stance and anchor at the bolts (80 feet, 5.11b).
FINISH: Rappelling off from here is recommended or you could continue up on some unaesthetic rubble.
SUGGESTED EQUIPMENT: Many small stoppers, medium RPs, and a few 3/4" Stoppers.
NOTE: This is a fun route involving wild stemming, enduring Fire Toes, and a big thanks to Dennis. Good protection. The Rosen Variation starts one crack left of One Way Sunset and goes straight up to the Approaching Lavender crack (5.10d) and takes small to medium nuts. Two stars.

122. APPROACHING LAVENDER (Rosen Variation): I, 5.10d
Note: Little is known about this short pitch, except that it was first climbed by Danny Rosen and takes small to medium nuts. Two stars.

123. ONE-WAY SUNSET: III, 5.10c
FIRST ASCENT: June 15, 1977, by Dennis Horning and Jim Slichter.
APPROACH: Take the West Face Approach until you are directly below the double roofs on the north end of the West Face. This route starts in the crack that leads up between the two roofs. Climb to the base of Carol's Crack (Route 118) and traverse down and right to the start of the climb. It is one crack left of Wrong Way (Route 126).
PITCH 1: Feather Fingers. Climb this thin crack 20 feet. Traverse right (5.9) to the crack on the face. Climb this crack (crux) with finger jams to the semi-hanging belay on a sloping ledge below a small roof (160 feet, 5.10c). **PITCH 2:** Jam. Climb this hand and fist crack through a roof to a good belay ledge with bolts. Sections of the crack are parallel sided and this crack is a rope eater, so use care pulling up ropes (130 feet, 5.9). **PITCH 3:** Degeneration. Continue up the line to a big belay ledge with bolts (70 feet, 5.9). **PITCH 4:** Overhanging. Climb the chimney crack to its end. A belay cave on the left offers a comfortable belay (80 feet, 5.8).
FINISH: Escape. Traverse left from the belay cave to the obvious crack which leads to the summit (70 feet, easy fifth class).
SUGGESTED EQUIPMENT: Standard rack, lots of #4 to #10 Stoppers, #5 to #11 Hexcentrics and a few large pieces.
NOTE: Most climbers only do the first two pitches and rappel.
A three star route.

124. BUSTER CATTLEFIELD: I, 5.11d
FIRST ASCENT: September 3, 1985, by Tom Kalakay, Mal Ham, Bill Dockins and Kristen Drumheller.
APPROACH: Take the Northeast Buttress Approach traversing right to the Northwest Shoulder. Start on One-Way Sunset (Route 123) but continue straight up the crack above the bent pins where One-Way Sunset traverses right one crack.
PITCH 1: Start on One-Way Sunset and continue up past the bent pins where Buster Cattlefield starts. Climb up on stemming and good locks to a good hand jam. From here the difficulty goes up a grade. Climb the next thirty feet or so on very thin fingertip jamming and liebacking. This section protects well with RPs and #1 and #2 Rocks. Finish the pitch by traversing right to the One-Way Sunset Pitch 1 belay stance (155 feet, 5.11d).
FINISH: Rappel off or continue up on One-Way Sunset.
SUGGESTED EQUIPMENT: Many #2, #3, and #4 RP's; extra #1 and #2 Rocks and #2, #2-1/2 and #3 Friends.
NOTE: This is an excellent thin-tip, liebacking pitch with good protection according to Tom Kalakay. Two star.

125. CALIFORNIA DREAMING: II, 5.11b
FIRST ASCENT: July ?, 1989, by Frank Sanders and Liana Kirk.
APPROACH: Take the Northeast Buttress Approach, traverse right to the northwest shoulder, and then up to the base of One-Way Sunset (Route 123).
PITCH 1: This is Pitch 1 of One-Way Sunset (160 feet, 5.10c), or you can take the Buster Cattlefield pitch (Route 124) (155 feet, 5.11d) to the belay stance. **PITCH 2:** Stem. Two face moves traverse you left to the corner above Buster Cattlefield. California Dreaming starts here. Climb this exquisite dihedral with delicate moves that are well protected. The initial 50 feet is the crux stem, and is protected by five bolts. The rest of the pitch yields to a more conventional style and protection to reach a bolt belay (100 feet, 5.11b).
FINISH: Rappel from the bolt belay.
SUGGESTED EQUIPMENT: Quick draws, RPs, small nuts, and TCUs to #1 Friend size. Check equipment for the first pitch you take.

NOTE: Frank Sanders says, "This route is a three-star classic. As the best protected, hard stemming pitch on this rock, it should be on your Tower itinerary".

126. WRONG WAY: I, 5.12 (Variation of One-way Sunset)
FIRST ASCENT: June 27, 1986, by Jim Brink and Dick Holm.
APPROACH: Take the Northeast Buttress Approach and traverse to the northwest corner. Climb up to the big ledge where the route starts. This climb is a direct start variation of One-way Sunset (Route 123) and starts one crack right of One-way Sunset.
PITCH 1: Climb via face holds and a thin (fingertips) crack to the belay bolt at the end of the first pitch of One-way Sunset. The crux is the final 15 feet before joining the original route (70 feet, 5.12).
FINISH: Continue up One-way Sunset and rappel from the bolts at the end of the second pitch or continue to the summit.
SUGGESTED EQUIPMENT: Many RPs (including five #3s) and quickdraws. See One-way Sunset for equipment list.
NOTE: Reported as a fine route with good protection.

127. SYNCHRONICITY: I, 5.11d
FIRST ASCENT: July 14, 1983, by Todd Skinner and John Rosholt.
APPROACH: Take the West Face Approach to the north end of the west face. The route starts one crack right of One-Way Sunset (Route 123) and left of Fractal (Route 128).
PITCH 1: Belay at the headwall. Ascend into the right-facing corner (crux). Continue up the crack to a semihanging belay (130 feet, 5.10). **PITCH 2:** Move up on desperate, endurance stemming. Two ropes are helpful as you need to protect in two separate cracks; or bring long runners. Continue up until the crack opens up enough to accept good Friends and Stoppers. Set up a hanging belay here (130 feet, 5.11d). **PITCH 3:** Continue stemming up the same crack system until the left crack turns left and joins the top of Pitch 2 of One-way Sunset (120 feet, 5.10c).
FINISH: It would be possible to continue in dirty dihedrals to the summit. You may want to rappel off or go to the summit via One-way Sunset.
SUGGESTED EQUIPMENT: Two ropes or plenty of long slings, a set of Friends, a set of Stoppers with extra small Stoppers.
NOTE: According to Todd, this route makes El Matador (Route 170) look like an off-width! A two star route.

128. FRACTAL: I, 5.10a
FIRST ASCENT: July 19, 1986, by Thomas and Rainer Malzbender.
APPROACH: Take the West Face Approach and traverse low past Deli Express (Route 132). The climb follows the dihedral to the right of Synchronicity (Route 127) and one crack left of the start of The Chipmunk (Route 130) which leads to Phase Locking With Strange Attractors (Route 131).
PITCH 1: Climb the dihedral via face hold using the crack primarily for protection. The crux is approximately 25 feet below the belay and consists of stemming with small face holds. Belay bolts are found beneath a small roof to the left of the corner (130 feet, 5.10a).
FINISH: Rappel from the belay bolts or continue up on Refractal (Route 129) (5.11c).
SUGGESTED EQUIPMENT: Standard rack with doubles on #1 to #4 small rocks, Stoppers, and a #4 Friend.
NOTE: Two star route.

129. REFRACTAL: II, 5.11c
FIRST ASCENT: Est. 1991, by undisclosed climbers.

APPROACH: Take the West Face Approach to the north side of the west face. This pitch starts at the top of Fractal (Route 128) which is four cracks left of Deli Express (Route 132).
PITCH 1: Fractal. Climb this pitch to the belay bolts on your left with stemming (5.10a). **PITCH 2:** Refractal. Continue up this face and thin crack to the bolted belay left of the crack (5.11c).
FINISH: Rappel off.
SUGGESTED EQUIPMENT: Standard rack, #4 Friend, a set of Rocks, and RPs.
NOTE: The first ascent party did not turn in any information on this route. For more information contact the first ascent party. If you have more information on this route contact the National Park Service. Reportedly two to three stars.

130. THE CHIPMUNK: IV, 5.10a, A2
FIRST ASCENT: September 9, 1986, by Janko Humar and Edo Kozorog
APPROACH: Take the West Face Approach past Deli Express (Route 132). Start one crack right of Fractal (Route 128) or three cracks left of Deli Express to start the route.
PITCH 1: Free climb up this easy crack to a small ledge for your belay (60 feet, 5.7). **Pitch 2:** Continue aiding directly up the crack using two sets of Rocks (up to #5), RPs and twenty knifeblade pitons (165 feet, A2). (This has now been done free as Phase Locking With Strange Attractors (Route 131) - II, 5.11). **PITCH 3:** Continue aiding directly up the crack sixty feet and traverse one crack left, then up fifty-five feet to a small ledge. Set up a half hanging belay from one bolt and nut. Use fifteen knifeblades and six angle pitons (140 feet, A2).
FINISH: Continue free climbing directly up the crack, made dangerous with loose rock and poor protection. Use a full set of Friends and belay from the top (165 feet, 5.10a).
SUGGESTED EQUIPMENT: Many knifeblades and angle pitons with a full set of Friends, small Rocks and RPs.
NOTE: This is a continuous climb with no particular crux. The finish has poor protection and dangerously loose rock. A two star route.

131. PHASE LOCKING WITH STRANGE ATTRACTORS: I, 5.11
FIRST ASCENT: September 9, 1986, by Janko Humar, and Edo Kosorog as The Chipmunk (Route 130) (IV, 5.10a, A2).
FIRST FREE ASCENT: Pitch 2 - May 1991, by undisclosed climbers.
APPROACH: Take the West Face Approach past the Nam Column. The pitch is on The Chipmunk aid route. It is one crack right of Fractal (Route 128) and three cracks left of Deli Express (Route 132).
PITCH 1: Climb the crack and face above until you are just below the Fractal belay bolts under a roof to your left. From here, start to move left and up the face past a bolt to the belay bolts (5.11).
FINISH: Rappel off.
NOTE: The first ascent party did not give the National Park Service a description of this route for its records.

132. DELI EXPRESS: II, 5.12a
FIRST ASCENT: June 26, 1983 by Mark Sonnenfeld and Steve Hong.
APPROACH: Take the West Face Approach until you are just left of center of the West Face. This crack is three cracks right of Phase Locking With Strange Attractors (Route 131) and two cracks left of Man Without A Planet (Route 133).
PITCH 1: Climb up easy bulges to a belay pod below the steep section (30 feet, 5.7). **PITCH 2:** Climb this long and increasingly difficult crack to one bolt on your right at a foot-hold hanging belay stance (165 feet, 5.11c). **PITCH 3:** Continue up

the crack to a two-bolt stance. Rappel off as the top rotten section is totally mungy (90 feet, 5.12a).
SUGGESTED EQUIPMENT: Two to four sets of RPs, over 30 carabiners, two #1 and #2 Friends, and 25 assorted small nuts.
NOTE: A three star route.

133. MAN WITHOUT A PLANET: I 5.10a
FIRST ASCENT: September 2, 1991, by Brent Kertzman, Dennis Horning, Steve Babbits and Sara Musel.
APPROACH: Take the West Face Approach past the Nam Column until you are two cracks right of Deli Express (Route 132).
PITCH 1: Start up the crack then move up and left onto the face. Continue climbing up the center of the face passing two bolts until you come to the two bolt belay (5.10a).
FINISH: Rappel off.
SUGGESTED EQUIPMENT: Standard rack, RPs, set of Rocks, Friends up to 3-inches, and quickdraws for the bolts.
NOTE: The first ascent party did not turn in a route description to the National Park Service. Rumor has it that this pitch was named after Scooter Metcalf.

134. LOSS OF ENTHUSIASM: II, 5.11a
FIRST ASCENT: Est. 1992, by undisclosed
APPROACH: Take the West Face Approach to the north end of the west face just before Deli Express (Route 132). Climb up to the start which is the bolted arete just right of the start of Man Without A Planet (Route 133).
PITCH 1: Follow the line of bolts up the arete and near the end move left until you reach the bolted belay (150 feet, 5.10a).
FINISH: Rappel off.
SUGGESTED EQUIPMENT: Quickdraws for the bolts.
NOTE: The first ascent party has not turned in any information to the National Park Service on this pitch. Anyone with further information should contact the National Park Service.

135. GOOD HOLDS FOR GODZILLA: I, 5.12d
FIRST ASCENT: July 30, 1985, by Kyle Copeland and John Gill as Verrouiller Letoit Pendang La Marche (Route 136) (II, 5.7, A3).
FIRST FREE ASCENT: September 19, 1987, by Andy Petefish and Kris Hjelle.
APPROACH: Take the West Face Approach until you are just past the Nam Column. The route is one crack left of Nam (Route 137) and Risque (Route 138).
PITCH 1: Climb up and surmount a difficult bulge. Continue up 15 to 20 feet where it thins. At this point, a 30 foot bridging must be tackled. Protection for this section is found in the right hand crack. After bridging, pull back into the right crack on finger jams and move up to a no-hands resting foot jam. The next 30 or 40 feet is the crux section. Many 5.11+ and 5.12 moves are protected by 3 bolts and a fixed pin (130 feet, 5.12d).
FINISH: Continue up on aid or rappel.
SUGGESTED EQUIPMENT: Two #3, #4, #5 RPs; one #4 Rock, three #5 Rocks; two #0 Met. three cam, two #1 Met. three cam, one #2 Met. three cam; #3, #5, #6 Stoppers; #0.5 and #1 Lowe Tricam; #1 Friend; and Quick Draws.
NOTE: This climb employs almost every technique used in climbing and rates three stars. A special thanks goes to Mike Robinson and Scott Croll for help on establishing this route. A two star route.

136. VERROUILLER LETOIT PENDANG LA MARCHE: II, 5.7, A3
FIRST ASCENT: July 30, 1985, by Kyle Copeland and John Gill.
FIRST FREE ASCENT: Pitch 1 as Good Holds For Godzilla (Route 135) (5.12d) - September 19, 1987, by Andy Petefish and Kris Hjelle.
APPROACH: West Face Approach. The climb is in the first corner left of Risque (Route 138) and right of Loss Of Enthusiasm (Route 134).
PITCH 1: Climb Good Holds For Godzilla (130 feet, 5.12d). **PITCH 2:** Climb up on aid in this thin crack through the crux about 20 feet up. Continue up past a set of double bolts using thin pins to the end of the pitch which only has two knifeblades and a sling to belay/rappel from. Set your own protection here (125 feet, A3).
FINISH: Rappel from here.
SUGGESTED EQUIPMENT: 40 Bugaboos and knifeblades, five Lost Arrows, a #1 Friend, two sets of RPs, #9 stopper, and a selection of small wires. Take lots of hero loops and about 50 carabiners. See Good Holds For Godzilla for freeing it.
NOTE: Falcon attacks limited the upward progress so bolts could not be placed at the end. Please do not aid with pins in any crack that has been free climbed. Pitch 1 is a one to two star pitch.

137. NAM: I, 5.8
FIRST ASCENT: July 7, 1985, by Richard Guilmette and Bruce Adams.
APPROACH: Take the West Face Approach to the base of the NAM Column. The route is just right of Verrouiller Letoit Pendang La Marche (Route 136) and below No Holds For Bonzo (Route 139) and leads up to it and the start of Risque (Route 138). The crack goes up the left side of the prominent NAM Column which looks like a knife sliced it off at a steep angle. Belay low in a left facing corner with a small tree on your right.
PITCH 1: Climb up on friction about 45 feet to the crux of the pitch. This awkward bulge can be climbed by stepping up left and twisting to the right and up on awkward moves. Easy climbing brings you to the belay under a bulge that starts No Holds For Bonzo (90 feet, 5.8). **PITCH 2:** This was aided easily (A1) but now goes free as No Holds For Bonzo (110 feet, 5.11b).
FINISH: Rappel off.
SUGGESTED EQUIPMENT: Small to medium Stoppers.
NOTE: If you plan to do Pitch 2 (originally aided), see the No Holds For Bonzo equipment list. One star.

138. RISQUE: I, 5.12b
FIRST ASCENT: August 10, 1985, by Todd Skinner, Beth Wald, Jim Schlinkmann and Bill Hatcher.
APPROACH: Take the West Face Approach to the base of the NAM Column. The route is the arete on the left side of Nam (Route 137) and No Holds For Bonzo (Route 139). Belay high in a cleft (NAM) fifteen feet below the first bolt. You will be just above and left of a lone tree.
PITCH 1: Follow the sharp arete past seven protection bolts using everything except the dihedral. Set up a hanging belay at the bolts (80 feet, 5.12b).
FINISH: Rappel down.
EQUIPMENT: Seven quick draws and a level head.
NOTE: Two to three star pitch.

139. NO HOLDS FOR BONZO: I, 5.11b
FIRST ASCENT: July 7, 1985, by Richard Guilmette and Bruce Adams (A1).
FIRST FREE ASCENT: July 16, 1985, by Mateo Pee Pee and Jim Schlinkmann.

APPROACH: Take the West Face Approach until you are below the Nam Column. Scramble up and left above an obvious pine tree and set up a belay.
PITCH 1: Surmount the overhang and follow the left facing corner to a small belay ledge with bolts. The climbing is fun and sustained, with stemming, face climbing and great finger locks. The crux is a thin section 15 feet from the end of the pitch (110 feet, 5.11a).
FINISH: Rappel from the bolts.
SUGGESTED EQUIPMENT: Many small to medium Stoppers, RPs, and at least one medium Hexcentric or #2 Friend for the flake midway up the pitch.
NOTE: Belay 20 feet below the overhang in order to watch the leader climb. Excellent protection. Destined to become a one pitch, West Face classic. Three stars.

140. HIGH NAM: II, 5.12b, A0
FIRST ASCENT: June, 1987, by Bill Dockins and Kristen Drumheller (II, A1).
FIRST FREE ATTEMPT: June, 1987, by Kristen Drumheller (II, 5.12b, A0)
APPROACH: Take the West Face Approach until you are just past the center of the face, and then work up to the base of the Nam Column.
PITCH 1: Climb to the top of the Nam Column by using Potatoes Alien (Route 141) (5.10d) or No Holds For Bonzo (Route 139) (5.11a). Belay at the bolts. **PITCH 2:** If you aid, use the right crack for straightforward aiding (160 feet, A1); and if you climb utilize the right crack as much as possible and also for placing protection. This pitch calls for enduro stemming with no move harder than 5.12b. The crux runs from 20 feet to 80 feet, after which some small edges can be found. Belay at the two chained bolts. See note below (160 feet, 5.12b, A0).
FINISH: Rappel off.
SUGGESTED EQUIPMENT: Assorted pitons if aiding or small to medium pieces.
NOTE: This route was worked on over a two year period. Kristen Drumheller has done all the moves and says none are harder than 5.12b. Because of falls and hanging on pieces, Kristen is not considering it a free climb. This route has yet to be done clean. If you do so contact the National Park Service and let them know and fill out a route description. Kristen says this will probably be a 5.12d when it is done clean.

141A. BLOTTER IS MY SPOTTER: I, 5.7, A3+
FIRST ASCENT: August 21, 1989, by Frank Sanders, solo.
APPROACH: Take the West Face Approach until you are two cracks left of Spank The Monkey (Route 142) and Bloodguard (Route 144) under the left facing dihedral. Start on Potatoes Alien (Route 141).
PITCH 1: Free climb up the start of Potatoes Alien until you can get into the dihedral, then aid up the dihedral. As height increases, the crack diminishes. The final one-third of the pitch is accomplished on hooks, RURPs and a few tied-off blades. There's air to catch, but nothing to hit. A three bolt belay rewards your efforts (140 feet, 5.7, A3+).
FINISH: Rappel from the bolts or explore upwards. Additional pitches in this incredible corner await your inquiries.
SUGGESTED EQUIPMENT: Standard aid rack.

141. POTATOES ALIEN: I, 5.10d
FIRST ASCENT: July 10, 1985, Mateo Pee Pee, Steve "Barney" Fisher and Jim Schlinkmann.
APPROACH: Take the West Face Approach. The route follows the right edge of the NAM Column. It is just right of NAM (Route 137) and No Holds For Bonzo (Route 139). Begin the route below a four foot flake slightly to the right of the upper crack that marks the right side of the column.

PITCH 1: Climb the flake then slightly up and left to a bulge which is surmounted directly by using face holds (5.8). Follow the curving crack above first to the right and then to the left. Belay on a superb ledge using nut anchors (110 feet, 5.8).
PITCH 2: Follow the crack above for approximately 20 feet then traverse left onto a large ledge. A couple of face moves lead back right to the thin crack which leads to the top of the column. Belay at the bolts (60 feet, 5.10d).
FINISH: Rappel from the bolts.
SUGGESTED EQUIPMENT: Small to medium Stoppers, #1 to #5 rocks, RPs, and a #1 Friend.
NOTE: A one to two star climb.

142. SPANK THE MONKEY: I, 5.10d
FIRST ASCENT: April 26, 1964, by Layton Kor and Tex Bossier as Saber (IV, 5.6, A3).
FIRST FREE ASCENT: Pitch 1 - August 22, 1985, by Jim Schlinkmann, Mateo Pee Pee, and Carl Coy.
APPROACH: Take the West Face Approach until you are left of Brokedown Palace (Route 146). The climb follows the first pitch of the aid route Saber (Route 143), and is one crack left of Bloodguard (Route 144).
PITCH 1: Climb the dihedral to a double bolt hanging belay. The lower half of the climb is a tricky 5.8+ hand crack. The remaining 80 feet follows a beautiful dihedral, and utilizes intermittent cracks on the right face. Climbing involves fingerlocks, face moves, and strenuous stemming. The crux is cranking on fingertips off a good rest ledge about 20 feet below the bolts. Good rests and excellent protection (140 feet, 5.10d).
FINISH: Rappel from the bolts.
SUGGESTED EQUIPMENT: #3 to #3-1/2 Friends for lower hand crack, two full sets of Rocks and RPs, Stoppers and sliders are helpful.
NOTE: Destined to become another short West Face classic, similar in flavor to No Holds For Bonzo (Route 139). A three star pitch.

143. SABER: IV, 5.6, A3
FIRST ASCENT: April 26, 1964, by Layton Kor and Tex Bossier.
FIRST FREE ASCENT: Pitch 1 - August 22, 1985, by Jim Schlinkmann, Mateo Pee Pee, and Carl Coy as Spank The Monkey (Route 142) (5.10d).
APPROACH: Take the West Face Approach until you are two cracks left of Brokedown Palace (Route 146) and one crack left of Bloodguard (Route 144). This is the start and is Spank The Monkey. Saber starts 140 feet up this crack. Belay high.
PITCH 1: Spank The Monkey. Climb this hand crack for 60 feet then the dihedral the rest of the way, utilizing intermittent cracks on the right face. Use stems, fingerlocks, and face moves. The crux is fingertips just off a good ledge 20 feet below the bolts. Good rests and protection (140 feet, 5.10d). **PITCH 2:** Continue up the crack on aid, setting up a hanging belay a few feet below the roof (130 feet, A2). **PITCH 3:** Continue up on aid and pass the roof on the left. Use aid up this crack until it becomes possible to free climb to a hanging belay (150 feet, 5.6, A3).
FINISH: Free climb the large diagonal crack on your left until it becomes possible to scramble to the summit (75 feet, 5.6).
SUGGESTED EQUIPMENT: A generous selection of pins, including many blades and several bongs for protection on the upper portions. Nuts may work well on the upper half of this route, and may help eliminate the need for the constant cleaning of pigeon dung from the crack and cleaning tool. See Spank The Monkey for equipment for it.
NOTE: Since Pitch 1 has been done free, if you aid it please do not use pitons to mar the climb. Spank The Monkey is a three star pitch.

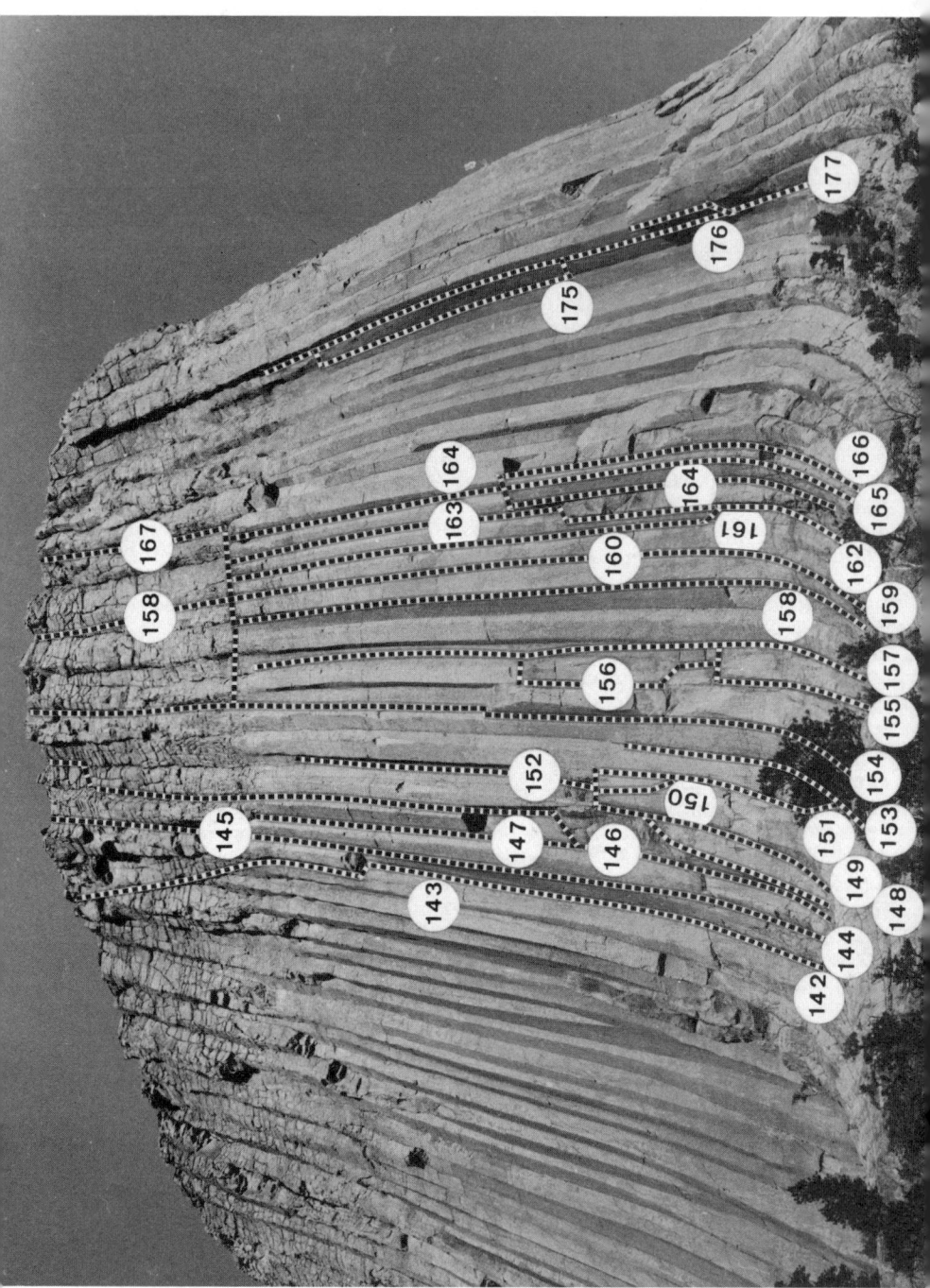

144. BLOODGUARD: I, 5.11d
FIRST ASCENT: As Non-Dairy Creamer, October 12, 1977, by Chris Ballinger, Jim Lynch and Frank Sanders (III, 5.8, A3).
FIRST FREE ASCENT: July 19, 1984, by Todd Skinner, Beth Wald, Bob Cowan and Paul Piana.
APPROACH: Take the West Face Approach. This route is between Spank The Monkey (Route 142) and Brokedown Palace (Route 146) and consists of one pitch.
PITCH 1: This is an amazing, straight-in, finger crack with perfect protection and several hands-down rests. It is exhilarating and exposed with the crux at the end. Very thin, steep tip jamming on the last 20 feet adds a full grade to the pitch (160 feet, 5.11d).
FINISH: Rappel off or climb Non Dairy Creamer (Route 145) to the summit.
SUGGESTED EQUIPMENT: Many medium Stoppers on the first 140 feet and several RPs on the last 20 feet.
NOTE: Any parties wishing to aid this, please use nuts, so as not to destroy the superb, free climbing. A three star route.

145. NON-DAIRY CREAMER: III, 5.12a, A3
FIRST ASCENT: October 12, 1977, by Cris Ballinger, Jim Lynch and Frank Sanders.
APPROACH: Take the West Face Approach. The route starts one crack right of Saber and one crack left of Brokedown Palace (Route 146). Belay high.
PITCH 1: Same as Bloodguard (Route 144) (160 feet, 5.12a). **PITCH 2:** Continue up the crack on aid, setting up a hanging belay a few feet below the roof (110 feet, A2). **PITCH 3:** Climb to the roof and pass it on the right. Continue up on aid until you have to hang a belay near the end of your rope (155 feet, A3).
FINISH: Continue up the same crack to the summit.
SUGGESTED EQUIPMENT: No list given.
NOTE: If you aid Pitch 1 Bloodguard, use nuts to protect this superb free climb.

146. BROKEDOWN PALACE: III, 5.12a
FIRST ASCENT: August 10, 1973, by Bruce Price and Mike LaLone as Conquest of Tillie's Lookout (III, 5.8, A2).
FIRST FREE ASCENT: October 2, 1981, by Steve Hong and Mark Sonnenfeld.
APPROACH: Take the West Face Approach past Vulture (Route 154) until you are below a prominent roof in the middle of the West Face. The crack is below the left side of the overhang and one crack right of Bloodguard (Route 144).
PITCH 1: Climb the left crack leading to a small belay ledge below the roof. Protection is difficult. Belay at the double corner bolts (160 feet, 5.11a). **PITCH 2:** Climb the right crack and out the right lip of the roof and up the crack 20 feet to small foot holds for a hanging belay at a bolt and fixed pin (70 feet, 5.12a). **PITCH 3:** Climb up the chimney above to the base of the exit chimney and an awkward belay which you will have to set up (130 feet, 5.11c). **PITCH 4:** Climb the grotesque chimney above about 100 feet to a bolt under the crux bulge. Traverse right here and continue up somewhat easier climbing to the summit. This pitch has marginal protection and very loose rock (130 feet, 5.7).
SUGGESTED EQUIPMENT: Three sets of medium RPs, numerous #4 to #8 Stoppers, #1 Friends and perhaps large Sliders (25 pieces).
NOTE: Steve Hong considers this a three star classic route but recommends rappelling after pitch three although there are no bolts here so use your own gear. Because of much better protection, some climbers recommend starting on Up In Smoke (Route 148) or Jerry's Kids (Route 149) (both 5.10b) to reach the first belay.

147. AVALON: II, 5.11d
FIRST ASCENT: July 26, 1984, by Todd Skinner and Beth Wald.
APPROACH: Take the West Face Approach to the base of Brokedown Palace (Route 146) below a prominent roof.
PITCH 1: Follow pitch 1 of Brokedown Palace to a belay ledge and bolts (150 feet, 5.11a). **PITCH 2:** Take the left crack off the ledge, using very thin fingerlocks and stemming to small edges to reach a stance underneath the roof. Make a classic 5.10 move to pull the roof and continue up a beautiful finger crack to a hanging belay with fixed pins and a fixed nut (80 feet, 5.11d). **PITCH 3:** Continue the wild finger crack which becomes significantly harder, involving continuously desperate stemming and thin fingers with a few rests, to a welcome ledge and pin belay (100 feet, 5.11c).
FINISH: Rappel from here or face the wrath of loose boulders.
SUGGESTED EQUIPMENT: Many RPs and small to medium Stoppers.
NOTE: A three star route.

148. UP IN SMOKE: I, 5.10b
FIRST ASCENT: August 18, 1988 by Kris Hjelle and Andy Petefish.
APPROACH: Take the West Face Approach until you are between Brokedown Palace (Route 146) and Jerry's Kids (Route 149).
PITCH 1: Face climb up the arete. The crux consists of a face move at the first bolt. The seam on the left provides some holds, jams, and good placement. After reaching the ledge at the top of the arete, traverse up and right on friction (protected by a bolt on the slab) to finish on Jerry's Kids. Good protection and six bolts (120 feet, 5.10b).
FINISH: Rappel from the two bolt belay on Jerry's Kids.
SUGGESTED EQUIPMENT: One #3 TCU, #4 and #5 RPs, one #2 TCU, one #1 Tricam, quickdraws, plus Stoppers for the finish on Jerry's Kids.
NOTE: This is a fun route with tricky technical moves. A two star route.

149. JERRY'S KIDS: I, 5.10b
FIRST ASCENT: July 21, 1985, by Jim Schlinkmann, Mateo Pee Pee, and "Barney" Fisher.
APPROACH: West Face Approach. The same as Brokedown Palace (Route 146). The route follows the crack right of pitch 1 of Brokedown Palace.
PITCH 1: Follow the crack in the left-facing corner to a comfortable belay ledge with bolts. Climbing involves fingertips, face moves, and stemming. The crux is a continuous thin section for 20 feet above the second bolt in the lower half of the pitch, until you reach a bomber #2-1/2 Friend placement. Three bolts help protect this pitch. Overall protection is good, but strenuous to place. Good rests (120 feet, 5.10b).
FINISH: Rappel from bolts.
SUGGESTED EQUIPMENT: Wired Stoppers, two sets of RPs, #1-1/2 and #2-1/2 Friends, sliders and quickdraws.
NOTE: Belay comfortably at the Juniper tree at the base of the route. Two to three stars.

150. DOUBLE FEATURE: I, 5.11d (A variation of Captain Video)
FIRST ASCENT: July 24, 1988, by Andy Petefish and Kris Hjelle.
APPROACH: Take the West Face Approach and belay below Pee Pee's Plunge (153). This route takes off from the Captain Video (Route 151) crack which lies between Jerry's Kids (Route 149) and Pee Pee's Plunge.
PITCH 1: Climb up to the second bolt on Captain Video (5.11d) to start on Double Feature. Traverse left and follow a thin seam up past two more bolts to the belay

on top of Jerry's Kids (5.11). Save a #1.5 Lowe Tricam for use after the fourth bolt. The crux is below the second bolt on Double Feature and consists of a thin face crack (145 feet, 5.11d).
FINISH: Rappel off.
SUGGESTED EQUIPMENT: Three sets of RPs #3 to #5, #3 HB, #4 steel, #1 slider, #1 and #2 Metolius TCU, #7 and #9 Newstyle Stoppers, #5 and #9 Rocks, #0.5 and #1.0 and #1.5 Lowe Tricam, and a #3 Friend.
NOTES: This pitch is destined to become a classic, and gets a three star rating. Protection is good. Double Feature and Captain Video are easily top-roped from the top of Jerry's Kids. There is a good directional bolt for top roping just out of sight around the corner to the right of the belay bolts.

151. CAPTAIN VIDEO: I, 5.12b
FIRST ASCENT: July 18, 1987, by Andy Petefish, belayed by Mike Robinson.
APPROACH: Take the West Face Approach. The crack is one crack left of Pee Pee's Plunge (Route 153) and one crack right of Jerry's Kids (Route 149) on the West Face.
PITCH 1: Start as if doing Pee Pee's Plunge. However, at the first fixed pin on Pee Pee's Plunge, traverse left (15 feet) on a ramp, to where two thin face cracks lie. Climb 20 to 25 feet up these thin face cracks to a ledge on the left. From this ledge, continue up and slightly right to a bolt and through a small roof to a good finger crack. Continue up this thin crack past two more bolts (crux) and belay from the two bolts on a ledge about 20 feet above the last bolt. This ledge is also the belay ledge for Jerry's Kids (110 feet, 5.12b).
FINISH: Rappel off.
SUGGESTED EQUIPMENT: #3 and #4 HBs; four #3 RPs; one #5 RP, one #1 slider; one #2 Metolius TCU, one .5 TCU, one #1 TCU, one #2 rock (first piece); one #4 rock; two #5 rocks; one #9 Stopper (new style); one #10 Stopper; one #9 rock. This is the exact gear rack which was used on the first ascent. Extra gear may be desired on repeated ascents.
NOTE: It is all thin tips and face climbing. Bolts were placed on rappel and the first lead was done after several top rope rehearsals. A special thanks goes to Mike Robinson, Scott Croll, Kris Hjelle, and Mal Ham for help on establishing this route. A two star route.

152. SCOTTFREE: II, 5.11b
FIRST ASCENT: October 11, 1992, by Carl Coy belayed by John Plotke.
APPROACH: Take the West Face Approach to Jerry's Kids (Route 149) which is where you have to start. Scottfree starts on top of Jerry's Kids.
PITCH 1: Jerry's Kids **PITCH 2:** Climb up off the middle of the belay ledge past a bolt, move right, up to another bolt, left, and then up and right to a small stance (no belay) at the base of the left facing corner. This is where the real climbing starts. The first 50-60 feet are thin stemming with only the occasional finger lock. The crack then opens up into nice fingers, with an occasional hand jam. Continue up to the chained bolts at the hanging belay (150 feet, 5.11b).
FINISH: Rappel off.
SUGGESTED EQUIPMENT: Many RPs, Stoppers, and Friends up to #2. See Jerry's Kids for it's equipment list.
NOTE: This pitch requires a nice diversity of techniques and protects reasonably well in the thin sections. A two star route.

153. PEE PEE's PLUNGE: I, 5.12a
FIRST ASCENT: August 7, 1986, by Carl Coy, Mateo Pee Pee, Stu Ritchie, Rob Adair, and Dan Hutchens.

APPROACH: West Face Approach. The climb ascends the crack left of Vulture (Route 154) and one crack right of Captain Video (Route 151).
PITCH 1: Belay from a fixed pin. Stemming a flared corner takes one past a fixed pin and bolt to a finger crack. Climb the crack using small pockets, face holds, and thin stemming through several difficult sections. Belay from double bolts placed to the right of the crack (140 feet, 5.12a).
FINISH: Rappel from the belay bolts.
SUGGESTED EQUIPMENT: Four sets of RPs (#2 to #5), two sets of wired rocks (#1 to #6), two #1 and #2 sliders, a #1 and #2-1/2 Friend, and three quick draws.
NOTE: This is a very technical pitch with few rests. A two star pitch.

154. VULTURE: IV, 5.12a, A3
FIRST ASCENT: May 13, 1961, by Layton Kor and Bob LaGrange (IV, 5.8, A3). Finish variation to the West Face Ledge - June 28, 1976, by Glen Banks and Paul Horak.
FIRST FREE ASCENT: Pitch 1 and 2 - July 9, 1985, by Steve Hong, Karin Budding, and Beth Wald.
APPROACH: Take the West Face approach until you are between Double Feature (Route 150) and One O'clock Demo (Route 155). It follows the crack up the left side of a column that ends halfway up the route.
PITCH 1: Climb up the left side of the Vulture Pillar, an incipient crack and face climb. Set up a belay at a stance. Protection is poor (50 feet, 5.7). **PITCH 2:** Continue up the crack with finger locks, face moves and laybacking to the comfortable ledge on top of the Vulture Pillar. The crux is a short distance below the top. Protection is poor at the start (165 feet, 5.12a). **PITCH 3:** Sustained difficult aid for about 100 feet leads to a not-so-reassuring belay from tied-off pins in a horizontal crack. This pitch takes lots of tied-off Knifeblades, and Crack-n-ups help considerably (100 feet, A3). **PITCH 4:** Continue up on shakey aid about 70 feet to where it becomes possible to climb free. Kor went straight up to very poor rock. It is best to traverse right (free) at this point, several columns, and belay at the West Face Ledge (90 feet, 5.8, A3). **PITCH 5:** Climb straight up Mr. Clean (Route 158) to the summit. There is loose rock and poor protection (160 feet, 5.8).
FINISH: Climb straight up Mr. Clean to the summit (160 feet, 5.8).
SUGGESTED EQUIPMENT: (for Pitches 1 and 2 free): Three sets each of RPs and #1, #2, #3, and #4 Rocks. One set medium Stoppers, two #2-1/2 Friends for first belay, and two #1, #2, and #1-1/2 Friends. Equipment for aid: #1 to #9 Hexcentrics, #1 to #4 wired Stoppers, #1 to #4 Copperheads, #1 to #4 Crack-n-ups, and assorted pitons from knifeblades to a 3/4-inch angle.
NOTE: Protection is poor in places. A one star route (free portion). Not recommended above the free portion.

155. ONE O'CLOCK DEMO: I, 5.9-
FIRST ASCENT: August 9, 1988, by Michael Sammis and Bob Gaines.
APPROACH: Take the West Face Approach to the Left of Mr. Clean (Route 158). Start on the Arete between the second and third crack left of Mr. Clean or just left of The Howling (Route 157).
PITCH 1: Climb up the Arete with a low angle runout to a ledge. Step left into a thin corner crack with good protection but difficult placement. Continue up this crack to the belay bolts on a ledge. The last fifteen feet is the crux of the climb (80 feet, 5.9-).
FINISH: Climb Some Like It Hot (Route 156) 5.12b, The Howling 5.11d or rappel off. One 165 foot rope will get you off the right (south) side.

SUGGESTED EQUIPMENT: Standard rack, RPs, small to medium Stoppers, two #2 Friends, and one #2-1/2 Friend.
NOTE: This is a one star pitch.

156. SOME LIKE IT HOT: I, 5.12b
FIRST ASCENT: August 11, 1988, by Paul Van Betten, Bob Gaines, Jay Smith and Robert Finlay.
APPROACH: Take the West Face Approach to the left of Mr. Clean (Route 158). The climb is one crack right of Vulture (Route 154).
PITCH 1: Climb either One O'clock Demo (Route 155) (5.9 -) or The Howling (Route 157) (5.10a). **PITCH 2:** Climb 15 to 20 feet up the crack just left of the bolts. Traverse up and left to the next crack. Climb this finger-tips crack to a two bolt belay on the right. The crux is 15 feet of thin edges and stemming (90 feet, 5.12b).
FINISH: Rappel off or climb The Howling.
SUGGESTED EQUIPMENT: Several sets of Friends with extra #4s and two sets HB nuts. See the Pitch 1 equipment list for that.
NOTE: A one to two star route. Fun if you have TCUs. Harder with HB nuts. Led on sight with one fall and one lower off.

157. THE HOWLING: II, 5.11d
FIRST ASCENT: August 18, 1988, Pitch 1 by Jay Smith and Paul Van Betten; Pitch 2 by Jay Smith, Bob Gaines, Paul Van Betten; and Pitch 3 by Jay Smith and Jo Bentley.
APPROACH: Take the West Face Approach. The route starts two cracks to the left of Mr. Clean (Route 158).
PITCH 1: Climb the thin finger crack until it pinches together, then use force holds and stemming to do the crux and reach the bolts at the belay ledge. Protection is OK (80 feet, 5.10b). **PITCH 2:** Continue up the same crack with good protection. Use thin fingers, lay back moves, and some stemming to reach the belay bolts at a ledge on the left (110 feet, 5.11c). **PITCH 3:** Climb, using only stemming techniques, the whole way with excellent protection to a two bolt stance. The crux of the climb here is height dependent (162 feet, 5.11d).
FINISH: You can rappel off with two rappels.
SUGGESTED EQUIPMENT: Three sets of HBs #3 to #6, two sets of RPs, three to four sets of TCUs, two #1-1/2 Friends and one each #1, and #2 Friend. A couple of quickies and several medium Stoppers.
NOTE: The third pitch is similar to A Bridge Too Far (Route 162), but longer. Technically not difficult but an endurance problem. Double ropes are nice for Pitch two and three. Jay gives it three stars, others two stars.

158. MR. CLEAN: III, 5.11a
FIRST ASCENT: July 30, 1976, by Curt Haire and Dennis Horning (III, 5.10, A1).
FIRST FREE ASCENT: August 14, 1977, by Henry Barber and Chip Lee.
APPROACH: Take the West Face Approach. The line follows the crack just left of Dead Point (Route 159) and two cracks right of The Howling (Route 157). Begin the route below a bright yellow one-foot-wide roof at a bolt. You may want to fourth class the 30 feet (5.6) up to the bolt.
PITCH 1: Climb up through the roof (5.10d) and the long finger crack above it until you get to the belay bolts on your left. This is strenuous with the only true rest halfway up, a small ledge on the right face (160 feet, 5.11a). **PITCH 2:** Continue up the same line with hand and fist jams to the West Face ledge (160 feet, 5.10a).
FINISH: Move one column right and follow the large crack to the summit (160 feet, 5.9).

SUGGESTED EQUIPMENT: Standard rack, #1 to #8 Hexcentrics, #3 to #12 Stoppers with many extra #7 to #10s. Friends helpful.
NOTE: Most climbers do pitch 1 only, then rappel off. A three star classic route.

159. DEAD POINT: I, 5.11b
FIRST ASCENT: June 1, 1980, by Steve Gardiner, Frank Sanders, and Mark Brackin as the aid route Misty Morning Melody (Route 160) (II, 5.8, A2).
FIRST FREE ASCENT: August 19, 1988, of Pitch 1, by Jay Smith and Jo Bentley.
APPROACH: Take the West Face Approach to Mr. Clean (Route 158). The route is one crack right of Mr. Clean which is on the old aid route Misty Morning Melody.
PITCH 1: Climb this very thin finger crack, using face holds, thin finger locks, and some layback holds to the two bolt belay (90 feet, 5.10d).
FINISH: Rappel from the two bolt belay.
SUGGESTED EQUIPMENT: RPs, #3 to #6 HB nuts, small TCU's, one #1-1/2, one #2 Friend and one set of Stoppers to #6.
NOTE: Although a short route, it is a good climb with excellent protection. The lower portion of the pitch may have been free climbed by the original party. A two star route.

160. MISTY MORNING MELODY: II, 5.8, A2
FIRST ASCENT: June 1, 1980, by Steve Gardiner, Frank Sanders and Mark Brackin.
FIRST FREE ASCENT: Pitch 1 - August 19, 1988, by Jay Smith and Jo Bentley as Dead Point (Route 159) (I, 5.11b).
APPROACH: Take the West Face Approach. Climb up to the base of the route which lies one crack right of Mr. Clean (Route 158).
PITCH 1: Dead Point. Free climb up the crack to the end of Dead Point (100 feet, 5/11b). Climb on aid to a hanging belay at a point where the crack widens slightly (150 feet from start, 5.11b, A2). **PITCH 2:** Continue on aid until you run out of rope and hopefully reach the West Meadows Ledge (165 feet, A2).
FINISH: Traverse to the right and finish the climb free, using the last two pitches of McCarthy West Face (Route 167) to the summit (100 feet, 5.8) and (70 feet, 5.5).
SUGGESTED EQUIPMENT: Full rack of Stoppers and Hexcentrics plus a good selection of knifeblades, Lost Arrows and angles. Take some RPs, TCUs, one #1-1/2 and one #2 Friend, with #3 to #6 HB nuts if you do Pitch 1 free.
NOTE: Dead Point is a two star route.

161. INDEPENDENCE: III, 5.8, A3
FIRST ASCENT: July 4, 1980, by Frank Sanders (solo).
APPROACH: Take the West Face Approach. This route is one crack left of Tulgey Wood (Route 164).
PITCH 1: Work your way up this crack until it is feasible to move left one crack just over half way up the Tulgey Wood Column. Continue up until you are out of rope and set up a hanging belay (160 feet, A2). **PITCH 2:** Stay in the same crack and aid up to the end of your rope and hang a belay (155 feet, A2). **PITCH 3:** More of the same except the last 20 feet to the West Face Ledge which is hard to figure out. Belay here (60 feet, A3).
FINISH: Rappel down or climb to the summit on McCarthy West Face (Route 167) (100 feet, 5.8).
SUGGESTED EQUIPMENT: Lots of knife blades, Bugaboos and Lost Arrows. Add a standard rack if you go to the summit.
NOTE: Hanging belays are quite secure. The first portion of pitch one has been climbed free as A Bridge Too Far (Route 162) (5.11d).

162. A BRIDGE TOO FAR: I, 5.11d
FIRST ASCENT: June 27, 1983, by Todd Skinner, Mark Sonnenfeld and Steve Hong.
APPROACH: Take the West Face Approach. Same as Tulgey Wood (Route 164). The two cracks used are one and two cracks left of Tulgey Wood and stemming between them. "It is impossible for people under 5.6," says Steve Hong.
PITCH 1: This is in the first corner left of Tulgey Wood. Work up until you can stem one crack left. Climb on desperate stemming past a bolt to Tulgey Wood's first belay on a column top (140 feet, 5.11d).
FINISH: Rappel down or continue to the summit on other routes.
SUGGESTED EQUIPMENT: Double 9mm rope recommended because you need to protect in both cracks; or bring runners if you're poor. Two sets of RPs and #6-#8 Stoppers for the upper portion of the pitch.
NOTE: Harder if you are short and tight. A one or two star route.

163. ADVENTUROUS DAZE: IV, 5.10a, A2
FIRST ASCENT: June 4, 1983, by Frank Sanders and Chris Engle.
APPROACH: Take the West Face Approach to Tulgey Wood (Route 164) or A Bridge Too Far (Route 162).
PITCH 1: Take A Bridge Too Far (140 feet, 5.11d) or Tulgey Wood Pitch 1 (130 feet, 5.10a) which is easier. **PITCH 2:** Aid up the left crack from the first belay ledge of Tulgey Wood then hang a belay (160 feet, A2). **PITCH 3:** Continue on aid up the same crack until you reach the West Face Meadows (60 feet, A2).
FINISH: Finish the climb on McCarthy West Face to the summit.
SUGGESTED EQUIPMENT: The aid cracks need a standard aid rack, wide assortment of Lost Arrows and knife blades. Also take small to medium pieces for the free portion of the climb and a few larger pieces for the top.

164. TULGEY WOOD: II, 5.10a
FIRST ASCENT: June 2, 1972, by Mark Hesse and Dan McClure.
APPROACH: Take the Durrance Approach a short distance and angle up left until you are just past of the McCarthy West Face (Route 167) roof. The climb is one crack left of Way Layed (Route 166) and Mystery Express (Route 165) in the obvious left facing dihedral.
PITCH 1: Climb this hand and finger crack to the column top bolts on your left (130 feet, 5.10a). **PITCH 2:** Climb the finger crack and stem to the column top bolts on your right (30 feet, 5.10a). **PITCH 3:** Climb the long fist crack to the large West Face Ledge (160 feet, 5.9). **PITCH 4:** Take the McCarthy West Face (Route 167) to the summit (160 feet, 5.8).
SUGGESTED EQUIPMENT: Standard rack, plus extra small to medium Stoppers, about five 2- to 3-inch pieces, and #4 Friends help on pitch three.
NOTE: Many climbers rappel after pitch 2, and avoid the long fist crack of pitch 3. A three star classic.

165. MYSTERY EXPRESS: I, 5.13a
FIRST ASCENT: September 26, 1988, by Andy Petefish and Kris Hjelle.
APPROACH: Take the West Face Approach to Tulgey Wood. This pitch follows the arete right of Tulgey Wood (Route 164) and left of Way Layed (Route 166).
PITCH 1: Face climb up the arete on continuous small holds. Numerous 3/8th inch bolts protect the pitch. There are repeated cruxes of 5.12 difficulty on this pitch. Continue up until you reach the column top and the Tulgey Wood bolts (150 feet, 5.13a).
FINISH: Rappel off or finish Tulgey Wood.
SUGGESTED EQUIPMENT: Eighteen quick draws.

NOTE: This is a two to three star pitch in a spectacular setting and the first 5.13 pitch put up on the Tower.

166. WAY LAYED: I, 5.11b
FIRST ASCENT: June 30, 1981, by Eric Rhicard and Mark Smedley.
APPROACH: Take the West Face Approach. The pitch is just right of Mystery Express (Route 165) and left of McCarthy West Face (Route 167).
PITCH 1: Climb the right-facing corner crack to the top of the Tulgey Wood Column. This crack is sustained thin fingers and stemming, with the crux at the roof (155 feet, 5.11b).
FINISH: Rappel from here or continue up on Tulgey Wood (Route 164) to the summit.
SUGGESTED EQUIPMENT: Small Stoppers, Friends, and RPs. See Tulgey Wood if you go higher.
NOTE: A three star pitch.

167. McCARTHY WEST FACE: III, 5.11c
FIRST ASCENT: July 26, 1955, by Jim McCarthy and John Rupley. This was the first route established on the West Face (5.8, A3).
FIRST FREE ASCENT: August 11, 1979, by Steve Hong and Karin Budding.
APPROACH: Take the West Face Approach and climb up and slightly left until you are below the prominent gray roofs on the West Face. This route is two cracks right of Tulgey Wood (Route 167) and one crack left of El Matador (Route 170).
PITCH 1: Belay from the ledge below the first bulge. The crux is 15 feet above here. Climb the left crack to the top of a column which forms a large, prominent flake (110 feet, 5.9+) **PITCH 2:** From the belay, climb the rightmost of the three cracks to belay on top of the right column (95 feet, 5.11c). **PITCH 3:** Hand jam to a ledge directly below the ceilings (60 feet, 5.8). **PITCH 4:** This pitch can be done two ways: immediately traverse left from the ledge and fist jam the crack, turning roofs on the left; or climb directly up the center crack to a fixed pin and hand traverse left, also turning ceilings on the left. Belay on the West Face Ledge (65 feet, 5.7).
PITCH 5: Climb the rightmost crack through two overhanging squeeze chimneys, the second of which is the crux of the pitch. Belay on a broad ledge directly after the last overhang (100 feet, 5.8).
FINISH: Climb the crack to the summit, traversing slightly left (70 feet, 5.5).
SUGGESTED EQUIPMENT: Standard rack, full set of Hexcentrics and Stoppers, with extra #5 to #12 Stoppers and runners. A four inch piece is helpful on Pitch 5.
NOTE: You can reach the top of Pitch 2 of Tulgey Wood by climbing up and left from the top of Pitch 1 of McCarthy West Face. This small traverse was first done July 7, 1976, by Greg Newth and Dave Hoag and is called the McCarthy West Face Heads Up Variation (Route 168). You can rappel from here or continue up on Tulgey Wood (Route 164) (30 feet, 5.10a). Three stars.

168. McCARTHY WEST FACE FREE VARIATION: II, 5.10b
FIRST ASCENT: July 1, 1978, by Chris Ballinger, Dennis Horning and Steve Gardiner.
APPROACH: Take the West Face Approach to the start of McCarthy West Face (Route 167).
PITCH 1: Same as McCarthy West Face Pitch 1 (5.9+). **PITCH 2:** Climb the left crack (McCarthy West Face - Heads up variation) halfway. The route starts here. Climb up and pass the roof on the right using a finger crack. A 1/4 inch bolt protects the roof move. Avoid rope drag under the roof and use wide stemming to reach the top of Pitch 3 of McCarthy West Face (155 feet, 5.10b). **PITCH 3:** Climb El Matador (Route 170) up and right through the gray roofs (5.10a)

FINISH: Continue to the summit (5.4).
SUGGESTED EQUIPMENT: Standard rack, full rack of Stoppers and Hexcentrics, extra medium and large Stoppers.
NOTE: After Pitch 2, you can climb McCarthy West Face to the top. A three star variation.

169. McCARTHY WEST FACE - HONG VARIATION: I, 5.11b (one Pitch)
FIRST ASCENT: May 11, 1979, by Steve Hong and Karin Budding.
APPROACH: Take the West Face Approach up to McCarthy West Face (Route 167).
PITCH 1: Start at the base of the McCarthy West Face crack and climb straight up to the overhang and pass it on the right, which is the crux. Continue straight up the thin crack with finger locks to a belay at the bolts above the flake (130 feet, 5.11b).
FINISH: Rappel off or go to the summit via any of the routes above.
SUGGESTED EQUIPMENT: For the Hong Variation, many RPs and small wired Stoppers.
NOTE: Grade III if you go to the summit. A two star pitch.

170. EL MATADOR: III, 5.10d
FIRST ASCENT: September 24, 1967, by Fred Beckey and Eric Bjornstad (IV, 5.7, A3).
FIRST FREE ASCENT: August 6, 1978, by Bob Yoho and Chick Holtkamp.
APPROACH: Take the West Face Approach. This route leaves the shoulder of the Tower two cracks to the right of McCarthy West Face (Route 167).
PITCH 1: Follow the right hand crack up to the obvious belay at the two bolts below the chimney. The crux is a finger crack in the last 15 feet (80 feet, 5.11a). **PITCH 2:** Stem the chimney and jam the left crack, fingers and hand, to the top of the column. No move is harder than 5.9, but very continuous. Obviously a height-dependent pitch that is harder for short people (130 feet, 5.11a). **PITCH 3:** Climb straight up the obvious hand crack to the good belay ledge 40 feet below the first roof. This is Pitch 3 of McCarthy West Face (60 feet, 5.8). **PITCH 4:** Climb the Left hand crack to a fixed pin. Then traverse into the right hand crack. Climb the fingercrack through this roof (crux) to a second roof and through that one continue up the 5.7 chimney on good holds. Continue up a larger finger crack (5.9) to a stance with a bolt (160 feet, 5.10a).
FINISH: Climb the chimney to the summit (60 feet, 5.4).
SUGGESTED EQUIPMENT: Standard rack, #3 to #8 Hexcentrics, #1 to #3 Friends, runners for overhangs, and a full set of Stoppers. Also, extra small Stoppers and long slings to prevent rope drag over the gray roofs.
NOTE: Most people rappel off from pitch #2. If you do this, be sure to rappel down the face (not the crack) to prevent jamming your ropes. Pitch 1 is an excellent short finger crack climb, to do in the evening. A three star route.

171. LA VACA SOLITARIA: I, 5.11a
FIRST ASCENT: August 1, 1987, by Carl Coy and Mal Ham.
APPROACH: Take the West Face Approach to El Matador (Route 170). The climb starts at the top of the second pitch of El Matador. It is the right crack that forms the right side of El Matador.
PITCH 1: Climb pitch #1 of El Matador. **PITCH 2:** Climb pitch #2 of El Matador.
PITCH 3: Step right, off the top of the El Matador ledge to the right crack. Climb up this finger crack on excellent protection to the Grey Roofs. Move left into the El Matador crack and continue up through the roofs to a two bolt hanging belay. The crux is stemming with thin fingers. (130 feet, 5.11a)

FINISH: Climb up El Matador to McCarthy West Face (Route 167) and up to the summit or rappel to the start of this pitch. Another rappel down and right gets you to the base.
SUGGESTED EQUIPMENT: Standard rack, small to medium Stoppers and Friends to #2. Also see El Matador equipment list.
NOTE: This is a two star route.

172. DIGITAL EXTRACTION: III, 5.11d
FIRST ASCENT: October 25, 1977, by Keith Lober as Made For Aid (III, 5.8, A3).
FIRST FREE ASCENT: May 19, 1982, by Steve Hong and Mark Sonnenfeld.
APPROACH: Take the Durrance Approach until you reach the solid rock. Scramble mostly up and slightly left until you are just right of the start of El Matador (Route 170). The climb follows the first crack right of the El Matador box except for the first few feet, where it is two cracks right.
PITCH 1: Climb this severe, thin crack until you can set up a hanging belay at a bolt (110 feet, 5.11c). **PITCH 2:** This pitch is continuously sustained with thin jamming at the crux near the end of the pitch and the end of your strength. There are fixed pins at the hanging belay (140 feet, 5.11d). **PITCH 3:** Rappel (recommended) or climb up the crack until you can belay from two bolts on your right. Crux in mid-point (100 feet, 5.10).
FINISH: Climb the final chimney above to the summit (130 feet, 5.8).
SUGGESTED EQUIPMENT: Take three to four sets of large RPs and a double set of #3 to #7 Stoppers. Also #1 to #4 Friends or Hexcentrics, three #1 and two #3 Friends for the first two pitches. Take larger nuts for the upper pitches.
NOTE: A three star route.

173. THE THIN DAGGER: IV, A2
FIRST ASCENT: September 13, 1980, by Dan Grady and Rod Johnson.
APPROACH: Take the Durrance Approach a short distance then left of the Southwest Buttress. The route starts mid-face and gives the appearance of a thin dagger when viewed against Conquistador (Route 174). Start about two cracks left of the large, left-facing dihedral on your right.
PITCH 1 TO SUMMIT: Aid up the Conquistador crack until you come to the point of The Thin Dagger which is about 110 feet up. Take the left side. The entire crack is a thin knifeblade to Lost Arrow crack with an occasional baby angle or #1 to #2 wired Stopper. It continues for about 380 feet straight up with hanging belays. Now traverse left to a pitch of easy free climbing to the summit.
SUGGESTED EQUIPMENT: Plenty of blades and Lost Arrows with some small angles and wired Stoppers.
NOTE: Little is known about each pitch and the exact final pitches.

174. CONQUISTADOR: IV, 5.7, A3
FIRST ASCENT: May 3, 1964, by Tex Bossier and Steve Komito.
APPROACH: Follow the Durrance approach until you are near the top of the Southwest Shoulder. Climb up and just left of the Southwest Buttress onto a large belay ledge. This route starts about two cracks left of the large left facing dihedral on your right and leads to the Thin Dagger (Route 173) further up. See "Note" below. Looking up you will see a fairly uniform, continuous crack that starts in a small, right facing dihedral for a few feet and that higher up runs up the edge of the large, left facing dihedral on your right. This is the route.
PITCH 1: Aid up this thin crack until you see the Thin Dagger crack angling up to the left. Continue straight up to a hanging belay at the end of your rope (110 feet, A3). **PITCH 2:** Continue up the same crack until you reach the end of your rope and set up a belay (160 feet, A3). **PITCH 3:** Climb up on aid a short distance until

you reach the weathered portion about 170 feet below the summit. From this point traverse one crack left and climb up to an overhang (A3).
FINISH: Traverse left to a pitch of easy free climbing to the summit.
SUGGESTED EQUIPMENT: Take a selection of blades and tie offs, a standard selection of angles, and a few bongs for protection on the upper portions of the climb. Nuts can also be used.
NOTE: Some confusion has existed as to the exact crack this route followed. Park records (a marked photo) and the photo descriptions in "A Climbers Guide to Devils Tower" show the correct route which starts a few cracks left of the large left facing dihedral. This was confirmed October 28, 1984, when I (Richard Guilmette) talked to both of the original climbers by telephone. For some time several climbers had thought the route started in the corner of the large dihedral and ran up the dihedral and even onto it's face. This is not correct. The route gets into the dihedral after you have climbed up a ways. Some details about belay locations and crux information is vague, so anyone wishing to climb this route or The Thin Dagger should take extra precautions.

175. WHITE LIGHTNING: III, A2
FIRST ASCENT: September 1, 1985, by Mark Gordon and Kristi Rolf.
APPROACH: Take the Durrance Approach to just below the Southwest Buttress then move up and left to the corner where Conquistador (Route 174) and Abject Cathexis (Route 176) start. The pitch is between Conquistador and Abject Cathexis.
PITCH 1: Aid up the first pitch of Abject Cathexis, a left facing dihedral, until you can set up a hanging belay from fixed pins (140 feet, A2). **PITCH 2:** Pendulum one crack to the left to start White Lightning. Aid up this crack on knifeblades (crux) about thirty-five feet to where the crack opens up to small Stoppers and Lost Arrows. Continue aiding up this crack about 110 feet where you can see a "bucket hold" off to your right. Tension traverse back to Abject Cathexis one crack right. Aid this crack to the fixed pins hanging belay (about 15 feet). This is at the base of the broken section of the Tower rock (160 feet, A2).
FINISH: Rappel down to the anchors on the Thin Dagger (Route 173) (fixed pins) and down to the starting ledge from there. Due to the overhanging nature of the dihedral you can not rappel directly down the route you went up on.
SUGGESTED EQUIPMENT: Many #1 to #5 Stoppers and some larger Stoppers, steel nuts, knife blades and Lost Arrows.
NOTE: One could swing out of Abject Cathexis sooner into the hand crack, but this would definitely increase the difficulty. This climb was a gas. The pendulum and the tension traverse were great.

176. ABJECT CATHEXIS: III, A3
FIRST ASCENT: May 27, 1983, by Eric Breitenberger and William Trull.
APPROACH: Take the Durrance Approach onto the Tower base and then straight up to the high ledge that starts Conquistador (Route 174). You are also just left of the Southwest Buttress. The route is in the second main crack right of Conquistador. This is the outermost crack in the left facing dihedral between Conquistador and the Southwest Buttress.
PITCH 1: Aid up this dihedral. At the end of your rope set up a belay on nuts or pins (140 feet, A2). **PITCH 2:** Continue aiding up the same crack in the overhanging dihedral until you reach the broken rock. The crux is just below the end. Set up a hanging belay at the fixed pins (140 feet, A3).
FINISH: Rappel off or continue up on Conquistador or The Thin Dagger (Route 173) to the summit.
SUGGESTED EQUIPMENT: Nuts to #8, #1-1/2 Friends, and lots of RPs especially #5s.
NOTE: This is rated a very good aid climb.

177. BILLIE BEAR CRANKS THE RAD: I, 5.12c

FIRST ASCENT: August 12, 1985, by Bill Hatcher, Todd Skinner and Rick Erker.
APPROACH: Take the Durrance Approach onto the lower shoulder then straight up to a large ledge at the base of Conquistador (Route 174). The route follows the start of Abject Cathexis (Route 176), then traverse right into the crack that goes up the left side of the Southwest Buttress.
PITCH 1: Climb the Abject Cathexis crack 40 feet, then traverse right into the excellent fingertip crack that separates the Southwest Buttress from the main Tower. Protection is excellent and the crux is near the top. Belay at the bolts (80 feet, 5.12b).
FINISH: Rappel from the bolts. One 165 foot rope doubled will reach the bottom ledge.
SUGGESTED EQUIPMENT: Small nuts.
NOTE: Bill Hatcher says "the route is possibly the best thin fingertips route on the Tower despite its length. The route is an ideal direct start for Abject Cathexis". Some climbers say this route was not done in good style when it was put up? Other climbers think it may have been climbed prior to this date. Park records do not show a previous climb. If you have any information on the background of this route please contact the National park Service. A two star route.

178. A REACH TOO FAR: I, 5.10d

FIRST FREE ASCENT: August 7, 1988, by Bob Gaines, Paul Van Betten, Foster green, Fred Williams, Clell Williams, Don Mann, and Brad Tschetter.
APPROACH: Take the Durrance Approach. This climb is located on the Southwest Buttress. The pitch follows the first crack system left of Liken Lichen (Route 179).
PITCH 1: Climb up mainly on the face, using the thin crack for protection. The crux is the last ten feet with a long reach off of a fingerlock. At the top, one can move right (5.9) to escape the crux section (140 feet, 5.10d).
FINISH: Rappel from the two bolts.
SUGGESTED EQUIPMENT: Standard rack, small to medium nuts, three cams, #2 and #3 Friends. Bring one #2 RP, one #2 Stopper, one #2 HB nut and two #6 HB nuts.
NOTE: Protection is adequate. Bob gives it two stars and others give it one star.

179. LIKEN LICHEN: I, 5.9-

FIRST ASCENT: June 18, 1986, by Mateo Pee Pee and Barney Fisher.
APPROACH: Take the Durrance approach until you are on the southwest shoulder directly below the small southwest buttress. The route starts two cracks left of Accident Victim (Route 182) (two cracks left of the small roof on the broken column). Begin from the base of the crack (down and left). The obvious thin crack above marks the crux of the climb.
PITCH 1: Climb the finger crack about 75 feet to where it thins and steepens. Enjoyable face moves (up and left) takes one through this crux to easy climbing above. The last portion of this pitch finishes on the belay at the rappel bolts for Billy Bear Cranks The Rad (Route 177) (120 feet, 5.9-).
FINISH: Rappel off or continue up Accident Victim.
SUGGESTED EQUIPMENT: RPs (double on #3 and #4), small rocks, and a #2 Friend or #7 Hexcentric.
NOTE: It is possible to rappel down (over!) Billy Bear Cranks the Rad with a single 165 foot rope. This is a very enjoyable pitch. A one star route.

180. PORCUPINING AWAY: I, 5.7

FIRST ASCENT: August 20, 1988, by Andrew M. Artz.

APPROACH: Take the Durrance Approach up to the Southwest Buttress area. The route starts in a deep alcove that contains several boulders and slabs between Liken Lichen and Accident Victim (Route 182).
PITCH 1: Follow the alcove to it's top (part of Durrance Approach), then traverse left and follow the first crack right of Liken Lichen (Route 179) up until it runs into the first pitch of Accident Victim (155 feet, 5.7).
INISH: Rappel off or climb one of the routes above.
SUGGESTED EQUIPMENT: Small to medium Stoppers, #1-1/2 Friend, and slings to avoid rope drag.
NOTE: This pitch may have been climbed before but there is no record of it here. Poor protection, not recommended and no stars.

181. OBJECT CATHEXIS: III, 5.12b
FIRST ASCENT: September 29, 1981, by Steve Hong and Mark Sonnenfeld.
APPROACH: Take the Durrance Approach until you are on the top of the Southwest Shoulder and below the Southwest Buttress. Climb to the base of Accident Victim (Route 182) above you to set up a belay. This crack is the one that leads to the right side of the high point on the Southwest Buttress.
PITCH 1: Accident Victim. Climb this easy crack to the large column top belay ledge in a corner below the high point of the Southwest Buttress (120 feet, 5.6).
PITCH 2: Face climb up to the base of a prominent diagonal crack angling left (5.10-). Continue up the crack (just left of Accident Victim 125 feet and traverse back right where the crack deteriorates (crux) to the belay at the top of Pitch 2 of Accident Victim (155 feet, 5.12b).
FINISH: Rappel down or use Accident Victim to Direct Southwest (Route 185) to gain the summit. Grade II if you rappel and III if you continue to the top.
SUGGESTED EQUIPMENT: Standard rack, three #1 and #2 Friends, three sets of medium RPs, and two sets of medium Stoppers (25 pieces).
NOTE: A one star route.

182A. STEAL AWAY: I, 5.11b (variation is 5.12a)
FIRST ASCENT: August 6, 1992, by Dave Rone, Kimi Harrison, and Leslie Appling.
APPROACH: Take the Durrance Approach to the Southwest Buttress. The pitch starts on top of the buttress in the center just right of Accident Victim (Route 182).
PITCH 1: Take any of numerous routes to the top of the buttress. **PITCH 2:** Climb up and right a short distance following a right curving crack that merges with the main crack to the right of Accident Victim. From here climb up and left on the face, then up and right to the main crack under an overhang. Move up and right to pass the (crux) overhang on the right following a line of bolts then climb back left past the crack and above the overhang. See the note for doing the harder overhang variation. This puts you back on the face you started on. Climb straight up then traverse right past the crack all the way to the 411 Southwest belay bolts. This is sustained thin face climbing near a flared seam (80 feet, 5.11b).
FINISH: Rappel off.
SUGGESTED EQUIPMENT: Take ten Stoppers #3 to #7, a set of TCUs #1 to #4, and eleven quickdraws.
NOTE: This pitch reportedly has good rock with excellent protection. The crux overhang on Pitch 2 can be climbed direct instead of passing it on the easier right side and it is bolt protected. This is called The Lander Girls variation and is 5.12a.

182. ACCIDENT VICTIM: IV, 5.11d
FIRST ASCENT: August 25, 1980, by Kim Carrigan and Steve Levin.

APPROACH: Take the Durrance Approach until you are on the Southwest Shoulder directly below the small buttress. The route starts at the base of the small buttress five columns left of Direct Southwest (Route 185).
PITCH 1: Climb up this easy corner crack to a belay ledge on the buttress top (120 feet, 5.6). **PITCH 2:** Climb up the leftward leaning flake then step right into the main line. Hard stemming leads to thin fingers, then hands to a good belay ledge on your left (147 feet, 5.11d). **PITCH 3:** Climb up this corner about 33 feet to a ledge on your right. Continue up and right around the next column past scary moves under a small roof and to the right, crossing three columns with poor protection to a good flake belay (85 feet, 5.11a). **PITCH 4:** Traverse up and right one crack which puts you just above and left of a large roof. Climb up this thin crack a ways then traverse left one crack and set up a belay where the crack curves to the left (160 feet, 5.9). This pitch can also be done straight up the Direct Southwest crack (150 feet, 5.10).
FINISH: Same as Direct Southwest Finish (70 feet, 5.6).
SUGGESTED EQUIPMENT: Full set of Hexcentrics, small to medium Stoppers and lots of wired nuts. Five sets of RPs were used by the first ascent team.
NOTE: Climber Dennis Horning reports that Mark Hudon (leader) and Max Jones actually climbed pitch #2 free prior to the reported party listed above? National Park Service records do not show this but Dennis could be correct. One star route.

183. SOUTHWEST BUTTRESS CRACKS: I, 5.6 to 5.7
FIRST ASCENT: Unknown
APPROACH: Take the Durrance Approach to the top of the shoulder. The Southwest Buttress Cracks are the easiest ones that go to the top of the Southwest Buttress.
NOTE: These heavily used cracks have been named to prevent confusion, and are used to reach the ledges at the top of the Southwest Buttress (85 feet, 5.6 to 5.7).

184. 411 SOUTHWEST: II, 5.12
FIRST ASCENT: Pitch 2 - June 12, 1991, by Dave Rone, George Kremer, and Mary Jo Rone. Pitch 3 - June 18, 1991, by Dave Rone and George Kremer.
APPROACH: Take the Durrance Approach to the Southwest Buttress. Start the climb one crack left of Direct Southwest (Route 185).
PITCH 1: Climb this finger crack to the crux at the top and belay on a comfortable ledge with two bolts on top of the Southwest Buttress (130 feet, 5.8) **PITCH 2:** Face climb left following bolts then up the arete which is on the third column left of the Direct Southwest crack. Very steep face climbing with occasional holds in the crack. There are some flaky holds and the crux is about half way up. Climb up to the hanging belay at two bolts right of the crack (70 feet, 5.12). **PITCH 3:** Hard face climbing off the belay (crux) through two bolts then continuous 5.10 to 5.11 moves to the next hanging belay at a bolt and fixed pin (80 feet, 5.12)
FINISH: Rappel off.
SUGGESTED EQUIPMENT: Nine quickdraws, #1 to #9 Stoppers, set of RPs, Two sets of camming units #0 to #4, and #1 to #3 Lowballs.
NOTE: Avoid the loose rock at the top of Pitch 3 by stemming.
Pitch one has been climbed many times before along with the cracks left of it, but there is no record on them. This is the first time Pitch 1 has been reported and named.

185. DIRECT SOUTHWEST: III, 5.11b
FIRST ASCENT: July 1, 1962, by John Evans and Dick Long (IV, 5.9, A3).
FIRST FREE ASCENT: July 17, 1978, by Henry Barber and Ajax Green.

APPROACH: Take the Durrance Approach until you are on the Southwest Shoulder and on the right side of the base of the prominent Southwest Buttress.
PITCH 1: Climb the right crack to the top of the buttress and belay at the upper right bolts (75 feet, 5.7). **PITCH 2:** Climb the large finger crack leading up the left side of a broken column to its top. Belay at the bolts here (90 feet, 5.11b). **PITCH 3:** Climb the left crack past a bush to a ledge on the left. Traverse right across the face to a crack above and left of the large roofs. Climb up, traverse back left, and move up a short distance to belay. The original aid climb went straight up without a traverse right (150 feet, 5.9).
FINISH: Climb the crack to the summit (70 feet, 5.6).
SUGGESTED EQUIPMENT: Standard rack with extra small to large Stoppers and #1 to #1-1/2 Friends.
NOTE: A very strenuous lead with few rests. A three star route.

186. RANGERS ARE PEOPLE, TOO: I, 5.9-
FIRST ASCENT: June 14, 1985, by Jim Schlinkmann, Steve Gardiner, and Richard Guilmette.
APPROACH: Follow the Durrance Approach until you are on top of the southwest shoulder and below the Southwest Buttress. The route follows the right side of the buttress (right-facing dihedral) and is one crack right of the first pitch of Direct Southwest (Route 185).
PITCH 1: Climb the moderate low angle finger crack that leads through two bushes for 70 feet (5.4). Continue up the steep portion with fingerlocks, lieback and stemming moves to the top of the buttress (120 feet, 5.9-).
FINISH: Rappel off or climb up on another route.
EQUIPMENT: Small to medium Hexcentrics, medium to large Stoppers and #1 and #2 Friends.
NOTE: This is a fun pitch with excellent protection. A two star pitch.

187. SPACE RANGER: I, 5.12a
FIRST ASCENT: September 28, 1987, by Jack Roberts and Pam Ranger.
APPROACH: Take the Durrance Approach until you are just past the Southwest Buttress. The pitch is between Rangers Are People Too (Route 186) and Space Challenger (Route 188).
PITCH 1: Begin this climb from a small belay stance 10 feet above a large ledge between Space Challenger and Rangers Are People Too. Begin at a fixed pin at the base of this crack. Corner stem and lie back until a good rest is found on top of a large flake. Wide stemming to the arete on the left, face moves, and strenuous lie back moves on the right allow one to ascend past a few rests and several fixed pins. The pitch is best exited left from the last fixed pin 20 feet from the top where a finger to hand size, flake crack can be reached (165 feet 5.12a).
FINISH: Rappel from the bolts on top of the column.
SUGGESTED EQUIPMENT: #1, #3\4, #4 TCUs, three sets of Rocks, #1 through #5; RPs: 2-#1, 6-#2, 7-#3, 3-#4, 2-#5; two 9 mm 165 foot ropes are necessary to protect this route well.
NOTE: This route has superb protection. The climb involves cerebral stemming combined with technical and finger face moves.

188. SPACE CHALLENGER: II, 5.12c
FIRST ASCENT: June 22, 1980, by Steve Gardiner and Mark Brackin as the aid route Acrophobia (Route 189) (IV, 5.7, A2+).
FIRST FREE ASCENT: August 23, 1986, by Tim Toula belayed by Paul Chamberlain.

APPROACH: Take the Durrance Approach to the southwest shoulder. The route lies three columns right of the first pitch of Direct Southwest (Route 185) and one crack left of Butterfingers (Route 190). Approximately 40 feet of easy fifth class climbing (5.6) leads to a belay stance one crack right of the route on a ledge below a small pillar. A #2-1/2 friend and a #3 RP provide a belay anchor for the pitch above.

PITCH 1: Climb the beautiful but relentless corner above using the "utmost" in classic palming and stemming. The crux of the pitch is the first 50 feet and is protected by three fixed pins and a bolt. Continued difficult climbing leads to thin parallel cracks and the end of the pitch (160 feet, 5.12c).

FINISH: Rappel from a fixed pin and a bolt at the end of the pitch, or continue on aid up Acrophobia (Route 189).

SUGGESTED EQUIPMENT: #1 to #5 RPs, #1 to #5 Rocks, 1/2, 3/4, 1-1/2 Friends, #1 slider, and eight quickdraws.

NOTE: "This route is dedicated to the crew of the Challenger and all those men and women who seek to defy gravity - Remain in Flight! Anyone looking up at this corner with thoughts of leading it is bound to say 'UH-OH'. An All-American corner."—Tim Toula

189. ACROPHOBIA: IV, 5.7, A2+

FIRST ASCENT: June 22, 1980, By Steve Gardiner and Mark Brackin.
FIRST FREE ASCENT: Of pitch 1 - August 23, 1986, by Tim Toula belayed by Paul Chamberlin as Space Challenger (Route 188) (5.12c).
APPROACH: Take the Durrance Approach until just around the corner from Direct Southwest (Route 185) (one crack left of Butterfingers (Route 190) or three right of Direct Southwest) then scramble to a good belay.
PITCH 1: Aid up the thin, but widening crack in the right facing dihedral to a hanging belay (150 feet, A2 or free at 5.12c). **PITCH 2:** Continue up the crack and set up a belay on top of a column on the left (75 feet, A1). **PITCH 3:** Climb the same crack until it ends, then traverse to the right under two roofs into Butterfingers. Set up a hanging belay 20 feet above the roof. This section is flaring and full of rotten rock (150 feet, A2+). **PITCH 4:** Continue up the flaring crack on aid to a good belay marked by a fixed standard angle (75 feet, A2). **PITCH 5:** Climb the squeeze chimney and blocks to the summit (120 feet, 5.7).
SUGGESTED EQUIPMENT: Bugaboos, Lost Arrows, baby angles, angles, and a full set of Stoppers and Hexcentrics.

190. BUTTERFINGERS: IV, 5.7, A2

FIRST ASCENT: July 15, 1979, by Steve Gardiner and Mark Brakin.
APPROACH: Follow the Durrance Approach onto the Southwest Shoulder. Proceed just past the Southwest Buttress. The route lies four cracks right of the base of Direct Southwest (Route 185) and bisects the right half of the double roof 250 feet up.
PITCH 1: Climb on direct aid using blades and Bugaboos. A rotten pin was left to mark the first belay because it would be difficult to establish a belay higher (110 feet, A2). **PITCH 2:** Continue on aid to a point where the crack widens about 15 feet below the roof and belay in slings. Much of this pitch goes clean (140 feet, A2). **PITCH 3:** Climb to the roof and turn it on the right. Be sure to find the textbook pocket for a medium Stopper around the corner of the roof. Aid on Stoppers to a ledge where free climbing becomes obvious. Continue 20 feet to a belay at the fixed standard angle (140 feet, 5.6, A2). **PITCH 4:** Climb the squeeze chimney and large blocks to the summit (120 feet, 5.7).

SUGGESTED EQUIPMENT: A large selection of blades, Bugaboos, and Lost Arrows, plus a full rack of Stoppers and Hexcentrics. Large Hexcentrics are needed to protect the upper leads.

191. KIRK-SANDERS WEST FACE CLASSIC: III, 5.8, A3+
FIRST ASCENT: July, 1989, by Liana Kirk and Frank Sanders.
APPROACH: Take the Durrance Approach until you reach Butterfingers (Route 190). This climb starts one crack right of Butterfingers.
PITCH 1: Thin to Win. Free climb, then aid up the crack that ascends the leaning, two-tiered overhang on its left side. Increasingly difficult nailing leads to the inevitable RURP just over the lip of the second roof. Placements then improve radically and lead you to a three-bolt belay (140 feet, 5.7, A3+). **PITCH 2:** Thick to Stick. Arrows and angles lead ever upward. The aiding is easy and the view is just fine. Higher, as the crack withers, traverse left to Butterfingers and follow that to a splendid, three-bolt belay just under the roof (135 feet, A2). **PITCH 3:** Easy aid climbing around the roof takes you to a ledge where free climbing is obvious, though wide and awkward. Take this classic "Top of Devils Tower Chimney" to the summit belay with a #4 Friend (170 feet, 5.8, A1).
FINISH: Walk to the top.
SUGGESTED EQUIPMENT: A standard rack, lots of blades, angles and some RURPS with plenty of slings.
NOTE: The third pitch, Butterfingers, is a long one and takes all your rope and then some. Save a #4 Friend for the last belay. Adequate protection for Pitch 3 can be had by creative use of slings, big pieces and a hammer to reset critical "fixed" pins.

192. BLADE CITY: IV, 5.7, A3+
FIRST ASCENT: September 7, 1980, by Frank Sanders and Steve Gardiner.
APPROACH: Follow the Durrance Approach onto the Southwest
Buttress. Continue four cracks to the right of Butterfingers
(Route 190) and locate a long, direct crack leading straight to the summit. This is Blade City. Scramble up to a suitable belay.
PITCH 1: Climb on direct aid using knifeblades and bugaboos for a rope length until it is possible to get in a couple of bigger pins and construct a hanging belay (155 feet, A3). **PITCH 2:** Continue up the same crack on thin aid to a hanging belay where the Tower rock begins to crumble (160 feet, A3). **PITCH 3:** Climb the same crack to the summit. This last pitch opens and closes many times and requires a variety of creative placements (150 feet, 5.7, A3+).
SUGGESTED EQUIPMENT: Take along as many blades and bugaboos as you can beg, borrow, or steal as the first 300 feet will accept little else.
NOTE: On leading the third pitch, Frank Sanders commented, "That's as scared as I remember being."

193. BLUE STEM SKYWAY: II, 5.12c
FIRST ASCENT: October 3, 1987, by Andy Petefish and Kris Hjelle.
APPROACH: Take the Durrance Approach just past the Southwest Buttress. This climb lies two cracks right of Blade City (Route 192) and two cracks left of the start of Tunnel Vision (Route 195), and one crack left of the aid route, Soon To Be Free (Route 194). Belay on a small ledge approximately 40 feet below the first bolt.
PITCH 1: Climb up slabs until you are below a bolted face between two dihedrals. A #1.5 Friend can be placed before the first bolt. Stem upward past nine bolts and up to a three bolt belay. Protection after the ninth protection bolt is found in the right crack. This pitch has no 5.12 moves on it, but if done without falls or hangs

it makes for a lactic nightmare (150 feet, 5.12c). **PITCH 2:** Continue up a beautiful finger crack which thins out in a few places. The climbing becomes easier after the first 80 feet. Belay on a large ledge on the right (160 feet, 5.11c).
FINISH: Continue up Zephyr (Route 196) or do two rappels down Tunnel Vision.
SUGGESTED EQUIPMENT: Three sets of RPs, #1, #2, and #3 Rocks; #1 Slider; two #0-2 Met. TCUs; many small to medium Rocks; Friends #0.5-#3, maybe doubles on #1's and #1.5s.
NOTE: A two star route.

194. SOON TO BE FREE: I, A2
FIRST ASCENT: October 25, 1987, by Scott C. Robertson and Lysle Carter.
APPROACH: Take the Durrance Approach just past the Southwest Buttress. This pitch is one crack right of Blue Stem Skyway (Route 193) and one crack left of Tunnel Vision (195).
PITCH 1: Aid up this crack on very good protection until you reach the hanging belay bolts. This is a good clean pitch with some loose flakes and at times the main crack is hollow (140 feet, A2).
FINISH: Rappel down.
SUGGESTED EQUIPMENT: A good selection of blades with at least 15 standard knife blades, L.A.s, baby angles and smaller nuts.
NOTE: For an A2 route this one rates 2 stars out of a possible three stars.

195. TUNNEL VISION: I, 5.12b
FIRST ASCENT: June 9, 1979, by Jim Beyer (solo) as Zephyr (Route 196) (III, 5.9, A1).
FIRST FREE ASCENT: The first 85 feet - July 25, 1987, by Andy Petefish and Kris Hjelle.
FIRST FREE ASCENT: Pitch 1 (last part) and Pitch 2 - September 12, 1987, by Andy Petefish and Kris Hjelle.
APPROACH: Take the Durrance Approach to the southwest shoulder. The route lies three cracks left of Graeme's Line (Route 197) and two cracks right of Blue Stem Skyway (Route 193). Scramble up to a small ledge below a bush. This is the first belay stance.
PITCH 1: Continue to stem between the columns as you work your way up. Good but tedious protection is found in the right hand crack until a bolt is reached. Protection can be found in the left crack after passing the bolt. There are no single moves harder than 11a or 11b on the whole pitch, but it's very sustained nature warrants a 12b rating. Belay at the bolts (150 feet, 5.12b). **PITCH 2:** Continue to stem up as before. Protection is found in the left crack. The last 70 feet of the route is 5.9. Belay at the bolts on the ledge on your left (140 feet, 5.11a).
FINISH: Continue up Zephyr (Route 196) or rappel down the route.
SUGGESTED EQUIPMENT: Pitch 1 - RPs: one #2, seven #3s, four #4s, & two #5s. Rocks: two #1s, two #2s, and 3 #4s. Matolius 3 cams: one #0 and one #2. One #0.5 Tricam or #2 Matolius 3 cam for backing up the 1st belay. Pitch 2 - RPs: one #2, two #4s and one #1 5. Rocks: two #5s, one #6 and one #7. Stoppers: two #9s, two #10s, and two #11s. Lowe Tricams: one #1 and two #1-1/2s. Metolius TCUs: two #0s, one #1 and one #2. Friends: one #1, two #1-1/2s, one #2 and one #2-1/2 or #3 for use down low.
NOTE: A special thanks goes to Mike Robinson, Bryan Boretsky, Mal Ham, Shane Woodruff and Richard Guilmette for help on establishing this route. This is a super three star route out of a possible three stars.

196. ZEPHYR: III, 5.9, A1 (Free at 5.12b)
FIRST ASCENT: June 9, 1979, by Jim Beyer (solo).

FIRST FREE ASCENT: First 85 feet - July 25, 1987, by Andy Petefish and Kris Hjelle as Tunnel Vision (Route 195). Completion of Pitch 1 and all of Pitch 2 - September 12, 1987, by Andy Petefish and Kris Hjelle as Tunnel Vision (5.12b).
APPROACH: Take the Durrance Approach until you reach the middle of the southwest shoulder between Soon To Be Free (Route 194) and Graeme's Line (Route 197). This route climbs a prominent right facing dihedral.
PITCH 1: Tunnel Vision (150 feet, 5.12b). **PITCH 2:** Tunnel Vision (140 feet, 5.11a). PITCH 3: Tunnel Vision (first 40 feet). Face climb above the ledge to a roof. Traverse right into the dihedral and continue right to a 5.8 off-width. Head back into the corner to the crux, then climb a short hand crack to a small ledge to the left. Belay on #2 to #3" nuts (125 feet, 5.9).
FINISH: A couple of hard moves gets one to a fist crack. Traverse right and finish with a small overhang. (80 feet, 5.8,
SUGGESTED EQUIPMENT: See Tunnel Vision for a free ascent or use many assorted nuts, Stoppers, RPs and Friends to aid it.
NOTE: Once an aid route has been climbed free, the emphasis is on its being climbed free in the future or aided without the use of pins to protect the route. A three star route.

197. GRAEME'S LINE: II, 5.12b
FIRST ASCENT: August 16, 1979, by Frank Sanders and Steve Gardiner as Runner's World (Route 198) (IV, 5.6, A3).
FIRST FREE ASCENT: August 1, 1985, by Todd Skinner, Bill Hatcher and Beth Wald.
APPROACH: Take the Durrance Approach to the middle of the southwest shoulder and climb up to the base of the crack that leads to the only column-top ledge in the middle of the southwest face. This is on the old aid route Runner's World.
PITCH 1: Climb this thin crack utilizing many face flaws on good protection. Utilize both cracks left of the Runner's World Column. The crux of the climb is about 130 feet up near the end of the pitch. Climb through this on the right arete to a large column-top ledge and belay here at the bolts (150 feet, 5.12b). **PITCH 2:** Continue up on stemming moves in this box to a hanging belay from bolts at the end of the crack. Protection is fair and the crux of the pitch is the last 25 feet (85 feet, 5.11).
FINISH: Rappel down (recommended) or continue up Runner's World with aid.
SUGGESTED EQUIPMENT: Three sets of #2 to #5 RPs and many small to medium wired Stoppers. Also six quick draws and a #1/2 Friend and a #1 Friend.
NOTE: This is a three-star route that offers steep face climbing and balance rests on the right arete near the end. According to Todd Skinner it should become a classic. The route was named in memory of Graeme Aimer who died tragically in 1984 in the New Zealand Alps. Six fixed pitons are in pitch one and one piton is in pitch two. Two to three star route.

198. RUNNER'S WORLD: IV, 5.6, A3
FIRST ASCENT: August 16, 1979, by Frank Sanders and Steve Gardiner.
FIRST FREE ASCENT: Pitch 1 & 2 - August 1, 1985, by Todd Skinner, Bill Hatcher, and Beth Wald.
APPROACH: Take the Durrance Approach to the middle of the southwest shoulder and climb up to the base of the cracks that lead to the only column top ledge in the middle of the southwest face. The climb starts on the left side of the Runner's World Column and is right of Tunnel Vision (Route 195) and left of Centennial (Route 199).
PITCH 1: This has now been climbed free as Graeme's Line (Route 197) (150 feet, 5.12b). **PITCH 2:** This has been climbed free now as Graeme's Line (85 feet, 5.11).

PITCH 3: Get into the left crack and climb until an obvious ledge can take you right. The ledge is well defined, but has a poor bolt in the middle. Traverse to Centennial (Route 199) (130 feet, A2). **PITCH 4:** Last pitch of Centennial (100 feet, 5.6, A3).
SUGGESTED EQUIPMENT: See Graeme's Line for the free portion. Take lots of knifeblades as two pitches are very thin. Also, take extra Bugaboos and Lost Arrows.
NOTE: Anchors and belays are excellent and the top pitch is a bit loose. Have a good time. You've got to bop until you drop.

199. CENTENNIAL: III, A3
FIRST ASCENT: June 10 1978, by Terry Rypkema, Frank Sanders and Steve Gardiner.
APPROACH: Follow the Durrance Approach to the middle of the Southwest Face. Pass Graeme's Line (Route 197). Centennial is several cracks right of Graeme's Line and several cracks left of Unknown Route Left (Route 200). Start climbing in a shallow, right facing dihedral two cracks to the right of a broken off column.
PITCH 1: Aid this narrow crack to the end of your rope. The crack widens a little the last few feet so you can set up a solid, hanging belay with large angles (165 feet, A2+). **PITCH 2:** Continue up the same crack until a traverse to the next crack right is feasible. Climb this crack on aid until you are just beneath an overhang where flaky rock necessitates a leftward traverse across a horizontal crack. Better pins lead up to a good belay with a poor attempt at a bolt above the overhang (165 feet, A2). **PITCH 3:** Continue up until a secure hanging belay can be established in a horizontal crack to the left, just below a leftward arch (100 feet, 5.6, A3).
FINISH: Climb the arch to the summit (75 feet, A3).
SUGGESTED EQUIPMENT: Take lots of blades and small angles. The upper pitches use many large pieces.
NOTE: This is an excellent climb. It is long, sustained, offers secure belays, varied problems and spectacular views.

200. UNKNOWN ROUTE LEFT: Aid
EXPLANATION: This route is clearly marked on one of the Park's large route photos showing the east end of the Southwest Face. It lies between Centennial (Route 199) and The Last Laugh (Route 201). The line goes up a long crack that passes between a double roof on the left and a single roof on the right at the same level part way up the face. A little further up it passes another roof immediately on its right side and then continues on up to the summit in the obvious crack above.
SUGGESTED EQUIPMENT: Large aid rack with a few larger pieces for the top. Small to medium pieces should do most of the route.
NOTE: Not recommended.

201. THE LAST LAUGH: I, 5.10d
FIRST ASCENT: Time and climbers are unknown. Possibly climbed by Harvey T. Carter according to one old time climber at the Tower. The route was done on aid and we have called it Unknown Route Right (Route 202). Unknown Route Right was aided by Frank Sanders and Sue Gass September 14, 1988, and they completed the crack to the top by freeing the upper part.
FIRST FREE ASCENT: Of Pitch 1 of Unknown Route Right was October 2, 1988, by Kris Hjelle and Andy Petefish.
APPROACH: Take the Durrance Approach until you are on the east end of the Southwest Shoulder. The pitch starts on the old aid route Unknown Route right, and lies between Unknown Route Left (Route 200) and Romeo is Restless (Route 204).

PITCH 1: Belay from a ledge. Climb the crack with occasional finger pockets. The pitch progressively steepens and becomes an interesting stemming problem. Protection runs from fair to good. The crux is the overhang at the top of the pitch. Belay at the bolts (75 feet, 5.10d).
FINISH: Rappel from the bolts.
SUGGESTED EQUIPMENT: Standard rack, two #1 Rocks, two #3 RPs, one #4 RP, two #5 RPs, one #2 Metolius, one #1-1/2 Friend, one #.5 and one #1 Tricam.
NOTE: This is a two to three star route.

202. UNKNOWN ROUTE RIGHT: Aid
FIRST ASCENT: Unknown
FIRST FREE ASCENT: Pitch 1, as The Last Laugh (Route 201) (5.10d) - October 2, 1988, by Kris Hjelle and Andy Petefish. Pitch 3 and 4 as The Devil Made Me Do It (Route 203) - September 14, 1988, by Frank Sanders and Sue Gass.
EXPLANATION: This route is clearly marked on the Park's large route photo showing the east end of the Southwest Face. It lies between Unknown Route Left (Route 200) and is six cracks left of Romeo is Restless (Route 204). The photo shows the route continuing up to a point where the crack seems to close off at about the height of a large roof on the left. From this point climb a few feet and traverse left to the crack that passed the left roof on the right side. Continue up this crack to another large roof directly above you and pass it on the left. Climb up a short distance above you and then traverse right to a good crack between and above two roofs. From here you can rappel off as the original unknown climbers did or you can climb the easier appearing crack above you to the summit.
SUGGESTED EQUIPMENT: Lots of small to medium pieces and a few larger ones especially if you are going to the top.
NOTE: To get to Pitch 3 and 4, you have to aid Pitch 2. If you have any information on this route or other routes that we do not have, please write the Superintendent; Devils Tower National Monument; Devils Tower, Wyoming 82714.

203. THE DEVIL MADE ME DO IT: III, A2, 5.9+
FIRST ASCENT: September 14, 1988, by Frank Sanders and Sue Gass.
APPROACH: Take the Durrance approach until you are on the east end of the Southwest Shoulder. The route starts on the old aid route Unknown Route Right (Route 202) and lies between Unknown Route Left (Route 200) and Romeo is Restless (Route 204).
PITCH 1: The first 75 feet has been freed as The Last Laugh (Route 201) (5.10d). Aid up another 85 feet in a widening crack to a secure hanging 3 bolt belay (160 feet, 5.10, A2). **PITCH 2:** Aid up the ever narrowing crack on Unknown Route Right to where a traverse to the left crack is both feasible and wise. Continue up to a three bolt, secure hanging belay, directly under the large roof (120 feet, A2). **PITCH 3:** This starts the route. From the belay, free climb directly left, around the corner and across the face to a great hand crack. This is a beautiful, long crack with many sections similar to Assembly Line and some off-width. Continue up to a belay on a great ledge and good anchors (150 feet, 5.9+).
FINISH: Climb up on the best of several alternatives. Climbing is difficult for twenty feet and then becomes a scramble through loose rock (60 feet, 5.9).
SUGGESTED EQUIPMENT: Twelve knife blades, 12 Lost Arrows, four angles to 1 inch, nuts, Friends and tube chocks for the third pitch. If you do the bottom free see The Last laugh for Equipment.
NOTE: Route should some day go free. Two stars.

204. ROMEO IS RESTLESS: I, 5.12b
FIRST ASCENT: November 2, 1975, by Pat Padden and Rodney Johnson as Tower Direct (Route 205) (III, 5.8, A2).
FIRST FREE ASCENT: July 18, 1985, by Todd Skinner and Beth Wald.
APPROACH: Follow the Durrance Approach to the base of the Tower Direct. Scramble up and left to a small ledge below the route to start. This is on the old aid route Tower Direct and leads up to the lowest of five connected large roofs.
PITCH 1: Climb up this desperately thin crack with powerful yet delicate climbing. The crux is face climbing about halfway up the pitch. The crack widens eventually to a fist crack. There is a lot of 5.11 climbing and fair protection. Climb to a very unusual sitting belay at the bolts. This is on a ledge below the roof (150 feet, 5.12b).
FINISH: Recommend rappelling down. Todd says free climbing to the summit would be possible but dirty. To continue to the top follow the Tower Direct aid route.
SUGGESTED EQUIPMENT: Four or five sets of #3, #4, and #5 RPs, some small and medium wired Stoppers, two each #3 and #3-1/2 Friends, and one each #2, #2-1/2, and #4 Friends.
NOTE: Save one #3 RP for the last moves. A one star pitch.

205. TOWER DIRECT: III. 5.8, A2
FIRST ASCENT: November 2, 1975, by Pat Padden and Rodney Johnson.
FIRST FREE ASCENT: Pitch 1 as Romeo Is Restless (Route 204) - July 22, 1985, by Todd Skinner and Beth Wald.
APPROACH: Take the Durrance Approach until you are almost at the Leaning Column then traverse left and set up a belay. This route is the crack that runs up directly under the middle and lowest of five large roofs.
PITCH 1: This pitch has been climbed free as Romeo Is Restless (150 feet, 5.12b).
PITCH 2: Free climb with some aid up to the overhang and pass it on the left. Climb directly up to and over the next overhang. Continue up 50 feet to a belay stance (140 feet, A2). **PITCH 3:** Free Climb the crack above you to a good belay stance (130 feet, 5.8). **PITCH 4:** Free climb over an overhang to the top (100 feet, 5.7).
SUGGESTED EQUIPMENT: Set each of Hexcentrics and Stoppers. Lots of small nuts and Stoppers. Runners and Friends are helpful. (See Romeo Is Restless for equipment for freeing Pitch 1.
NOTE: Pitch one was originally done with many pitons (horizontals, angles, and bongs). Please do not use pitons to aid Pitch 1 since it has been climbed free, and this will help save the rock. A one star climb.

206. P.O.T.C.: II, 5.10d
FIRST ASCENT: August 24, 1965, by Pete Oslund and Tom Christensen (III, 5.7, A3).
FIRST FREE ASCENT: June 4, 1978, by Frank Sanders and Dennis Horning.
APPROACH: Take the Durrance Approach. The route lies three cracks left of the Leaning Column.
PITCH 1: Climb up the crack and belay below the roof (160 feet, 5.10d). **PITCH 2:** Climb up and over the left side of the roof to an off-width crack and chimney above. Belay on the column top (160 feet, 5.10b). **PITCH 3:** Traverse right and climb up to the Bailey Direct (Route 4) Finish of Durrance (Route 1). Climb this and belay at the Durrance rappel bolts (150 feet, 5.5). You can also traverse right to the Meadows and reach the summit by the Standard Meadows Finish.
SUGGESTED EQUIPMENT: Standard rack, full set of Stoppers and Hexcentrics with extra medium to large Stoppers. Take extra #5 to #12 Stoppers and 2- to 5-inch pieces.

NOTE: Initials stand for the first aid climbers (P.O.T.C.) Pete Oslund and Tom Christensen. A one to two star route.

207. BLACK-JONES DIRECT: II, 5.11b
FIRST ASCENT: Exact date and climbers unknown, but was climbed on aid prior to the establishment of Manifest Destiny (Route 208).
FIRST FREE ASCENT: July 7, 1979, by Steve Jones and Carol Black.
APPROACH: Follow the Durrance Approach to the base of the Leaning Column. The route starts one crack right of P.O.T.C. (Route 206) and two cracks left of the base of the Leaning Column.
PITCH 1: Climb up this thin crack until Manifest Destiny joins it. Continue up a little further to the belay/rappel bolts on your left (155 feet, 5.11b).
FINISH: Rappel off or continue up on Manifest Destiny and take any of the several options to reach the summit.
SUGGESTED EQUIPMENT: Take lots of medium to large Stoppers and see the equipment list for Manifest Destiny if you plan to go higher.
NOTE. Elvin (Al) Aaberg, former chief ranger at Devils Tower, said he spent a day watching some climbers aid up the crack (bottom to top) that starts at the base of Black-Jones Direct, then climb through what is now the end of Pitch 1 and all of Pitch 2 of Manifest Destiny before that route was put up. The climbers and date are not known. A three star route.

208. MANIFEST DESTINY: II, 5.9
FIRST ASCENT: See note below.
FIRST FREE ASCENT: August 21, 1973, by Bruce Bright and Dennis Drayna.
APPROACH: Follow the Durrance Approach to the base of the Leaning Column. The route starts one crack right of Black-Jones Direct (Route 207) and one crack left of the Leaning Column.
PITCH 1: Follow the ever-widening, extremely steep crack (fingers and fist) until the crack turns left and you can join the main crack on your left. Continue up this crack to a hanging belay at the bolts on your left (155 feet, 5.9). **PITCH 2:** Continue up this increasingly large crack chimney to the column tops for a belay (120 feet, 5.8).
FINISH: Follow the chimney above and climb to the summit (150 feet, 5.6). You can also traverse right to the Meadows for a Standard Meadows Finish or do the Bailey Direct (Route 4).
SUGGESTED EQUIPMENT: Take a full rack plus a number of large pieces (to 4") and runners.
NOTE: Mr. Elvin (Al) Aaberg, former Chief Ranger at Devils Tower, told me he spent a day watching some climbers aid up the crack (bottom to top) that starts at the base of Black-Jones Direct through Manifest Destiny end of Pitch 1 and all of Pitch 2 prior to Manifest Destiny being put up. The climbers and date are not known. A two star route.

209. DEDICATED TO THE GAME: I, 5.11c
FIRST ASCENT: September 5, 1991, by Nate B. Postma and Pam Postma.
APPROACH: Take the Southwest Buttress Approach. Follow the Tower Trail to the left until you reach the "Life on Top" interpretive sign. Walk up this ravine which takes you to the low point at the base of the Southwest Buttress. Traverse left a short distance and beyond Drilling Miss Daisy (Route 211) and Joe Kid (Route 210). The start is under a big roof.
PITCH 1: The route starts on layback flakes below the left side of the nose of the most prominent roof. The climb starts on fun gentle face climbing that is bolt

protected up to three roofs. The first roof is 5.11a, the second is 5.11c, and the last roof is 5.9+. Belay at two bolts (120 feet, 5.11c).
FINISH: Rappel off.
SUGGESTED EQUIPMENT: Take six quickdraws; one each 1-1/2, 2-1/2, and 3 inch camming units and maybe a couple of medium to large nuts if more intermediate placements are desired.
NOTE: Six bolts protect the face section and each roof is very different from the rest. Excellent and varied climbing with good rests and protection. Three Stars.

210. JOE KID: I, 5.9+
FIRST ASCENT: June 8, 1991, by Burton Lindquist and Tony Lindquist.
APPROACH: Take the Tower trail to the right until you come to the "Life On Top" interpretive sign. Follow the gully up to the base of the southwest buttress and go left until you are under the big roof. The route starts between Dedicated To The Game (Route 209) and Drilling Miss Daisy (Route 211).
PITCH 1: Climb up the obvious crack between Dedicated To The Game and Drilling Miss Daisy to a ledge and go right to the base of a vertical crack. Climb this crack to a flake which leads to an overhang. The crux is the roof and there is some loose rock here with marginal pro. Once over the roof, climb over some stacked blocks to a semi-hanging belay off your placed protection (120 feet, 5.9+). **PITCH 2:** Climb a large slot veering left, pull a 5.6 roof, and continue up a crack on good protection past large blocks on your left and right. The crux is one of the blocks. Set up a belay at the base of Rangers Are People Too (Route 186) below the southwest buttress (150 feet, 5.6).
FINISH: Down climb the Durrance Approach.
SUGGESTED EQUIPMENT: A standard rack with doubles of medium Stoppers and some large Friends/Camelots for the wide crack in the Pitch 2 slot.
NOTE: Some cleaning was done but more is needed. After pulling the first roof you can go left and up to the rappel bolts on Dedicated To The Game and rappel without doing Pitch 2. One star.

211. DRILLING MISS DAISY: I, 5.10a (A variation of Joe Kid)
FIRST ASCENT: July 3, 1991 by Nathan Postma and Paul Fritze.
APPROACH: Take the Tower Trail right across the boulder field to the "Life On Top" interpretive sign. Walk up the ravine to the base of the southwest shoulder at its' low point. Go left a short distance until you are under a large roof just right of Joe Kid (Route 210).
PITCH 1: Start just right of Joe Kid and climb straight up through the 5.10a crux, then left to a ledge where you join Joe Kid. Continue up on Joe Kid to the right side of the large overhang then rejoin Joe Kid just right of Drilling Miss Daisy. Climb up to where you can set up a belay (110 feet, 5.10a).
FINISH: Climb up and left to the top of the face (40 feet) where you can downclimb the Durrance Approach, or rappel from the Dedicated To The Game (Route 209) belay bolts, or you can continue up Joe Kid.
NOTE: A one star route.

212. DOWN AND OUT: I, 5.7
FIRST ASCENT: November 6, 1988, by Brad Solon and Jenny Silbernagel.
APPROACH: Take the Tower Trail and go right to the "Life on Top" interpretive sign. You will be directly south of the Southwest Buttress. Walk up the gully to the buttress at the low point in the boulder field. The climb starts approximately thirty feet to your right where you can belay from the third large tree from the low point in the boulder field.

PITCH 1: Follow the crack up and left on easy climbing to a pocket at the base of the prominent, right-facing dihedral below a bulge. This starts the crux and the main line of the climb. Surmount the bulge and continue up the crack in the dihedral to the column top on your left (80 feet, 5.7).
FINISH: Rappel off using your own gear.
SUGGESTED EQUIPMENT: Take #1 to #13 Stoppers plus extra #4 to #7s. Also three runners.
NOTE: Protection is very good but there are no bolts to rappel from. One star route.

213. TINTIN DOES DOUGHNUTS: I, 5.9 (Not Shown On Photo)
FIRST ASCENT: July 31, 1989, by Martin Ziebell belayed by Joel Barnett.
APPROACH: Take the Tower Trail right until you reach the "Life On Top" interpretive sign. Climb up the gully to the base of the buttress then go right past Down And Out (Route 212) and stop under the Park Service rescue training ledge. The pitch starts 20-30 left of Flight 714 (Route 214) whose bolts are easily seen. This climb starts three feet right of a tree that brushes up against the cliff.
PITCH 1: Climb directly up the face through four protection bolts. The crux is at bolt one and four. This pitch has good protection and rests. Face moves and edging (60 feet, 5.9).
FINISH: Rappel down. The wall was fully climbed above but is not recommended.
SUGGESTED EQUIPMENT: Four quick draws for the bolts.
NOTE: A good warm up climb for those short of time or for beginners. Two stars.

214. FLIGHT 714: I, 5.11a (Not Shown on Photo)
FIRST ASCENT: October 25, 1990, by Martin Ziebell.
APPROACH: Take the Tower trail, go right and through the boulder field until you come to the "Life On Top" interpretive sign. Walk up the gully to the base of the southwest shoulder, then go right well past Down And Out (Route 212) until you are a short distance below the top of the talus. The route is between Tintin Does Donuts (Route 213) and Lakota (Route 215).
PITCH 1: Climb the face through the roofs, clipping four bolts. The crux (5.11a) comes after the second bolt, making the balance swing to the right. Belay at the two bolt anchor (55 feet, 5.11a).
FINISH: Rappel, a single rope should do it.
SUGGESTED EQUIPMENT: Four quickdraws for the bolts and runners for the anchor.
COMMENTS: This route is a lot of fun. At the second bolt, it is possible to avoid the crux by moving to the left (5.10b). You would then have to move back right. Two stars.

215. LAKOTA: I, 5.11a (Not Shown On Photo)
FIRST ASCENT: August 18, 1988, by Jean Christople Berrard, Michel Miconi, and Eric Poncet.
APPROACH: Take the Tower trail to the right until you reach the Life On Top interpretive sign. Climb up the gully to the base of the southwest buttress then go up and right past Down And Out (Route 212) until you see the crest of the talus slope. The route is 50 feet left of the talus slope crest and between Flight 714 (Route 214) and Tiny's New Shoes (Route 216).
PITCH 1: Face climb straight up past three bolts to the chained rappel bolts (50 feet, 5.11a).
FINISH: Rappel off or continue up to the large Petzl rappel bolts on the NPS Practice Ledge.

SUGGESTED EQUIPMENT: Four quick draws for the bolts.
NOTE: A two star route. Good if you are short of time.

216. TINY'S NEW SHOES: I, 5.6 (Not Shown On Photo)
FIRST ASCENT: Local warm-up area. First ascent unknown. It was named September 5, 1990, by Shawn Garner and Mark Beluscak for convenience. The pitch starts just right of Lakota in an obvious dihedral.
PITCH 1: Climb the crack with good holds and fun stemming to an overhang. This is the crux. Above the overhang, climb up and slightly right along obvious holds to the large Petzl eye bolts belay on a large ledge (80 feet, 5.6).
FINISH: Rappel off.
SUGGESTED EQUIPMENT: Standard rack.
NOTE: This area is great for top roping three other pitches and is a good rescue practice area for training. The obvious areas in this area have been climbed many times but no records have been kept on them.

217. LITTLE DEBBIE: I, 5.7 (Not Shown On Photo)
FIRST ASCENT: June or July, 1978, by Debbie Berglund and another climber.
APPROACH: Take the Tower trail right and go to the Life On Top interpretive sign. Walk up the gully to the base of the southwest shoulder. Go right past Down And Out and Lakota to the top of the talus slope. Start on the easy ledges in front of you.
PITCH 1: Climb up and left on the easy ledges to the large NPS Practice Ledge. Continue up and left along a small ramp to a corner where you can set up a belay with your own pieces (5.6). **PITCH 2:** Climb up the obvious line above you to the top of the shoulder and set up a belay (5.7).
FINISH: Downclimb the Durrance Approach.
SUGGESTED EQUIPMENT: Standard rack with good medium size pieces.
NOTE: It may be better to belay at the two large Petzl eye bolts at the top of the Practice Ledge. A rope length may not reach to the top. A one star route.

218. ONE DIET COKE FOR FAT "JICE": I, 5.11b/c (Not Shown On Photo)
FIRST ASCENT: August 19, 1988, by Jean Christople Berrard, Michel Miconi, and Eric Poncet.
APPROACH: Take the Tower Trail to the right past the Belle Fourche River overlook by 70 yards. Climb up past the start of Little Fingers (Route 220) to the start of Little Creatures (Route 219) in a corner. It is 175 feet right of Lakota (Route 215).
PITCH 1: Climb 15 feet up Little Creatures and traverse left to the first bolt. Face climb straight up past three more bolts to the fourth bolt. The crux is from the third through the fourth bolt (50 feet, 5.11b/c).
FINISH: Rappel off.
SUGGESTED EQUIPMENT: Four quick draws for the bolts.
NOTE: The rappel is suspect because it is only from one bolt. A two star pitch.219.

219. LITTLE CREATURES: I, 5.9+
FIRST ASCENT: October 6, 1985, by Carl Coy and Keith Pike.
APPROACH: Take the Tower trail to the right, and 70 yards past the Belle Fourche River Overlook. Climb over the boulders to the buttress in front of you. Climb up and left past Little Fingers (Route 220) a short distance until you reach a corner where the route starts. This is also the start of One Diet Coke For Fat Jice (Route 218).

PITCH 1: Using thin hands and fingers, climb up the crack and left facing dihedral to the top of the dihedral. Step off left and up to an overhang. Continue up and right through the roof to the bolts at the belay. You will have to tandem climb several feet in order to complete this pitch (170 feet, 5.9).
FINISH: Rappel off.
SUGGESTED EQUIPMENT: Standard rack, small to medium Stoppers, and a full set of Friends (#1-4).
NOTE: A two star climb. This route has been greatly confused with Little Fingers, but is further north and west. Use caution and two long ropes for the rappel.

220. LITTLE FINGERS: I, 5.9-
FIRST ASCENT: Possibly in 1986, by unknown climbers thinking it was Little Creatures (Route 219). It was climbed by several parties before the error was pointed out by Carl Coy, who put up Little Creatures.
APPROACH: Take the Tower trail to the right and 70 yards past the Belle Fourche River Overlook. Climb over the boulders to the group of trees at the base of the wall in front of you. This route starts behind those trees.
PITCH 1: Climb up the chimney to a roof (crux) which is negotiated using thin finger jams and delicate footwork. Continue up to the obvious ledge (60 feet, 5.9-).
FINISH: Rappel off with one rope or continue up and left to join Little Creatures.
SUGGESTED EQUIPMENT: A standard rack.
NOTE: It is not known if bolts are at the top of this pitch so be prepared. A one star route.

221. HUBBA BUBBA: I, 5.11a (Not Shown On Photo)
FIRST FREE ASCENT: August 7, 1988, by Paul Van Betten and belayed by Fred Williams.
APPROACH: Take the Northeast Buttress Approach to the base of the Hourglass then follow the talus slope down and west to the overhang. This climb is at the base of the Northeast Buttress.
PITCH 1: Face climb up to a good finger crack that goes over a four foot roof, which is the crux. Excellent protection (50 feet, 5.11a).
FINISH: Rappel
SUGGESTED EQUIPMENT: One set of Rocks, Friends to three inches, and TCU's.
NOTE: This is not on the Tower proper, but is easily seen from the Northeast Buttress Approach. This short pitch is not shown on any photos. A one star pitch.

Jim Schlinkmann leading first free ascent of "Rangers Are People Too."

APPENDIX

Climbing History

DATE	RTS./CLIMBS/PITCHES	GRADE/RATING	PIONEERED BY
06-28-1937	WIESSNER	II, 5.7	Fritz Wiessner, William House, Lawrence Coveny
09-08-1938	DURRANCE	II, 5.7	Jack Durrance, Harrison Butterworth
07-02-1948	CONN TRAVERSE	5.5	Herb Conn, Jan Conn
08-30-1951	SOLER First Free Ascent 05-02-1959	II, Aid	Anton (Tony) Soler, Art Lembeck, Herb Conn, Ray Moore, Chris Scordus
08-10-1954	PSEUDO-WIESSNER	II, 5.8	Ray Northcutt, Harvey T. Carter
07-26-1955	McCARTHY WEST FACE First Free Ascent 8-11-1979	IV, 5.8, A3	Jim McCarthy, John Rupley
06-07-1956	CASPER COLLEGE First Free Ascent 06-01-1979	III, 5.7, A2	Dud McReynolds, Walt Bailey, David Sturdevant, Bruce Smith
07-09-1956	M&CWTC #1 (DEVILS DELIGHT) First Free Ascent 07-02-1962	II, Aid	Cecil Ouellette, Charles Kness
07-10-1956	M&CWTC #2 (TAD) First Free Ascent 07-03-1973	II, Aid	Dale Gallagher, Jack Morehead
07-12-1956	M&CWTC #3 First Free Ascent 07-03-1973	II, Aid	Cecil Ouellette, Charles Kness,
07-14-1956	M&CWTC #4	II. Aid	Marcus Russi, John Callahan
07-16-1956	M&CWTC #5	II, Aid	Exact Army Climbers Unknown
08-05-1957	McCARTHY NORTH FACE First Free Ascent 05-28-1978	III, 5.7, A2	Jim McCarthy, John Rupley

Date	Route	Rating	Party
02-02-1958	BAILEY DIRECT (Of Durrance)	5.6	Walt Bailey, Raymond Jacquot, Jim Kothel, Richard Williams, Kenneth Johnson
08-17-1958	SUNDANCE	II, 5.7	Bob Kamps, Dave Rearick, Verena Frymann
08-20-1958	BON HOMME	II, 5.8+	Bob Kamps, Don Yestness
05-02-1959	FIRST FREE ASCENT OF SOLER	II, 5.9-	Layton Kor, Raymond Jacquot
07-23-1959	GOOSEBERRY JAM	III, 5.9-	Bob Kamps, Don Yestness
07-26-1959	WALT BAILEY MEMORIAL First Free Ascent 05-27-1974	II, 5.8, A2	Gary Cole, Raymond Jacquot, Charles Blackmon
05-08-1960	HOLLYWOOD AND VINE First Free Ascent 05-26-1974	III, 5.5, A1	Gary Cole, Raymond Jacquot
05-13-1961	VULTURE	IV, 5.8, A3	Layton Kor, Bob La Grange
05-28-1961	BELLE FOURCHE BUTTRESS First Free Ascent 10-16-1977	III, 5.8, A3	Don Ryan, Gary Cole
07-16-1961	NORTHWEST CORNER First Free Ascent 07-09-1985	III, 5.8+, A3	Layton Kor, Herb Swedlund
07-01-1962	DIRECT SOUTHWEST First Free Ascent 07-17-1978	II, 5.9, A3	John Evans, Dick Long
07-02-1962	DEVILS DELIGHT (First Free Ascent of M&CWTC #1)	II, 5.8+	John Evans, Dennis Becker
04-26-1964	SABER First Free Ascent 08-22-1985	IV, 5.6, A3	Layton Kor, Floyd Tex Bossier
05-03-1964	CONQUISTADOR	IV, 5.7, A3	Floyd Tex Bossier, Steve Komito
06-02-1964	NORTHEAST CORNER	III, 5.7, A3	Dean Moore, Paul Stettner
08-19-1964	DANSE MACABRE	II, 5.10d	Royal Robbins, Peter Robinson
08-20-1964	THE WINDOW	IV, 5.6, A4	Royal Robbins, Peter Robinson
10-31-1964	DELTA I First Free Ascent 09-15-1976	II, 5.8,	Bob Schlichting, Bill Heatley

Date	Route	Grade	First Ascent
05-01-1965	DIRECT SOUTHEAST First Free Ascent 08-24-1978	II, 5.5, A2	Peter Oslund, John Horn
08-24-1965	POTC First Free Ascent 06-04-1978	III, 5.7, A3	Peter Oslund, Tom Christensen
08-26-1965	CAVE First Free Ascent 09-20-1976	II, 5.5, A2	Peter Oslund, Dave Ingalls
09-04-1967	THE D.O.M. (DIRTY OLD MAN)	II, A2 or A3	Ron Howe, Terry O'Donnell, Evans Winner
09-24-1967	EL MATADOR First Free Ascent 08-06-1978	IV, 5.7, A3	Fred Beckey, Eric Bjornstad
07-06-1968	EXIT-US First Free Ascent 09-27-1976	II, 5.5, A2	Dave Ingalls, Roy Klingfield
10-06-1968	SECOND CAVE (LAST COWGIRL CAMP) First Free Ascent 08-27-1979	II, 5.7, A2	Peter Oslund, John Chuta
07-24-1969	THE ROUTE OF ALL EVIL (DR. ZEN) First Free Ascent 09-01-1983	III, 5.8, A3	David Lunn, John Luz, Bruce Morris
10-18-1970	B.O. PLENTY First Free Ascent 09-16-1976	III, A2	Charles Bare, Jim Olson
04-22-1971	TROGLODYTES TRAUMA First Free Ascent 06-14-1979	II, A3	Ian Wade, Barbra Euser Walter Fricke
05-08-1971	PATENT PENDING First Free Ascent 08-17-1972	III, 5.7, A1 or A2	Charles Bare Jim Olson
06-02-1972	TULGEY WOOD	III, 5.10a	Mark Hesse, Dan McClure
07-10-1972	CARPENTERS CAPER	II, 5.7, A2	Terry Rypkema, Roger Holtorf, Bruce Bright
08-17-1972	FIRST FREE ASCENT OF PATENT PENDING	III, 5.8+	Bruce Bright, Dennis Drayna
09-14-1972	UNCLE REMUS DIRTY VEGETABLE GARDEN	II, 5.4, A2	Mike Brown, Frank Sanders
11-05-1972	BON HOMME, HORNING VARIATION	II, 5.8	Dennis Horning, Howard Hauck
07-03-1973	TAD (FIRST FREE ASCENT OF M&CWTC #2)	II, 5.7	Dan Burgette, Charles Bare

Date	Route	Rating	First Ascent
08-10-1973	CONQUEST OF TILLIE'S LOOKOUT (BROKE DOWN PALACE) First Free Ascent 10-02-1981	III, 5.8, A2	Bruce Price, Mike LaLone
08-21-1973	MANIFEST DESTINY	II, 5.9	Bruce Bright, Dennis Drayna
10-21-1973	EL CRACKO DIABLO	II, 5.8	Rod Johnson, Pat Padden
05-26-1974	FIRST FREE ASCENT OF HOLLYWOOD AND VINE	II, 5.10c	Jeffery Overton, Scott Woodruff
05-27-1974	FIRST FREE ASCENT OF WALT BAILEY MEMORIAL	II, 5.9	Jeffery Overton, Scott Woodruff
06-02-1974	SUCHNESS First Free Ascent 09-07-1976	II, 5.8, A1	Dennis Horning, Paul Piana
09-08-1974	DEVILS DELIGHT DIRECT	I, 5.7	Dennis Horning, Judd Jennerjahn, Rob Wheeler
05-18-1975	ASSEMBLY LINE	III, 5.9-	Dennis Horning, Judd Jennerjahn
08-31-1975	SUNFIGHTER	II, 5.9	Dennis Horning, Jim Slichter
08-31-1975	WITCHIE	III, 5.10a	Geoffrey Conley, John Pearson
11-02-1975	TOWER DIRECT First Free Ascent 07-22-1985 of Pitch 1	III, 5.8, A2	Pat Padden, Rodney Johnson
05-01-1976	TODTMOOS	II, 5.9-	Dennis Horning, Jim Slichter
05-31-1976	WATERFALL	II, 5.9	Dennis Horning, Skip Fossen, Mark Santangelo
06-09-1976	JOURNEY TO IXTLAN	II, 5.10b	Dennis Horning, Perry Ohlsen
07-02-1976	CROCODILE	III, 5.10d	Dennis Horning, Curt Haire
07-07-1976	McCARTHY WEST FACE HEADS UP VARIATION	I, 5.10a	Greg Newth, Dave Hoag
07-30-1976	MR. CLEAN First Free Ascent 08-14-1977	III, 5.10, A1	Curt Haire, Dennis Horning
09-07-1976	FIRST FREE ASCENT OF SUCHNESS	III, 5.10b	Dennis Horning, Frank Sanders

Date	Route	Grade	Party
09-15-1976	FIRST FREE ASCENT OF DELTA 1	II, 5.9-	Dennis Horning, Frank Sanders
09-16-1976	FIRST FREE ASCENT OF B.O. PLENTY	II, 5.8+	Frank Sanders, Dennis Horning
09-20-1976	FIRST FREE ASCENT OF CAVE	II, 5.9	Dennis Horning, Frank Sanders
09-24-1976	BEELZEBUB	II, 5.10b	Dennis Horning, Frank Sanders
09-27-1976	FIRST FREE ASCENT OF EXIT-US	II, 5.9	Frank Sanders, Dennis Horning
09-28-1976	KAMA SUTRA	III, 5.10a	Dennis Horning, Cody Paulson, Frank Sanders
UNKNOWN	UNKNOWN ROUTE LEFT	Aid	Unknown
UNKNOWN	UNKNOWN ROUTE RIGHT First Free Ascent Pitch 1 as The Last Laugh 10-02-88, and Pitch 3&4 as The Devil Made Me Do It 09-14-88	Aid	Harvey T. Carter?
06-15-1977	ONE-WAY SUNSET	III, 5.10c	Dennis Horning, Jim Slichter
06-25-1977	EXTENDED WIESSNER	I, 5.8	Unknown
08-14-1977	FIRST FREE ASCENT OF MR. CLEAN	III, 5.11a	Henry Barber, Chip Lee
09-25-1977	BITTERSWEET	II, 5.10c	Dennis Horning, Frank Sanders
09-28-1977	SECOND THOUGHT Bon Homme Variation	II, 5.7	Dennis Horning Howard Hauck
10-12-1977	NON-DAIRY CREAMER First Free Ascent Pitch 1 Blood- guard 07-19-1984	III, 5.8, A3	Chris Ballinger, Jim Lynch, Frank Sanders
10-16-1977	FIRST FREE ASCENT OF BELLE FOURCHE BUTTRESS	III, 5.10b	Dennis Horning, Dave Rasmussen
10-25-1977	MADE FOR AID First Free Ascent Digital Extraction 05-19-1982	III, 5.8, A3	Keith Lober solo
10-30-1977	BURNING DAYLIGHT	II, 5.10b	Dennis Horning, Mike Todd
04-02-1978	AFTERNOON DELIGHT First Free Ascent The Power That Preserves 07-12-1983	II, A2	Terry Rypkema, Frank Sanders

Date	Route	Grade	Party
05-07-1978	GOOSEBERRY JAM PETERSON VARIATION	III, 5.10a	Don Peterson
05-13-1978	MAID IN THE SHAID First Free Ascent 06-25-1983	III, 5.8, A2	Terry Rypkema, Frank Sanders, Steve Gardiner Debbie Bergland
05-14-1978	SPEEDWAY First Free Ascent as English Beat 07-22-1984	II, A3,	Terry Rypkema, Steve Gardiner
05-28-1978	FIRST FREE ASCENT OF McCARTHY NORTH FACE	III, 5.11a	Dennis Horning, Frank Sanders
06-04-1978	FIRST FREE ASCENT OF POTC	II, 5.10d	Frank Sanders, Dennis Horning
06-10-1978	CENTENNIAL	III, A3	Terry Rypkema, Frank Sanders, Steve Gardiner
Summer 1978	LITTLE DEBBIE	I, 5.7	Debbie Bergland, Unknown
07-01-1978	McCARTHY WEST FACE VARIATION	II, 5.10b	Chris Ballinger, Dennis Horning, Steve Gardiner
07-17-1978	FIRST FREE ASCENT OF DIRECT SOUTHWEST	III, 5.11b	Henry Barber, Ajax Green
07-22-1978	PHILLIP'S RETREAT	I, 5.9+	Dennis Horning, Phillip Chandler on belay
07-27-1978	TWO LEFT SHOES	III, 5.8, A1	Jim Beyer (solo)
08-06-1978	FIRST FREE ASCENT OF EL MATADOR	III, 5.10d	Bob Yoho, Chick Holtkamp
08-19-1978	CAROL'S CRACK	III, 5.11a	Bob Yoho, Carol Black, Chick Holtkamp, Jeff Baird
08-24-1978	FIRST FREE ASCENT OF DIRECT SOUTHEAST	II, 5.11d	Steve Hong, Mark Smedley, Karin Budding
10-21-1978	TOWER CLASSIC First Free Ascent as Let Me Go Wild Pitch 1 9-20-80 Pitch 2 8-15-84	III, 5.7, A2	Steve Gardiner, Terry Rypkema, Frank Sanders
10-29-1978	LUCIFER'S LEDGES	III, A3	Frank Sanders, Steve Gardiner, Terry Rypkema Mark Brackin
05-11-1979	McARTHY WEST FACE HONG VARIATION	I, 5.11c	Steve Hong, Karin Budding

Date	Route	Rating	First Ascensionists
06-01-1979	MORCHELLA ESCULENTA First Free Ascent 09-06-1980	II, 5.7, A3	**Larry Wydra,** Tom Ptacek
06-01-1979	FIRST FREE ASCENT OF CASPER COLLEGE	III, 5.10d	Jim Beyer, Dennis Horning
06-09-1979	ZEPHYR First Free Ascent Pitch 1 07-25-87 Pitch 2 09-12-87	III, 5.9, A1	Jim Beyer (solo)
06-14-1979	TROGLODYTES TRAUMA	II, 5.11c	Jim Beyer, Dennis Horning
07-07-1979	FIRST FREE ASCENT OF BLACK-JONES DIRECT	II, 5.11b	Steve Jones, Carol Black
07-15-1979	BUTTERFINGERS	IV, 5.7, A2	Steve Gardiner, Mark Brackin
07-30-1979	PATH OF DISSENT	II, 5.9	Mark Smedley, Jim Black, Rich Jaskiewiez
08-11-1979	FIRST FREE ASCENT OF McCARTHY WEST FACE	III, 5.11c	Steve Hong, Karin Budding
08-16-1979	RUNNER'S WORLD First Free Ascent 2 Pitches Graeme's Line 08-01-1985	IV, 5.6, A3	Frank Sanders, Steve Gardiner
08-27-1979	THE LAST COWGIRL CAMP First Free Ascent of Second Cave	II, 5.11b	Dennis Horning, Jay Smith
05-17-1980	PERSISTENCE	II, 5.9	Steve Gardiner, Frank Sanders
05-24-1980	DOUBLE INDEMNITY	II, 5.11a	Steve Hong, Karin Budding, Mark Smedley
05-25-1980	FOUR PLAY	III, 5.11c	Steve Hong, Karin Budding, Mark Smedley, Bill Feiges
06-01-1980	MISTY MORNING MELODY	II, 5.8, A2	Steve Gardiner, Frank Sanders, Mark Brackin
06-22-1980	ACROPHOBIA First Free Ascent Pitch 1 08-23-1986	IV, 5.7, A2+	Steve Gardiner, Mark Brackin
07-04-1980	INDEPENDENCE	III, 5.8, A3	Frank Sanders (solo)
08-25-1980	ACCIDENT VICTIM	IV, 5.11d	Kim Carrigan, Steve Levin

Date	Route	Grade	Party
09-06-1980	FIRST FREE ASCENT OF MORCHELLA ESCULENTA	II, 5.11c	Dennis Horning, Mark Smedley
09-07-1980	BLADE CITY	IV, A3+	Frank Sanders, Steve Gardiner
09-13-1980	THE THIN DAGGER	IV, A2	Don Grady, Rod Johnson
09-20-1980	DUSK IN DOGTOWN First Free Ascent Pitch 1 Tower Classic	II, 5.10c	Mark Smedley, Jim Black
05-21-1981	EMOTIONAL RESCUE	III, 5.7, A3+	Frank Sanders, Chris Engle
05-29-1981	GIMME SHELTER Var. Emotional Rescue	III, 5.7, A3	Frank Sanders
06-30-1981	WAY LAYED	I, 5.11b	Eric Rhicard, Mark Smedley
08-29-1981	JUMPIN' JACK FLASH First Free Ascent Pitch 2 & 3 Daredevil Index 06-18-1985 First Free Ascent Pitch 1 Leaping Lizards 8-3-1985	III, 5.7, A2	Frank Sanders, Dale Chamberlain
08-29-1981	DUMP WATT	II, 5.10b	Mark Smedley, Dave Larsen, Eric Rhicard
09-05-1981	SYMPATHY FOR THE DEVIL First Free Ascent Pitch 2 6-27-1982 First Free Ascent Pitch 3 8-6-1985	III, 5.9, A2	Frank Sanders, Cris Engle
09-29-1981	OBJECT CATHEXIS Var. of Accident Victim	III, 5.12b	Steve Hong, Mark Sonnenfeld
10-02-1981	BROKEDOWN PALACE First free ascent of Conquest of Tillie's Lookout	III, 5.12a	Steve Hong, Mark Sonnenfeld
03-??-1982	SEAMSTRESS First Free Ascent 06-13-1982	II, A2	Chris Engle, Dave Johnson
05-19-1982	DIGITAL EXTRACTION First Free Ascent of Made For Aid	III, 5.11d	Steve Hong, Mark Sonnenfeld
06-13-1982	FIRST FREE ASCENT OF SEAMSTRESS	II, 5.12a	Steve Hong, Karin Budding
06-10-1982	NEW WAVE	I, 5.10a	Dave Larsen, Dennis Horning

Date	Route	Grade	Party
06-22-1982	BROKEN TREE	I, 5.10a	Dennis Horning, Dave Larsen
06-27-1982	BACK TO MONTANA First Free Ascent Pitch 2 Sympathy For The Devil	II, 5.10d	Dennis Horning, Monte Cooper
07-11-1982	THE CHUTE	I, 5.10d	Dennis Horning, Hollis Marriott
05-27-1983	ABJECT CATHEXIS	III, A3	Eric Breitenberger, William Trull
06-04-1983	ADVENTUROUS DAZE	IV, 5.10a, A2	Frank Sanders, Chris Engle
06-25-1983	FIRST FREE ASCENT OF MAID IN THE SHAID	III, 5.11d	Steve Hong, Andy Hong, Karin Budding
06-26-1983	DELI EXPRESS	II, 5.12a	Mark Sonnenfeld, Steve Hong
06-27-1983	A BRIDGE TOO FAR	I, 5.11d	Todd Skinner, Mark Sonnenfeld, Steve Hong
07-12-1983	THE POWER THAT PRESERVES First Free As of Afternoon Delight	II, 5.12a	Todd Skinner, Moana Roberts (jumared)
07-14-1983	SYNCHRONICITY	I, 5.11d	Todd Skinner, John Rosholt
07-24-1983	TWO MOONS OVER HULETT Parts of this route follows Emotional Rescue	II, 5.11b	Dennis Horning, Dave Larsen
08-13-1983	EVERLASTING	I, 5.10c	Dennis Horning, Dave Larsen
08-15-1983	KLONDIKE	I, 5.10a	Dave Larsen, Dennis Horning
09-01-1983	DR. ZEN First Free Ascent of Route of All Evil	III, 5.11c	Steve Mankenberg, Dave Larsen
04-14-1984	PIGEON ENGLISH	II, 5.9-	Paul Piana, Bill Hatcher
06-02-1984	NORTHEAST CORNER	III, 5.7, A3	Dean More, Paul Stettner
07-02-1984	MATEO TEPEE	II, 5.7, A3	Steve Gardiner, Joe Sears
07-04-1984	SATAN'S STAIRWAY	III, 5.8, A3	Steve Gardiner, Joe Sears, Chris Engle, Dave Johnson

Date	Route	Grade	First Ascentionists
07-14-1984	SURFER GIRL Partly on M&CWTC Aid Route	II, 5.12c	Todd Skinner, Beth Wald
07-19-1984	APPROACHING LAVENDER	II, 5.11c	Paul Piana, Bob Cowan, Todd Skinner, Beth Wald
07-19-1984	BLOODGUARD First Free Ascent Pitch 1 Non-Dairy Creamer	I, 5.11d	Todd Skinner, Beth Wald, Bob Cowan, Paul Piana
07-20-1984	THE BEST CRACK IN MINNESOTA	I, 5.9	Paul Piana, Bob Cowan, Todd Skinner, Beth Wald
07-22-1984	ENGLISH BEAT First Free Ascent of Speedway	II, 5.12b	Todd Skinner, Paul Piana, Bob Cowan, Frank Hill, Kevin Lindorff
07-26-1984	AVALON	II, 5.11d	Todd Skinner, Beth Wald
08-01-1984	ANIMAL CRACKER LAND	I, 5.12b	Todd Skinner, Beth Wald
08-15-1984	LET ME GO WILD First Free Ascent Pitch 2 Tower Classic	II, 5.12b	Todd Skinner, Beth Wald
08-15-1984	PSYCHIC TURBULENCE	I, 5.11a	Todd Skinner, Daniel Rosen, Beth Wald
06-14-1985	RANGERS ARE PEOPLE TOO	I, 5.9-	Jim Schlinkmann, Steve Gardiner, Dick Guilmette
06-15-1985	McCARTHY'S BROTHER	II, 5.10a	Dennis Horning, Jim Schlinkmann
06-18-1985	DAREDEVIL INDEX First Free Ascent Pitch 2&3 Jumpin' Jack Flash	III, 5.12a	Paul Piana, Steve Petro
07-07-1985	NAM	I, 5.8	Dick Guilmette, Bruce Adams
07-09-1985	First Free Ascent Pitch 1 & 2, VULTURE	IV, 5.12a	Steve Hong, Karin Budding Beth Wald
07-10-1985	POTATOES ALIEN	I, 5.10d	Mateo Pee Pee, "Barney" Fisher, Jim Schlinkmann
07-16-1985	NO HOLDS FOR BONZO First Free Ascent of NAM	I, 5.11a	Mateo Pee Pee, Jim Schlinkmann,
07-17-1985	RAINDANCE	I, 5.10b	Carl Coy, Beth Wald

Date	Route	Grade	Climbers
07-18-1985	SPINEY NORMAN	I, 5.12b	Todd Skinner, Beth Wald
07-21-1985	JERRY'S KIDS	I, 5.10b	Jim Schlinkmann, Mateo Pee Pee "Barney" Fisher
07-21-1985	EXTENSION	II, 5.11a	Dennis Horning, Jim Schlinkmann
07-22-1985	ROMEO IS RESTLESS First Free Ascent Pitch 1 Tower Direct	I, 5.12b	Todd Skinner, Beth Wald
07-27-1985	MYSTIC AND THE MULCHERS	I, 5.8-	Jim Schlinkmann, Dick Guilmette, "Barney" Fisher, Mateo Pee Pee
07-30-1985	VERROUILLER LETOIT PENDANG LA MARCHE First Free Ascent Pitch 1 9-19-87	II, 5.7, A3	Kyle Copeland, John Gill
08-01-1985	NITRO EXPRESS Pitch 2	II, 5, 11c	Steve Petro, Todd Skinner, Beth Wald
08-01-1985	GRAEME'S LINE First Free Ascent of the lower half of Runners World	II, 5.12b	Todd Skinner, Bill Hatcher, Beth Wald
08-03-1985	LEAPING LIZARDS First Free Ascent of Pitch 1 Jumpin' Jack Flash	I, 5.10b	Carl Coy, Mark Jacobs
08-06-1985	HOLLOW MEN First Free Ascent Pitch 3 Sympathy For The Devil	II, 5.12c	Todd Skinner, Beth Wald
08-10-1985	RISQUE	I, 5.12b	Todd Skinner, Beth Wald, Jim Schlinkmann, Bill Hatcher
08-12-1985	BILLIE BEAR CRANKS THE RAD	I, 5.12c	Bill Hatcher, Todd Skinner, Rick Erker
08-14-1985	SEE YOU IN SOHO	I, 5.12b	Todd Skinner, Beth Wald
08-22-1985	SPANK THE MONKEY First Free Ascent Pitch 1 Saber	I, 5.10d	Jim Schlinkmann, Mateo Pee Pee, Carl Coy
08-26-1985	NEVERLASTING	I, 5.9-	David Kozak, Denny Hochwender
09-01-1985	WHITE LIGHTNING	III, A2	Mark Gordon, Kristi Rolf
09-03-1985	BUSTER CATTLEFIELD	I, 5.11d	Tom Kalakay, Mal Ham, Bill Dockins, Kristin Drumheller

Date	Route	Grade	Climbers
10-06-1985	LITTLE CREATURES	I, 5.9+	Carl Coy, Keith Pike
03-30-1986	LIFE DURING WARTIME	II, 5.10d	Mike Friedrichs, Dennis Horning
05-25-1986	OLD GUYS IN LYCRA	I, 5.10d	Carl Coy, Bill Pelander
06-18-1986	LIKEN LICHEN	I, 5.9-	Mateo Pee Pee, Barney Fisher
06-27-1986	WRONG WAY Direct start to One-way Sunset	I, 5.12	Jim Brink, Dick Holm
(est) 1986	LITTLE FINGERS	I, 5.9-	Unknown
07-19-1986	FRACTAL	I, 5.10a	Thomas and Rainer Malzbender
07-23-1986	NO KISS FOR DOG LIPS	II, 5.9	Mateo Pee Pee, David Ek, Barney Fisher
08-07-1986	PEE PEE'S PLUNGE	I, 5.12a	Carl Coy, Mateo Pee Pee, Stu Ritchie, Rob Adair, Dan Hutchens
08-23-1986	SPACE CHALLENGER First Free Ascent Pitch 1 of Acrophobia	II, 5.12c	Tim Toula, Paul Chamberlain (belayed)
09-08-1986	THE SKUNK	IV, 5.6, A3	Igor Jamnikar, Matjaz Ravhekar
09-09-1986	THE CHIPMUNK First Free Ascent Pitch 2, May 1991	IV, 5.10a, A2	Janko Humar, Edo Kozorog
09-11-1986	NITRO EXPRESS Pitch 1 & 3	II, 5.12a	Steve Petro, Paul Piana
05-27-1987	THE MAIDEN	I, 5.10a	Scott Flesner, Jim Swenson
05-28-1987	A PIECE OF THE ACTION	I, 5.10d	Jim Swenson, Scot Flesner
06-0?-1987	HIGH NAM	II, 5.12b, A1	Bill Dockins, Kristen Drumheller
07-18-1987	CAPTAIN VIDEO	I, 5.12b	Andy Petefish, Mike Robinson belayed
07-24-1987	SKINNY PUPPY	I, 5.10d	David Thomas, Seth Pierce, Mike Robinson
07-24-1987	SUICIDAL TEND- ENCIES	III, 5.10c, A3+	David Thomas, Seth Pierce
07-25-1987	TUNNEL VISION (1st 85 feet of Pitch 1)	I, 5.11d/12a	Andy Petefish, Kris Hjelle

Date	Route	Rating	First Ascent
08-01-1987	LA VACA SOLITARIA	I, 5.11a	Carl Coy, Mal Ham
09-12-1987	TUNNEL VISION Pitch 2	I, 5.12b	Andy Petefish, Kris Hjelle
09-19-1987	GOOD HOLDS FOR GODZILLA First Free Ascent of Pitch 1 of Ver-rouiller Letoit Pendang La Marche	I, 5.12d	Andy Petefish, Kris Hjelle
09-28-1987	SPACE RANGER	I, 5.12a	Jack Roberts, Pam Ranger
10-03-1987	BLUE STEM SKYWAY	II, 5.12c	Andy Petefish, Kris Hjelle
10-25-1987	SOON TO BE FREE	I, A2	Scott C. Robertson, Lysle Carter
07-24-1988	DOUBLE FEATURE (variation of Captain Video)	I, 5.11d	Andy Petefish, Kris Hjelle
08-07-1988	HUBBA BUBBA	I, 5.11a	Paul Van Betten, belayed by Fred Williams
08-07-1988	A REACH TOO FAR	I, 5.10d	Bob Gains, Paul Van Betten, Foster Green, Fred Williams, Clell Williams, Don Mann, Brad Tschetter
08-09-1988	ONE O'CLOCK DEMO	I, 5.9-	Michael Sammis, Bob Gaines
08-11-1988	SOME LIKE IT HOT	I, 5.12b	Paul Van Betten, Bob Gaines, Jay Smith, Robert Finlay
08-18-1988	THE HOWLING	II, 5.11d	(Pitch 1) Jay Smith, Paul Van Betten (Pitch 2) Jay Smith, Bob Gains, Paul Van Betten (Pitch 3) Jay Smith, Jo Bentley
08-18-1988	LAKOTA	I, 5.11a	Jean Christople Berrard, Michel Miconi, Eric Poncet
08-18-1988	UP IN SMOKE	I, 5.10b	Kris Hjelle, Andy Petefish
08-19-1988	ONE DIET COKE FOR FAT "JICE"	I, 5.11b/c	Jean Christople Berrard, Michel Miconi, Eric Poncet
08-19-1988	DEAD POINT	I, 5.11b	Jay Smith, Jo Bentley
08-20-1988	PORCUPINING AWAY	I, 5.7	Andrew M. Artz

Date	Route	Grade	First Ascent
09-14-1988	THE DEVIL MADE ME DO IT (on the old aid route Unknown Route Right	III, A2, 5.9+	Frank Sanders, Sue Gass
09-26-1988	MYSTERY EXPRESS	I, 5.13a	Andy Petefish, Kris Hjelle
10-02-1988	THE LAST LAUGH First Free Ascent of Pitch 1 of Unknown Route Right	I, 5.10	Kris Hjelle, Andy Petefish
11-06-1988	DOWN AND OUT	I, 5.7	Brad Solon, Jenny Silbernagel
05-21-1989	AERIAL BOUNDARIES	II, 5.11d	Layne Kopischka, Dennis Horning
05-27-1989	ADRENALIN SURFER	III, 5.12a	Nate Postma, Dan Meyer, Dan Feda assisted
06-06-1989	MY UNSUNG HERO	II, 5.10c	Dennis Horning, Frank Ducel
07-0?-1989	CALIFORNIA DREAMING	II, 5.11b	Frank Sanders, Liana Kirk
07-0?-1989	KIRK-SANDERS WEST FACE CLASSIC	III, 5.8, A3+	Liana Kirk, Frank Sanders
07-0?-1989	MARRIAGE WAS MY FIRST MISTAKE	II, 5.7, A3	Frank Sanders, solo
07-31-1989	TINTIN DOES DOUGHNUTS	I, 5.9	Martin Ziebell, belayed by Joel Barnett
08-23-1989	WHINE AND BRUISES First Free Ascent of Pitch 1 & 2 Northwest Corner	II, 5.12b	Carl Coy, Rick Hays
08-21-1989	BLOTTER IS MY SPOTTER	I, 5.7, A3+	Frank Sanders
09-28-1989	YOUNG MAN BLUES	II, 5.12b	Keith Pike
06-02-1990	ANTS ON ANGEL FOOD	II, 5.11d	Dennis Horning, Steve Babbits
Summer 1990	NATURAL PERVERSITY	I, 5.11a	Dennis Horning, Hollis Marriot
07-??-1990	FOUR WINZE	III, 5.10c	Dennis Horning, Robin Jones
07-??-1990	STRONGBACK	II, 5.11d	Dennis Horning, Steve Olson, Steve Babbits
07-??-1990	SOARING	II, 5.10d	Possibly Dennis Horning

Date	Route	Grade	First Ascent
09-01-1990	CALCULUS AFFAIR	III, 5.10d, A0	"Tintin" Ziebell, "Scooter" Metcalf, "Batman" Stevens
09-05-1990	TINY'S NEW SHOES	I, 5.6	Unknown (done yrs previously)
09-15-1990	CARL'S FACE	I, 5.10c	Danny Rosen, Dennis Horning
10-25-1990	FLIGHT 714	I, 5.11a	Martin Ziebell
05-??-1991	PHASE LOCKING WITH STRANGE ATTRACTORS First Free Ascent Pitch 2 of The Chipmunk	II, 5.11	Unknown
06-08-1991	JOE KID	I, 5.8	Burton Lindquist, Tony Lindquist
06-12-1991	411 SOUTHWEST Pitch 2	II, 5.12	Dave Rone, George Kremer, Mary Jo Rone
06-18-1991	411 SOUTHWEST Pitch 3	II, 5.12	Dave Rone, George Kremer
07-03-1991	DRILLING MISS DAISY	I, 5.10a	Nathan Postma, Paul Fritze
08/09-1991	ALL AMERICAN ECSTASY BOY	II, 5.11	Dennis Horning, Danny Rosen, Scott Brachtmann
Unknown	ROACH ADDITION	I, 5.7	Steve Roach
Unknown	REFRACTAL	II, 5.11c	Unknown
Unknown	SOLAR ECLIPSE	II, 5.11b	Eric Fazio-Rhicard, Dennis Horning, Brent Kertzman
Est. 1991	BUCKSPECK	II, 5.10c	Dennis Horning, Hollis Marriott
Est. 1991	STEPPING OUT OF FLATLAND	II, 5.11b	Unknown
09-02-1991	MAN WITHOUT A PLANET	I, 5.10a	Brent Kertzman, Dennis Horning, Steve Babbits, Sara Mysel
09-05-1991	DEDICATED TO THE GAME	I, 5.11c	Nate Postma, Pam Postma
08-06-1992	STEAL AWAY	I, 5.11b	Dave Rone, Kimi Harrison, Leslie Appling
10-24-1992	SCOTTFREE	II, 5.11b	Carl Coy, belayed by John Plotke
Est. -1992	LOSS OF ENTHUSIASM	I, 5.11a	Unknown
Est. -1992	ROCKSUCKERS	II, 5.11c	Unknown

Beth Wald belaying.

Climbing Route Index

#176	Abject Cathexis - 126		#151	Captain Video - 117
#182	Accident Victim - 128		#120	Carl's Face - 106
#189	Acrophobia - 132		#118	Carol's Crack - 104
#61	Adrenalin Surfer - 82		#30	Carpenter's Caper - 68
#163	Adventurous Daze - 121		#64	Casper College - 83
#51	Aerial Boundaries - 77		#47	Cave - 76
#87	All American Ecstasy Boy - 91		#199	Centennial - 136
#56	Animal Cracker Land - 79		#130	The Chipmunk - 109
#83	Ants on Angel Food - 90		#79	The Chute - 89
#121	Approaching Lavender - 106		#174	Conquistador - 125
#122	Approaching Lavender (Rosen Variation) - 106		#63	Crocodile - 83
			#16	Danse Macabre - 62
#91	Assembly Line - 93		#104	Daredevil Index - 98
#147	Avalon - 115		#159	Dead Point - 120
#100	Back to Montana - 97		#209	Dedicated to the Game - 141
#4	Bailey Direct - 57		#132	Deli Express - 109
#52	Beelzebub - 78		#20	Delta I - 65
#68	Belle Fourche Buttress - 84		#11	Devils Delight - 61
#14	The Best Crack in Minnesota - 62		#10	Devils Delight Direct - 61
#177	Billie Bear Cranks the Rad - 127		#203	The Devil Made Me Do It - 138
#18	Bittersweet - 63		#172	Digital Extraction - 125
#207	Black Jones Direct - 141		#32	Direct Southeast - 69
#192	Blade City - 133		#185	Direct Southwest - 129
#193	Blue Stem Skyway - 133		#35	The D.O.M. - 70
#141A	A Blotter is my Spotter - 112		#150	Double Feature - 116
#144	Blood Guard - 113		#28	Double Indemnity - 68
#22	B.O. Plenty - 66		#212	Down and Out - 142
#24	Bon Homme, Horning Variation - 66		#111	Dr. Zen - 101
#25	Bon Homme - 67		#211	Drilling Miss Daisy - 142
#162	A Bridge Too Far - 121		#70	Dump Watt - 85
#146	Brokedown Palace - 115		#1	Durrance - 56
#95	Broken Tree - 94		#53	Dusk in Dogtown - 78
#72	Buckspeck - 87		#44	El Cracko Diablo - 75
#65	Burning Daylight - 84		#170	El Matador - 123
#124	Buster Cattlefield - 107		#107	Emotional Rescue - 100
#190	Butterfingers - 132		#29	English Beat - 68
#74	Calculus Affair - 87		#97	Everlasting - 96
#125	California Dreaming - 107		#45	Exit US - 75

#9	Extended Wiessner - 59	#168	McCarthy West Face Free Variation - 122
#46	Extension - 75	#169	McCarthy West Face Hong Variation - 123
#214	Flight 714 - 144	#106	McCarthy's Brother - 99
#114	Four Play - 103		M&CWTC #3&4 - 55
#86	**Four Winze - 91**		M&CWTC #5 - 55
#128	Fractal - 108	#160	Misty Morning Melody - 120
#108	Gimme Shelter - 100	#19	Morchella Esculenta - 65
#135	Good Holds For Godzilla - 110	#158	Mr. Clean - 119
#66	Gooseberry Jam - 84	#165	Mystery Express - 121
#67	Gooseberry Jam—Peterson Variation - 84	#101	Mystic and the Mulchers - 98
#197	Graeme's Line - 135	#17	My Unsung Hero - 63
#140	High Nam - 112	#137	Nam - 111
#98	Hollow Men - 96	#84	Natural Perversity - 90
#39	Hollywood and Vine - 71	#102	Neverlasting - 98
#157	The Howling - 119	#94	New Wave - 94
#221	Hubba Bubba - 147	#81	Nitro Express - 89
#161	Independence - 120	#139	No Holds for Bonzo - 111
#149	Jerry's Kids - 116	#112	No Kiss for Dog Lips - 101
#210	Joe Kid - 142	#145	Non-Dairy Creamer - 115
#15	Journey to Ixtlan - 62		Northeast Corner - 55
#88	Kama Sutra - 91	#115	Northwest Corner - 103
#191	Kirk-Sanders West Face Classic - 133	#181	Object Cathexis - 128
#110	Klondike - 101	#77	Old Guys in Lycra - 88
#171	La Vaca Solitaria - 123	#218	One Diet Coke for Fat "Jice" - 145
#215	Lakota - 144	#155	One O'Clock Demo - 118
#48	Last Cowgirl Camp - 76	#123	One-Way Sunset - 107
#201	The Last Laugh - 136	#90	Patent Pending - 92
#103	Leaping Lizards - 98	#12	Path of Dissent - 61
#54	Let Me Go Wild - 78	#153	Pee Pee's Plunge - 117
#49	Life During Wartime - 77	#3	Persistence - 57
#179	Liken Lichen - 127	#131	Phase Locking With Strange Attractors - 109
#219	Little Creatures - 147	#34	Phillip's Retreat - 70
#217	Little Debbie - 145	#36	A Piece of the Action - 71
#220	Little Fingers - 147	#2	Pigeon English - 56
#134	Loss of Enthusiasm - 110	#206	P.O.T.C. - 139
#59	Lucifer's Ledges - 82	#180	Porcupining Away - 128
#93	Maid in the Shaid - 94	#141	Potatoes Alien - 112
#133	Man Without a Planet - 110	#31	The Power That Preserves - 69
#96	The Maiden - 96	#8	Pseudo Wiessner - 59
#208	Manifest Destiny - 141	#113	Psychic Turbulence - 103
#71	Marriage Was My First Mistake - 87	#119	Raindance - 106
#6	Mateo Tepee - 58	#186	Rangers Are People Too - 131
#105	McCarthy North Face - 99	#178	A Reach Too Far - 127
#167	McCarthy West Face - 122	#129	Refractal - 108

#138	Risque - 111	#99	Sympathy for the Devil - 97
#37	Roach Addition - 71	#127	Synchronicity -108
#38	Rocksuckers - 71	#43	Tad - 74
#204	Romeo is Restless - 139	#173	The Thin Dagger - 125
#198	Runner's World - 135	#213	Tin Tin Does Doughnuts - 144
#143	Saber - 113	#216	Tiny's New Shoes - 145
#60	Satan's Stairway - 82	#42	Todtmoos - 74
#152	Scottfree - 117	#55	Tower Classic - 79
#23	Seamstress - 66	#205	Tower Direct - 139
#26	Second Thought - 67	#50	Troglodytes Trauma - 77
#80	See You In Soho - 89	#164	Tulgey Wood - 121
#75	Skinny Puppy - 88	#195	Tunnel Vision - 134
#58	The Skunk - 81	#69	Two Left Shoes - 85
#85	Soaring - 90	#109	Two Moons Over Hulett - 101
#40	Solar Eclipse - 74	#27	Uncle Remus Dirty Vegetable Garden - 67
#41	Soler - 74	#200	Unknown Route Left - 136
#156	Some Like It Hot - 119	#202	Unknown Route Right - 138
#194	Soon To Be Free - 134	#148	Up In Smoke - 116
#184	411 Southwest - 129	#136	Verrouiller Letoit Pendant La Marche - 110
#183	Southwest Buttress Cracks - 129	#154	Vulture - 118
#188	Space Challenger - 131	#33	Walt Bailey Memorial - 70
#187	Space Ranger - 131	#21	Waterfall - 65
#142	Spank the Monkey - 113	#166	Way Layed - 122
#117	Spiney Norman - 104	#116	Whine and Bruises - 104
#182A	Steal Away - 128	#175	White Lightning - 126
#82	Strongback - 90	#7	Wiessner - 58
#73	Stepping Out of Flatland - 87	#57	The Window - 81
#89	Suchness - 92	#62	Witchie - 83
#76	Suicidal Tendencies - 88	#126	Wrong Way - 108
#5	Sundance - 57	#78	Young Man Blues - 89
#13	Sunfighter - 62	#196	Zephyr - 134
#92	Surfer Girl - 93		

About the authors:

Steve Gardiner, a teacher of English and journalism in Jackson, Wyoming, has made over 100 climbs on Devils Tower, including 15 first ascents. He has also climbed in the Andes, Alps, Alaska and throughout the western United States.

He is the author of *Why I Climb: Personal Insights of Top Climbers.*

Richard Guilmette is retired from the National Park Service where he had daily contact with visitors at Devils Tower National Monument, Grand Teton and Yellowstone National Parks, and at Denali National Park and Preserve. He is well versed in the needs of climbers and visitors within the National Park System. Richard has been an active climber and done many of the routes on the tower.

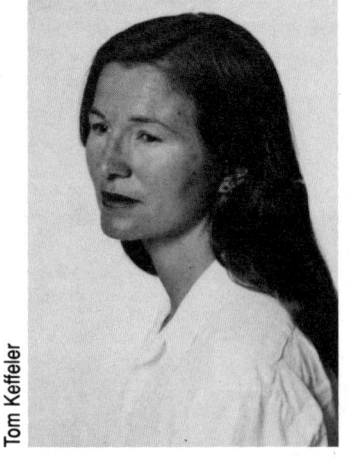

Renée Carrier lives and writes in northern Crook County, Wyoming, near the Bear Lodge Mountains and the Tower.

168